DESERT DRUMS

THE PUEBLO INDIANS OF NEW MEXICO
1540–1928

BY
LEO CRANE

WITH ILLUSTRATIONS

BOSTON
LITTLE, BROWN, AND COMPANY
1928

THE DRUMMERS
A ceremonial at Sandia pueblo

Copyright, 1928,
BY LITTLE, BROWN, AND COMPANY

All rights reserved

Published October, 1928

THE ATLANTIC MONTHLY PRESS PUBLICATIONS
ARE PUBLISHED BY
LITTLE, BROWN, AND COMPANY
IN ASSOCIATION WITH
THE ATLANTIC MONTHLY COMPANY

PRINTED IN THE UNITED STATES OF AMERICA

To the Franciscans

PIONEERS AND PRIESTS
MISSIONERS AND MARTYRS
SHEPHERDS OF DESERT SHEEP

CONTENTS

I	The Pioneer Official, James S. Calhoun	1
II	The City of the Holy Faith	19
III	Laguna: on the Feast of San José	34
IV	Laguna: the Landed Proprietors	59
V	The Man in the Golden Helmet	85
VI	Chauffeurs and Colonists	99
VII	A Mystery at Acoma	121
VIII	Christmas Revels	149
IX	Conquistadors!	181
X	The Crusader	210
XI	The Pueblo Indians of New Mexico	220
XII	"Infernal Affairs"	238
XIII	Friends at Court	257
XIV	The Riddle, the Bunk, and the Bursum Bill	275
XV	The People of the Little Island	312
XVI	Legends and Leases	338
XVII	The Indian Who Got Away	361
XVIII	"Mañana, and Mañana, and Mañana"	387

ILLUSTRATIONS

THE DRUMMERS	*Frontispiece*
MAP	x
A SANTA FE ADOBE	8
THE SANGRE DE CRISTOS	
A STREET IN THE JEMEZ PUEBLO	12
PHILOSOPHERS OF THE DESERT	
"EL PALACIO"	24
FIESTA SCENE, LAGUNA	36
"COMANCHE DANCE"	
THE OLD LAGUNA MISSION	40
RELIGIOUS PROCESSION, LAGUNA	
A GUEST OF THE FIESTA	44
INTERIOR OF THE OLD LAGUNA CHURCH	56
THE SANDIA MOUNTAIN	90
TAOS PUEBLO	
THE ACOMA MESA	114
AN ACOMA BLOCK	
THE MISSION OF SAN FELIPE	150
SANTO DOMINGO	160
THE MISSION OF SANTO DOMINGO	
A ROUND "KIVA"	174
CEREMONIAL DANCERS LEAVING A KIVA	
A JEMEZ DOORWAY	192
SIA MISSION	
THE BELLS OF COCHITI	196
THE ACOMA MISSION	206
ST. MICHAEL'S MONASTERY	

ILLUSTRATIONS

THE BLACK MESA OF SAN ILDEFONSO	218
THE PLAZA AT SIA	
JEMEZ INDIAN GIRLS	226
A TAOS DANDY	
THE EAGLE DANCE	234
SAN ILDEFONSO DANCERS.	236
STREET IN SANTO DOMINGO	242
HOUSE OF THE SACRISTAN, SANTO DOMINGO	
MONICA SILVA	246
A SQUARE "KIVA"	252
A MOUNTAIN HACIENDA	282
"HONEY," A SCHOOLGIRL OF TAOS	292
SANTA CLARA WOMAN IN FIESTA COSTUME	
CHURCH OF SAN BUENAVENTURA AT COCHITI . . .	304
THE NORTH PUEBLO AND BRIDGE AT TAOS	
THE PUEBLO OF ISLETA	314
PABLO ABEITA	316
THE MISSION OF SAN AGUSTIN AT ISLETA	332
FATHER ANTON DOCHER IN HIS GARDEN	
KIVA ENTRANCE AND SENTINEL, TAOS	356
JOHN CHAVEZ	378
JUDGE JOHN DIXON	
THE MISSION OF SAN GERONIMO, TAOS	388
MUSEUM AND ART GALLERY, SANTA FE	

DESERT DRUMS

I

THE PIONEER OFFICIAL, JAMES S. CALHOUN

IN CAMP NEAR SANTA FE
July 29, 1849

SIR:—

You are already advised of my departure from Fort Leavenworth on the 16th of May, and I have now to inform you that we reached Santa Fe on the 22nd of the present month, having been employed in marching 49 days, our halting days numbering 19. This you will perceive is the 8th day in camp at this place, not having been able to procure quarters elsewhere. I have the promise, however, of an adobe building at the enormous rent of $100 per month, to which an additional expenditure must be made to Americanize it so that it may be inhabited with any degree of comfort. All the buildings in Santa Fe are of mud, with floors and covering for the roof of the same material. . . .

— Extract from Calhoun's First Field Report

IN this manner the first and most picturesque of the Southwestern Indian Agents, the man who would become first Territorial Governor of New Mexico, reported his arrival at his designated post. He had been appointed April 7, 1849, and with his commission received, among other important enclosures, "a copy of the late Treaty with Mexico."

This Treaty — that of Guadalupe Hidalgo, marking the close of the War with Mexico — may be termed the Magna Carta of the Pueblo Indians; a document drawn by those who thought they were settling things of far greater moment than the future of a small group of Indians; a charter destined to cause dispute and dissension for sixty-five years and more, and to invite the scrutiny and study of many gifted advocates and jurists without bringing the Pueblo Indians peace of mind. It was, quite likely, Calhoun's lightest piece of baggage, — a simple pamphlet, — yet it would generate many kinds of mental indigestion, and in scope of time, bitter interest, and vehement partisanship would bulk perhaps the most important question that has commanded the attention of central New Mexico's diversified citizens.

As for Calhoun, many interesting figures had appeared on the Santa Fe stage as envoys of that growing power in the East — beginning with Baptiste La Lande, that doubtful French Creole who furnished Zebulon M. Pike with an excuse for his visit; then the long train of picturesque and daring Santa Fe traders, convoying Kit Carson and Josiah Gregg; then the soldiers — Kearny, and Doniphan, and Sumner, heroes of many fields; but in my judgment, with the possible exception of an advocate who emerged from Santa Fe in 1923 to defend them, no other American may be said to have so vitally affected the fortunes of the Pueblo Indians.

Calhoun's letter of appointment, signed by William Medill, then Commissioner of Indian Affairs at Washington, contains language to engage those who have known "the Pueblo Indians of New Mexico,"[1] and of especial

[1] There are in Arizona and New Mexico to-day, including the "reservation" Hopi and Zuñi tribes, about 12,800 "pueblo-type" Indians; but because of their confirmed and patented Spanish grants of land, bringing to them a unique status among Indian tribes, 8200 of these natives located in Valencia, Bernalillo, Sandoval, Santa Fe, Taos, and Rio Arriba counties are grouped and nominated by the Government as "the Pueblo Indians of New Mexico," a label having a precise legal and political meaning. Their problems do not include or affect the Zuñi and the Hopi tribes, and the term will not be

THE PIONEER OFFICIAL, JAMES S. CALHOUN 3

interest to the few who, like myself, have followed in Calhoun's footsteps.

My own survey and acquaintance with these curious people of the adobe towns began on September 1, 1919, seventy years after Calhoun pitched his camp on the dusty outskirts of the Villa Real de Santa Fe de San Francisco, and the comparisons I shall draw between the events of two so widely separated periods will prove, I think, that Pueblo conditions found by Calhoun in the year of the great Gold Rush had not been clarified or settled in the year of the Treaty of Versailles.

That camouflage of modesty devised for and meekly donned by those who have not engaged in battles or attained the wisdom of fourscore years (when it is often too late to assert anything) should restrain me from comparing my little work in a restricted field with that of the great Indian Agent, who had the "comprehension" of all the Southwest Indians, from the Jicarilla Apache and the Ute north of Santa Fe, westward through the vast Navajo and Hopi country to the Grand Cañon, thence along the Rio Colorado to the baking lands of the Mohave, and south from Santa Fe through Apache ranges to where the Rio Grande marked the new division with Old Mexico. But having had both Navajo and Hopi in charge for years, and having visited places of Calhoun's jurisdiction to which he did not dare venture (indeed, of which he never heard), including a more recent view of the Mohaves and Chemehuevis in their sun-scorched Colorado River domain, I may present views and draw conclusions that he was unable to procure, and certainly could not be expected to imagine.

---

used in this book to embrace any of the pueblo stock not possessed of this peculiar and unique Indian legal status.

In any event, whatever the value of my experiences elsewhere, we both observed most closely and administered the affairs of the Pueblo Indians of New Mexico; and as no other of their Agents serving between 1849 and 1928 has given a record of his service to the public, this present record may not be futile. H. L. Mencken has remarked that Indian Agents are doubtless able to read and write after a fashion. A bitter comment; but one they, with the exception of the late "Major" James McLaughlin and possibly myself, deserve. But they have not all been inarticulate. The examination of old reports has caused me amazement at the verity of their prophecies and the sanity of their conclusions. But these chronicles are buried in the files. For the most part they have been willing to accept silently the husks of office, and have permitted themselves to become inert, colorless, and mute through servitude.

Dr. Johnson once recalled a passage in Goldsmith's *Vicar of Wakefield*, which, in his opinion, the poet was fool enough afterward to expunge — "I do not love a man who is zealous for nothing!" Had Goldsmith been an Indian Agent, one could understand his erasing this very fine sentiment; but perhaps he was thinking only of some indifferent patron. There have been and are Indian officials zealous for nothing, but of these was not Calhoun. Hardly was he on the ground before he was investigating, reporting, advising, recommending. That was in 1849. Some of his most important proposals, wrenched back to life by the galvanic battery of public opinion, were beginning to function in 1924.

Calhoun's record, save for brief historical mention, would have been lost perhaps but for a peculiar combination of red-taped happenings. In 1913, the Bureau of Indian

THE PIONEER OFFICIAL, JAMES S. CALHOUN

Affairs, having failed to procure a sufficient appropriation of funds from Congress with which to classify properly and safeguard its historical records, wished to use what money was available, and, since it was prevented by the quirk of an auditor's mind from purchasing filing equipment, somehow had a stroke of genius in determining to have edited and published a set of historical papers. Aside from this fateful twisting of dollars and pink vouchers, the public and I are indebted to the excellent work of Miss Annie H. Abel, who retrieved Calhoun's reports from the dust-encrusted vaults of the Pension Office and prepared *The Official Correspondence of James S. Calhoun*, accompanied by old maps, and issued as a public document. The work is of great value to those who would know more of our colorful Southwest beginnings and who would gain a partial view of the natives who inhabit that area which I called, in an earlier volume, "the Enchanted Empire." I do not believe that the fullest value of Miss Abel's work has been appreciated, or may be, unless it is interpreted or illuminated by modern comparisons and illustrated by that wonderful little instrument, the camera obscura.

It is not possible to paint a modern picture of the Pueblo Indians of New Mexico without mentioning their appointed guardians — such men as James R. Garfield, the late Franklin K. Lane, John Barton Payne, and that recent and retired patron, Albert Bacon Fall. If criticism has snared any one of these former Great White Fathers, the public, always doubtful of criticism, has had time in which to judge of its value. Should I endeavor to procure for any one of them a just consideration, please do not accuse me of political partisanship. I was merely an Indian Agent in New Mexico, — a very simple one,—having been arbitrarily ordered there by Cato Sells, then Commissioner of Indian Affairs.

In the early months of 1919, while acting as Agent for the Hopi-Navajo province then known as the Moqui Reservation, I was offered the superintendency of the Mescalero Apache Indian Agency in southern New Mexico, an offer that was withdrawn after I had packed my gear, filed a $75,000 bond, and camped in Keams Cañon for months awaiting final orders. I rejoiced when relieved of this assignment. Many years before, the Mescalero Apache country had been described to me by its Agent as "the Switzerland of America," a sobriquet that it splendidly deserves; but in my time in the field, even before the passing of the Wilson Administration, no sane Indian Agent wished to administer affairs in Fall's back yard. I had no earnest wish to leave the Hopi Indians, but I did not protest the subsequent transfer to the Pueblo provinces, with Agency headquarters at Albuquerque, New Mexico, because my knowledge and appreciation of the pueblo type, gained from the Hopi, would be of value at a Pueblo post. I had studied with considerable interest the history of the Pueblo Indians, and could look forward with some pleasure to the job of advancing their well-being. It seemed to me that they had a future, whereas it would be generations before the Hopi and the Navajo, as tribes, would advance clearly within the zone of civilization according to our standards. And however one views the Indian, with whatever of sentiment or admiration or affection, he cannot be diverted from laboring toward this proposed destination.

It should not be odious to compare my brief work of 1919–1922 with Calhoun's of 1849–1852, since in entirely dissimilar times so many conditions were similar. He

THE PIONEER OFFICIAL, JAMES S. CALHOUN

found the frontier raw and crude, and its long delays and waiting and lack of support from Washington irksome and wearing.[1] Leave out the word "frontier," and that was my case exactly. All the forces opposed to Calhoun were more or less savage and untamed, but some small part of them had been civilized or beaten into submission in those seventy intervening years. Nevertheless, I faced people as ignorant and as unreasoning as did Calhoun, and the alcalde of remote New Mexican districts was no better in my day than in his.

But my office commanded both the telephone and the telegraph. Washington, and even some desert points, were but a few minutes or hours distant, while Calhoun must await the mail "from the States" moving under guard along those seven hundred and seventy miles of the Santa Fe Trail between his office and Independence, Missouri. Once he complained that forty-five days had passed without a mail, and, with its arrival, no advices from Washington.

Where he had but one interpreter and several assistants, I was responsible for the work and vagaries of about one hundred employees, and could influence that of unofficial

[1] Extract from Calhoun's commission as Indian Agent, evidencing Washington's knowledge of Southwest Indian conditions: "So little is known here of the condition and situation of the Indians in that region that no specific instructions relative to them can be given at present; and the Department relies on you to furnish it with such statistical and other information as will give a just and full understanding of every particular relating to them, embracing the names of the tribes, their location, the distance between the tribes, the probable extent of territory owned or claimed by each respectively, and the tenure by which they hold or claim it; their manners and habits, their disposition and feelings towards the United States, Mexico and whites generally, and towards each other, whether hostile or otherwise; whether the several tribes speak different languages, and when different the apparent analogies between them, and also what laws and regulations for their government are necessary, and how far the law regulating trade and intercourse with the Indian tribes . . . will, if extended over that country, properly apply to the Indians there and to the trade and intercourse with them, and what modification, if any, will be required to produce the greatest degree of efficiency."

helpers. Whereas he would have to spend fifteen days' hard travel with troops between the Jemez pueblo and the Cañon de Chelly, fast trains on the border and at least workable motors to the interior of these districts were at my disposal. He had lived in a mud hut, and I inherited an old mansion surrounded by a beautiful garden. Whereas his annual appropriation of funds was $3800 including his salary, mine was well above $100,000 yearly, and that was inadequate to maintain efficiently the activities supervised. To the itemizing observer, the only close similarity was to be found in our wages. He drew $1500 per annum at a time when mechanics were satisfied with a daily ration and forty dollars a month; I netted less than $2200 annually when mechanics demanded and received from eight to eleven dollars a day. Such is the progress of governmental standards, and an exact barometer by which to gauge its Civil Service efficiency.

It is my purpose to show — clearly, if that be not beyond me, and perhaps with some amusement and pleasure — just what forces had affected the Pueblo Indians of New Mexico from the time of their discovery by the great Conquistador, Don Francisco Vasquez de Coronado, in 1540-1541 (deceased), and the advent of Messrs. Fall and Bursum in 1921 (retired). There is an excuse for including Coronado, an historical character long undervalued — a king's protégé, a ruthless man in armor, a picaresque figure known in Mexico as early as 1535. He was ambitious and fearless, perhaps unscrupulous; but he is tempting to the imagination, for it was his tremendous fortune to swagger *first* across the vast stage of Arizona and New Mexico, a place then as unknown to white men as the planet Mars. His figure appears mistily

A SANTA FE ADOBE
Built in the 1860's

THE SANGRE DE CRISTOS

in the dawn of our American history, looks wonderingly at the fabled cities of Cibola, strides across the deserts, stalks up the Rio Grande, and passes a winter entrenched and barricaded at Tiguex or Puaray, as you will, somewhere close to the present little town of Bernalillo. His long march across the Plains into Kansas, through Texas and Oklahoma, is epic. His explorations, and those of his lieutenants, left footprints that have not been erased, as monumental as those of Columbus.

There is the dramatic excuse for once again picturing his vanguard of dons and scriveners, adventurers and tonsured prelates. More than one François Villon, more than one Don César de Bazan, followed in his train. His host included slaves and princes, gentlemen and bravoes, butchers and martyrs. Old Rio Grande, rolling its muddy floods along, looked on this curious company, and but for the quite similar *entrada* of Oñate, nearly fifty years later, has not seen the like since.

Save for a proper comprehension of Pueblo griefs of yesterday, however, there is no excuse for including Messrs. Fall and Bursum, unless it be that, in the course of otherwise brilliant careers, they too touched the empire of the Pueblo Indians, and, having planned a charitable campaign in a refined manner (Cardenas only tried to burn them at the stake), brought these simple *amigos* to plead before an American Congress for justice that had not been denied them by Spanish kings.

Many times, during my work in Arizona, I had encountered representatives of the Pueblo Indians of New Mexico. The Hopi-Navajo country had been the refuge of their ancestors after the great revolt of 1680; and the Tewas, who had settled at the First Mesa of the Hopi in 1700, and who came from the neighborhood of the San

Juan pueblo, maintained a link in language and sympathy with their distant kinsmen; and, too, there is a close link of clanship and ritual between the Hopi proper and the Laguna people. Whereas once the Hopi made toilsome pilgrimages to Santa Fe, their ancient capital, to present petitions and to invite controversy, in my time they traveled little. But the various pueblos, now and then, sent in visitors and traders, perhaps semidelegates. In this wise I met and talked with men from Taos, San Juan, and Laguna. The picturesque dress of the Taos Indians, the braiding of their hair, and the regularity of their handsome countenances, resembling the traditional warriors of the Plains, was in strong contrast with my Hopi and Navajo charges; and, too, I had heard, frequently and from afar, — the distance lending both interest and enchantment, — the legend of their ancient, honorable, and democratic form of pueblo government. Once to me came a traveler, armed with letters from the Commissioner, who wished to compare the sluggish Hopi civilization with that of the more advanced Pueblo people. She had devoted a monograph to the virtues of the Rio Grande organizations, and I devoured it. Then the government engineer, Herbert F. Robinson, having the direction of pueblo water development, also had charge of this same work in the Navajo-Hopi desert. I enjoyed many talks with him, and with his subordinates, read their reports, and without a twinge of conscience purloined many photographs from their unofficial files, some of which are reproduced in this volume.

Calhoun approached the pueblos from the East, from Washington via St. Louis and the Santa Fe Trail. He had to wait in St. Louis eight days for a military escort that would guarantee the safety of himself and two other officials en route to their respective posts, the Indian Agent to be stationed at "the Salt Lake, California," and the Collector appointed to that office at San Francisco. The Indian Agents were allowed one year's salary in advance, and "their traveling expenses from St. Louis to the place of rendezvous" by order of the Secretary. It is interesting to me, although it may not amuse those who have not served Uncle Sam, that Calhoun requested of the Military Department the use of two "ambulances," for himself, his daughters, and other members of his party. Ten days after his appointment he had notified the Secretary that provision must be made for the transportation of fourteen persons who would accompany him to the frontier post. These were not all members of his family, it appearing that a group of friends and former soldiers went with him, expecting, as did so many of the early Westerners, that the virgin territory would provide them opportunity and service. Some few of them may have counted on Calhoun's military dreams; others would grow up with the country.

And in 1851, or two years after his arrival in New Mexico, Calhoun was acridly debating with Washington auditors exceptions to his accounts, and especially to his having purchased an ambulance, since the Quartermaster at St. Louis had been unable to furnish him one. Calhoun stated that, aside from the need for transportation equipment to cross the Plains, unless he had acquired some such vehicle for the carrying of his camp outfit in the field it would have been impossible for him to have properly discharged his official duties. But you see, military ambulances were not being used then on Pennsylvania Avenue, and how was an auditing official, who hoofed through Washington mud, to know that the Santa

Fe Trail and the dim routes to the pueblos required anything other than "foot cavalry"? Calhoun was entirely too bitter and sarcastic when complaining of these exceptions. Why should he have found it necessary to purchase mules, or, once having purchased them, to feed them? Could he not have walked from Santa Fe to the Cañon de Chelly, via Jemez pueblo, and on occasion to Old Laguna, Zuñi, and Taos? Why was a teamster employed to wrangle his field equipment? Could he not have attended to these simple chores himself? I am inclined to think that this Calhoun, despite his military experience in the Mexican War, was a trifle indolent and fastidious. His statement that, had he dispensed with the teamster, he would himself have been useless as the Department's representative, strikes one as evasive and irrelevant, if not irreverent. Or, in any case, why did he not evidence a spirit of humility and due subordination, and permit the teamster to join with Lieutenant-Colonel Washington in making the first American Treaty with the Navajo Nation, while he (Calhoun) dutifully looked after those precious mules? So the first Governor of New Mexico, then installed in his high office, occupied himself with justifying items of horse feed, subsistence for menials and Indians, farrier's expenses, guide fees, and all the petty details that an auditor in the States could not understand, and therefore could not approve of, while turbulent New Mexico fomented around him.

My own journey in proceeding to my charge over the same people was from the West, across the painted Navajo desert, coming from the Hopi pueblos that Calhoun so often planned to visit and could not. It required a wagon for little more than one hundred miles, and I knew better than to buy the wagon or charge its hire. He

A STREET IN THE JEMEZ PUEBLO

had greeted Hopi delegations as strange and peculiar people from afar, whereas in my case they were friends, unconscious interpreters between me and my new charges; and, in a way, my sponsors, for the word is passed about the Indian country, one province to another, and woe to the white man who comes heralded by the smoke of suspicion.

And so I went from the warm, parched, and isolated country of the Hopi-Navajo in northern Arizona, a wondrous land of eroded cañons and rugged mesas and semiarid highlands, the whole having a general tone of saffron and red, to the blue-and-silver atmosphere of the New Mexican valleys, where once again I would see fog-like mists arising from rivers, and hear the constant murmur of streams, some of them babbling down through wooded fairylands. And instead of finding the crumbling foundations of long-lost pueblos, half obliterated by great drifting sand dunes, and speculating where Fray José de Espeleta, of the Kingdom of Navarre, had his bath at Oraibi, or just where Fray Francisco de Porras, of Villanueva de los Infantes, Spain, had lived at Awatobi in 1629, I would see the Franciscan ruins dating from the early seventeenth century, and move among a people whose modern history, at least, had been most thoroughly documented. In the Hopi country, standing on the edge of the First Mesa to overlook the orchards and desolation of sand in the plains below, one with a vivid imagination could picture those early padres at their orisons and tasks, and the occasional gleam of a Spanish spear; but in the Pueblo country — at the Jemez Abbey, for instance — one could find the ruined cloister of Fray Juan de Jesus, of Granada — perhaps the very cell in which that zealous monk, Fray Gerónimo Zarate-Salmeron, penned his *doctrina* in the Jemez language, and made the first drafts of his *Relaciones de Nuevo Mexico* in the period 1617–1626. It was not necessary to pause and imagine the sound of old mission bells emerging from the twilight of the past; they called to Mass and spoke eloquently of history in each pueblo.

The Territory of New Mexico, which included all of the present state of Arizona and a small bit of Colorado (nearly 240,000 square miles), was established by Act of Congress, September 9, 1850; and by letter of January 9, 1851, Daniel Webster, Secretary of State, notified James S. Calhoun that the President had, with the advice and consent of the Senate, appointed him Governor of the new Territory. It was not until March 2 that a military escort conducted the Indian Agent from his adobe Agency to his new chambers in the old adobe Palace. As the governors of the various territories were also Superintendents of Indian Affairs, Calhoun had added another nerve-racking job to his already harassed shoulders.

The scope of this volume does not admit of the inclusion of his record as Governor — scarcely an outline of his problems. Political conditions in the new Territory were most trying, and certainly the Governor, sick or well, was no Job. I have no space in which to analyze and justify his proposed, and of course rejected, military plans; his acrid correspondence with army officers he thought inert; the annoying politics being played by a peasant citizenry; the religious influences that were by no means sacrosanct and only a trifle removed from the mediæval; or the daily embarrassment of an empty treasury. Moreover, he was to suffer from private sorrow and physical disorders. In his second year as Governor, after having the scurvy, one of the then pleasant features of Santa Fe life, he wrote Colonel E. V. Sumner that for four weeks he had been unable to stand unassisted. Much of his acrimony and criticism of this officer may be ascribed to this condition. Calhoun was one of those men who manage to form a fairly accurate estimate of their own abilities; and he chafed from inaction and delay. Many of these have their specifications accepted after death, but the human race, devoted to submissive mediocrity, is bitterly opposed to honoring drafts on appreciation during the subject's lifetime. Calhoun's whole administration, his every report and suggestion, show that he was in spirit the military man first and the civil official afterward. Indeed, it was a job for a dictator.

But I am not confident that he would have found Sumner's task a simple one had it been given him, and had he had the health to prosecute it. In October, Sumner reported the scope of his work during the summer of 1851. He had reached Santa Fe in July, and he at once abolished its military post. Having established Fort Union in the Mora Valley, one hundred and ten miles east of Santa Fe and within striking distance of the Indian hostiles that terrorized the Santa Fe Trail, he proceeded to withdraw troops from other towns and to establish additional frontier posts — Fort Fillmore near El Paso and Fort Conrad at Valverde, both on the Rio Grande, and the famous Fort Defiance in the Navajo country, now the principal Navajo Indian Agency. He claimed that discipline and economy justified this change in methods, for he considered the towns vicious. He reported that if Fort Defiance did not stop Navajo depredations, nothing would but the extermination of the tribe. His views on Indian fighting in these deserts may cause a smile, but they were fundamentally sound when the type of cavalry mount used, the problem of field forage, and the protection of the animals are considered; and therefore he proposed to dot the frontier with posts apart from towns, from which shorter cavalry expeditions, with select mounts, could be made against the enemy, while infantry held the stations.

But my purpose is to show, not how Governor Calhoun disputed with Colonel Sumner, but how Indian Agent Calhoun viewed the Pueblo Indians of New Mexico in those parlous times of the frontier. If it should be advanced that my comment is prejudiced, in that I admire because I agree, then this charge will rest practically on all those who have faced the same problems with these Indians, their neighbors, and their local conditions; and may be as generously extended to the United States Supreme Court.

Having arrived at Santa Fe, July 22, 1849, we find that in October Calhoun transmitted to Washington a report of conditions that was singularly complete. Before the end of January 1850, having found that he would receive from Washington but little assistance, — and that little of no value, — he began legislating for himself, issuing without authority an order to control trade with the Indians. Somebody had to act. The populace was seething with resentment; even the peaceful Pueblo Indians were restless and suspicious; and traders were furnishing both whiskey and ammunition to savages. Traders are in the womb of every war.

Briefly, Calhoun appreciated promptly ten significant points with regard to the Pueblo Indians of New Mexico: —

THE PIONEER OFFICIAL, JAMES S. CALHOUN

He comprehended the peculiar compromise between mediæval Catholicism and paganism in their superficial religion, and the subtle influences of foreign priests and wily *caciques.*

He sensed at once the actual impotency for good in the Pueblo tribal governments.

He saw the necessity for a native court to adjudicate all cases purely Indian; and he pointed out where the Act of 1834 (government and control of Indian tribes) was inadequate, though even it did not apply then to New Mexico.[1]

He saw the evils of the liquor trade, and all the intrigue and menace of the traders who kept both tame and savage Indians fomented and equipped for warlike raids.

He understood clearly the exact feeling that has always existed between the Mexican-type citizen and the Pueblo Indian — one that exists to-day: "The Mexicans and the Pueblo Indians have not one feeling in common."

He refused to countenance the suggested consolidation of the Pueblo Indians, knowing they were not in spirit a tribe, but diversified factions of a similar people with their hearts and altars in certain fixed locations.

He witnessed the farcical features of Mexican alcalde courts, and declared that the Indian might as well expect the millennium as justice from an ignorant and prejudiced system.

He considered the Pueblo Indians unfitted to exercise the franchise, although he did not question that they

---

[1] The laws regulating trade and intercourse with the Indian tribes, "or such provisions of the same as may be applicable," were extended over the Indian country of New Mexico by Act of July 27, 1851. However, the fact that the "military law" of 1834, plainly enacted to govern *savage tribes*, was not in every particular applicable to the civilized (?) Indians acquired in 1848 (that is, the Pueblo Indians) has always hampered Indian Agents when seeking to control and protect them.

were entitled to it by the Treaty. He saw that such exercise would be farce in the face of opposing majorities surrounding them; and he feared that they would become the pawns of politicians.

He felt all the misunderstanding and bitterness that would arise out of garbled and prejudiced interpretation of the Treaty of Guadalupe Hidalgo, and he recommended that Congress accept the obligation to clarify the indefinite clauses as to citizenship.

But the most memorable of his warnings concerned the necessity for immediately settling the land problems — the clarification of Indian pueblo titles — at the beginning of the American administration.

In November, 1849, he reported: —

Various representations have been made to me by Pueblo Indians of Mexican and Spanish encroachments upon their grants, and it may be that many of these encroachments will be difficult of adjustment. There is no doubt that villages are built upon grounds rightfully belonging to Indian pueblos. These grounds were seized by those who now occupy them, at a moment when resistance by the legitimate owners was impracticable, and justice to the Indians is too often withheld. This subject, at this moment, is the cause of much anxiety and irritation with the Pueblo Indians.

Perhaps a Commission to examine the tenure by which the respective parties hold possession of their lands . . . would relieve the present anxiety of the Indians. . . . [1]

If I am correct in these observations and conclusions, culled from the mass of his correspondence, comment is superfluous.

[1] The Commission, to be known as the Pueblo Lands Board, was authorized by Congress, *June 7, 1924.*

II

THE CITY OF THE HOLY FAITH

> GREAT shadows fall across my floor —
> One Pike, a subtle, anxious guest;
> Calhoun, the troubled Governor,
> And Carson, on some Desert quest;
>   Then Sumner, from his forts, and he
>   Who penned the tale of Galilee.
>
>   — "El Palacio"

THE Santa Fe that received Calhoun in 1849 is described best by his own comparison of it with the adjacent Indian pueblos: "The general character of their houses are superior to those of Santa Fe."

It is likely that he was just getting miserably acquainted with the leaky propensities of an adobe roof, and, as he wrote this in October, I fancy that his rheumatism was bothering him. But there is something of critical justice in the picture when one examines the oldest of adobes to be found there to-day. Isleta pueblo has many finer houses.

This Santa Fe to which Calhoun introduced himself was little if at all different then from the Spanish frontier town of 1800 or the Mexican province capital of 1822, when it had less than 5000 inhabitants. When Gregg saw Santa Fe in 1831, he thought he approached a series of brick kilns. The low flat-roofed houses, irregular of line, having few windows but always a number of outer doors — one to each room — and smoke wreathing from many plastered chimney pots, are not unlike earthen ovens in appearance. Spanish-type towns do not change quickly. The race is not a hurried one, having a drowsy routine and many lackadaisical modes. It sincerely believes in and dogmatically practises its faith in fiestas, siestas, and mañanas. When Calhoun paid a call, he should have said at the door, "Deo gracias!" and, if his Spanish host had nothing against him, the answer would be a long recitative in praise of God and the Holy Virgin before reaching "Pase adelante." Those who have time to put a litany before a cheery good-morning are not likely to affect architecture in a hurry.

This was the northern metropolis of a republic still in swaddling clothes, and Calhoun found no considerable changes in the customs of the people or the atmosphere they had inherited from a semimediæval past. The inhabitants were not unfriendly; they were curious to know how this change in sovereignty would affect them and their daily routine; and of course, like children, they expected a golden future to arrive on the heels of the American cavalry, since the lusty East had in many ways flaunted its riches in their faces. The enormous trade of the Santa Fe Trail was still growing. Whereas in 1822 not more than sixty traders had transported $15,000 worth of merchandise to Santa Fe, in 1846 the cost of goods freighted was close to a million dollars, with $400,000 invested in wagons and outfits, wages and insurance, and the annual profits were estimated at an equal figure. In that year, 375 wagons, 1700 mules, 2000 oxen, and 500 men were employed in this trade. By 1866 there came into New Mexico 3000 wagons belonging to traders, exclusive of government transportation. Gregg's *Commerce of the Prairies* furnishes a virile picture of the times. And it must be kept in mind that the majority of these frontier people, whose former allegiance to Spain and Mexico had been abruptly severed, were of the mestizo class.

But however one may attempt to explain the local atmosphere, the fact remains patent that the prospect could not have been inviting to an official of the American temperament; and I cannot refrain from repeating my own comment with respect to those who approach the fatalistic Hopi Indian of to-day and propose to change everything in an afternoon. Such a job is too large for an afternoon, and in Santa Fe the environment was that of dawdling coöperation, procrastination, and smouldering intrigue. In the centres of the population, and in strict accordance with Spanish habit and usage, a few prominent men, whose wealth commanded respect, and the army officers and the clergy, had been the ruling power; and naturally what remained of their former influence would continue to pervade the diffident subject. For many years money had been the passport to judicial and executive favors, and the thing known as "justice" had been invoked and procured by those who could pay for it. Those who ruled had exercised a monopoly of it. The peon class seldom sought it.

Given a populace of this type, that influence which should have been for the greatest possible educational good, if intelligently used and directed, had been practically destroyed about the year 1829 through the banishment of the Franciscans as an organization. Many of the missions were then secularized and many others left without priests. Iturbide's revolution had alienated that royal support which had sustained the friars and maintained the missions. With the birth of the Mexican

Republic a great hostility toward them had become manifest. Therefore one stable element, and perhaps the only dependable one, of the means of government had disappeared. A people of this sort, unlettered, attenuated by distances, having no means toward a cultivation of what little patriotism and imagination it possessed, must be sustained by something; and its old sustenance and leaven, even among the Pueblo Indians, had been religion — the only religion that had ever been presented to it. The people had no choice in the matter. They were yet to be educated in the separation of Church and State. One might say that religion had been their sole source of entertainment even. So, in the circumstances, there could result nothing but a period of stagnation that would generate resentment and suspicion toward any government not ready to supply an acceptable equivalent. Even the secular branch of the Church had its political terrors. In 1846, when the Mexican Governor, Armijo, busied himself to resist the American forces, he demanded all the money, plate, and live stock in the possession of the vicar-general, and then promptly departed from the scene of possible hostilities to find himself something of sanctuary in the remote distances. Indeed, this sounds very Mexican, if not modern.

Referring to the early stage of this period, Bancroft states that the Mexican Government still paid, or at least made appropriations for, the *sinodos* of from twenty-three to twenty-seven Franciscan friars, who acted for the most part as curates at the Mexican settlements and made occasional visits to the Indian pueblos. Thus, as late as 1847, we find the very last of the Franciscans located at Isleta, having the remote districts of Laguna and Acoma as *visitas*.

Conditions had little improved at the time of the American occupation. And Calhoun, always most vigorous and patriotic in his impulses, plunged against this wall of native construction for nearly three years, to dash himself to pieces eventually. This was not the West that Boone and others had opened up; it was "the Southwest," a marvelously different thing.

Its patch-quilt of civilization had journeyed through three hundred years by southern routes from the Iberian Peninsula, and into its motley Mediterranean temperament had absorbed everything of the semitropics, including that curious alloyage of the desert Indian. Any vigorous effort was met and enervated by the patient psychology that sun and sand and alkali and wind and long summer days and toilsome distances had produced. It was like trying to hustle the red-hot sunset, murkily obscured by a swirling dust storm. This Spanish sun was setting, but it would require its every measured second of inexorable time.

To present a sketch of the Pueblo Indians of New Mexico, Santa Fe — and whatever of civilization it reflected — must be taken as the hub about which they revolved. During three several periods — Spanish, Mexican, American — it had been their capital, the seat of whatever of order, justice, and intelligence was available to protect or to guide them. To-day, one of the two Pueblo Indian Agencies is to be found there, and when Indian Agent at Albuquerque, having quite three fourths of the Pueblo population in charge, I found it most necessary to visit frequently the Holy City in connection with their business. In their last revolt — that of 1922-1923 against the Bursum Bill — the three distinguished advocates who sought to educate two the air as the guards assumed their duties on each side of the shrine. The Gobernador, bare of head, and his civic assistants, having made obeisance, took up stations too for appointed periods, and the faithful of the community approached to pay homage to this representation of their Saint, who, for one long day, would bless their plaza with his presence. They brought gifts of many sorts to litter the carpet of the shrine. The candles burned and guttered in the sunlit desert air. And one act of the fiesta had reached its dramatic crisis.

On this particular day a new feature was scheduled. At the far end of the plaza, where the dance floor had been laid, the Hopi band announced a patriotic air and flags were raised. The terraces and house tops filled as I had seen them so many times among the Hopi when the pagan rites of snake worship were enacted. All save the guards left the shrine to hear Agent Lonergan's farewell. With the respectful silence and courteous attention that especially mark the Pueblo Indian in council, they listened. They had suffered Agents before, and have endured them since, to whom they cheerfully would have tied a can. But Philip T. Lonergan had been more than their appointed head — he had been their friend, and had been with them in the front line of their battles. They bore him both respect and affection. There was a deep quiet in the plaza, for this Chief was about to say "Adiós."

Then with a reference to their new Agent, who, having been so long with their Hopi brothers, could be expected the better to understand them, I was introduced, and, in accordance with our traditions as well as theirs, had to make a speech. I am not well trained in the art of making speeches, but somehow I plunged through it, stressing the continued education of their children, and

EL PALACIO

The old adobe palace of the Conquistadors, built in 1609

THE CITY OF THE HOLY FAITH

rough-hewn logs for pillars, and its grated prisonlike windows. Down its side street ambles a burro, prodded by the staff of a figure whose dark face and unweeded beard show foreign blood; and in the shade of the Plaza edge is parked a load of firewood, racked on an ancient wagon, having a team of these patient animals, leaning together, somnolent, dreaming on their possible chance for rations once this cargo is sold. They are solidly blocked-out creatures, seldom looking gaunt or undernourished, thanks to that ability to absorb life from the dregs of civilization.

> I can go a day on a sardine can,
>   And two on a scrap of leather;
> I have lived a week on a Chinese fan,
> And 't is even plain that I sometimes gain
>   On only a change of weather.

On the wagon seat the owner sleeps, knowing that a purchaser will come when he will come. It is the past, drifting back, except that the Palace no longer exhibits those strings of Indian ears — bounty-vouchers — once so prominent.

Beside the Palace the towers of Santa Fe's new museum rise, the replica of an old mission and its *convento*, and farther down the street one can view crumbling adobes where once the caravans halted. The little crooked alleys, just wide enough for one vehicle, have not all disappeared, and they end in dusty lanes lined with lilacs and tamarisks, and lead to rising slopes set with vineyards. The Rio de Santa Fe purls under bridges down a glenlike arroyo, a brook but a handsbreadth wide. The Cathedral, a mass of saffron sandstone, lifts its bell tower as a watch above the city.

And beyond the Villa de Santa Fe is the glory of the eternal hills. There, arising in unexcelled splendor, lifts the snow-crowned diadem of the Sangre de Cristo Range. The newcomer may wonder at this name. Through a lens of crystal air and sunlight, these mountains show an ethereal blue, like some blue-robed saint in a snowy halo; and with approaching night they turn to vague masses of violet and purple and deepest green. But once in so often, as if to quiet critics, there steals over the Sangre de Cristos a strange and beautiful radiance. I fancy that some early cavalcade of the Spanish first viewed them in this startling transformation. For the whole vast bulk suddenly burns in the red of sacrifice, as if a flow of richest blood had instantly bathed it. Those sanguinary peaks, hovering over the old Villa, where so much of blood has been shed, cause one to think of the many years when the vesper bell sounded through a quiet that was simply a mask, smiling in the faces of brooding enemies. The Blood of Christ is no idle name.

The exact age of Santa Fe has interested all those who have written of New Spain. Twitchell says there is mention of Oñate leaving Santa Fe for his western tour, 1604–1605; but he concludes: "It is abundantly proved, by documentary evidence, that from San Gabriel the seat of government was moved to Santa Fe, and this appears to have been done in 1605." However, the latest Franciscan historian, Father Zephyrin Engelhardt, in the *Franciscan Herald* of July 1920, quoting from original documents in the Ayer collection at Chicago, reaches the following conclusions: that Oñate resigned in 1607; that his resignation was accepted in January 1609 with instructions that he should await the arrival of his successor; that the orders to Don Pedro de Peralta included

THE CITY OF THE HOLY FAITH 27

directions for the founding of "a Villa," a matter that was known at the time of Oñate's resignation, but the execution of which had been delayed; that Peralta could not have arrived in New Mexico until late in the autumn of 1609, and that the "Villa" could not have been organized until the autumn of that year; and that such "Villa," there being no other, must be the city of Santa Fe, the exact date of its founding being unknown.

This was in the reign of Philip III. Great Philip II had been in the grave but little more than a decade, and Elizabeth of England had died only six years before. When the Spanish officials gathered to the founding of Santa Fe, a little craft named the Half Moon was cautiously feeling its way through the waters of New York Harbor to explore the Hudson; Jamestown was but a doubtful experiment in colonization; Quebec had been established in name only; and the Mayflower's passenger list was a thing yet to be. In London, a new play, *Cymbeline*, was being enacted by the King's men at the Globe, and perhaps Peralta passed more than one Santa Fe siesta reading in the first edition of *Don Quixote de La Mancha*, the author of which, having failed to gain a post in the New World, was living in Spain in poverty.

The old Palace on the Plaza embraces with its four walls Santa Fe's whole saga. It is the heart of the historic Southwest. Its roof sheltered Spanish councils coincident with that first stormy one on the James River, and before there was government at New Amsterdam and Plymouth. Its audience chamber has seated the Conquistador, the captain-general, the military dictator, the *jefe politico*, the Indian Agent, and the governors of four nations. Here the Spaniards were beleaguered in the revolt of 1680, and their harassed leader gave the order to execute forty-seven of the Pueblo insurgents in the Plaza, only to decide on evacuation of the town a few days later. Here the triumphant Pueblo Indians, headed by their war captains and caciques, burned the Spanish archives and destroyed the sacred vessels of the Church; here they cried that they had killed God and the Virgin Mary, and, arrayed in the vestments of the friars, rode through the town sounding their war chants, after having scrubbed away the effects of baptism with amole in the waters of the Rio de Santa Fe. Here, in 1693, De Vargas gave thanks to this same Virgin for having aided him to recapture the city, and the despairing Pueblo chieftain hanged himself from the Palace rafters, while seventy of his followers were executed in the Plaza. Here, more than a century later, one Pike, an American officer, red-haired, smiling, and almost impudently confident, was brought a prisoner before the Spanish Governor, Alencaster, charged with being an invader of Spanish soil; and Don Facundo Melgares, who would be the very last of the Spanish Governors, was directed to take Pike as a prisoner into Mexico. Here, in 1822, a new nation raised its eagle-and-cactus banner to signify that the Spanish Bourbons no longer ruled New Spain and Santa Fe. From these doors, in 1837, the Mexican Governor Perez started to suppress insurrection in the north, at the pueblo of Taos, where that turbulent faction had been joined by warriors of San Juan, San Ildefonso, Nambe, Santa Clara, and other pueblos now extinct. Shortly thereafter the victorious Indians carried Perez's head in triumph to their camp, not five hundred yards from the Palace, and on the succeeding day a Pueblo Indian, one José Gonzalez, entered it as Governor of New Mexico, his brief reign ending early in 1838 when, being caught after a farcical battle, he was instantly shot without trial. In the principal reception room, Governor Martinez, in 1844, killed the chief of the Utes by one crushing blow of his chair.

But the era of violence was approaching its end, and the curtain slowly descending on Indian and Spanish and Mexican plays. The pennon of the savage, the red-and-gold oriflamme of royal Spain, the green-and-white Mexican standard, were soon to be succeeded by a star-spangled banner not seventy years old. In 1846 these Palace doors admitted Captain Philip St. George Cooke, who was received by the Mexican Governor as an American envoy. Six days later, August 18, 1846, the leading cavalry of the American Army of Occupation picketed their mounts in the streets; Brigadier-General Stephen Watts Kearny ordered the American flag raised over the old adobe Palace; a roar of guns in salute sounded from the batteries on the hills, and "the States" had come to Santa Fe!

These events may have startled the drowsy Villa momentarily, but it quickly resumed its routine of religious festivals and processions and siestas. Officials and money had changed, but values were still the extraordinary ones fixed by the frontier and the Santa Fe Trail trade. One can imagine Calhoun's consternation on a salary of $1500 per annum. Flour, bacon, and pork could be had only of the military commissaries, and more than once there was dispute as to supplying him. Sugar, fifty cents a pound; tea, one dollar and a quarter, and he describes it as "a poor article of gunpowder." In reporting these prices he states that he will have to expend another $1500 from private funds to supplement his salary, and he comments that "what would be quite liberal in the United States would be wholly inadequate in this Territory." He compares costs at Leavenworth and at Santa Fe, the transportation across the Plains being more than the value of the goods: —

	Leavenworth	Santa Fe
Lard	$.07½	$.17½
Flour	.02½	.12½
Bacon	.05	.15
Hams	.07	.17
Rice	.06	.16
Molasses	.44	1.44
Soap	.06	.16
Whiskey	.52	1.52
Value of five months' subsistence		$423.19
Transportation charges on same		528.49
Total cost at Santa Fe		$951.68

There were received 82½ gallons of whiskey, should any prohibition officer wish to investigate; and look at the Leavenworth price of it! This item, which should be strange to the "Indian country," he explains and justifies in his report of April 29, 1851: —

The Indians (Pueblos) are moody when they come to the Agency, if you do not give them sugar, coffee, and whiskey. The market retail price for sugar and coffee, fifty cents per pound each, and whiskey, $3.50 per gallon.

It was with the greatest reluctance that I gave them whiskey. There are several distilleries in the Territory which supply them with ardent spirits in exchange for their grain. In addition to which, unless I gave it to them at the Agency, they would roam through Santa Fe until they could find a small grocery that would indulge them. Thefts and bloody contests ensued, and I found it would be a matter of economy to give them a little at the Agency, and cause them to be watched until they were beyond the limits of the town. If Congress has passed laws sufficiently stringent, this pernicious habit may be abandoned.

Sixty-two years later this "habit" of the Pueblo Indians would invite attention to them, and result finally in the "Sandoval Decision" of the United States Supreme Court.

One of Governor Calhoun's last letters was directed to Colonel Sumner at Albuquerque, April 18, 1852, requesting troops to assist the civil authorities in maintaining order in Santa Fe. Owing to the lack of means to furnish them food in prison, a number of criminals had been turned loose on the public, and this, taken with the general attitude of disgruntled and believed disloyal citizens and rumors of Indian "devilment," to use Greiner's words, presented an alarming state of affairs. On the twenty-first of April, Calhoun as Governor and Sumner as Commander of the Ninth Military Department issued a joint notice to the public, stating that, should Calhoun be obliged to leave for the States, no interregnum would take place in the office of Governor, since the military authority would take charge of the executive office to make the preservation of law and order absolutely certain. The bitterness that had existed for a short time between Calhoun and Sumner was now at an end. The officer suggested that the Governor go to Fort Union and rest for a few days before starting on his long journey. In accordance with these arrangements, Calhoun shortly thereafter left the Territory of New Mexico. He had been at its head, as either Indian Agent or Governor, for two years and ten months.

Dry official reports are sometimes interesting, if not pathetic: —

SANTA FE, NEW MEXICO
May 31, 1852

HON. L. LEA
Commissioner of Indian Affairs
SIR : —

On Wednesday last Governor Calhoun left Fort Union for the States with very little probability of ever reaching there alive. He takes his coffin along with him.

Mr. Love, his son-in-law, and Mr. Whiting, his private secretary, are in company with him, and should he die on the road, will take charge of all his effects — the books and papers belonging to this office, and deliver them at the Department. ...

Very respectfully,
Your ob.'t Svt.
JOHN GREINER
Act. Supt. Ind. Aff. New Mexico

So Calhoun retraced his journey of '49, eastward, going home. Competent to the last, he carried his coffin with him. Somewhere close to Independence, Missouri, at the end of the long, dusty Santa Fe Trail, he reached his goal, probably in the shade of cottonwood trees as the military escort halted. He was buried with Masonic rites. The exact place of his grave is unknown.

Civil officials may have records as fine, were they understood, as their military contemporaries. The verity of Calhoun's Indian visions has outlived the effects of Sumner's desert activities. Had Calhoun been permitted to carry out his suggestions for the best interests of the Pueblo Indians of New Mexico, and for the organization of the embryonic state, his figure might grace the Santa

THE CITY OF THE HOLY FAITH

Fe Plaza as New Mexico's first and ablest administrator. As it is, a compilation of his reports, published when the purchase of filing cabinets was forbidden, reveals the official who without an army, and, one may say, without arms, sought to quiet and command a suspicious and hostile territory — an empire that contained four dissimilar and contentious races — that had been Indian and Spanish, and was Mexican; his task to Americanize it, as he had to Americanize his first adobe apartment.[1]

[1] Little known of Calhoun's early life or family. Believed to have been born near Abbeville, South Carolina, 1802 or 1803, although he referred to himself as a native of Georgia. In one family record he is shown as a brother of John C. Calhoun, in another as a half brother, and in still another as a first cousin. Married, December 1822, to Caroline Ann Simmons, of South Carolina, who died in 1828; and in February 1830 to Mrs. Annie V. Williamson, of Greene County, Georgia. In 1913 but two of his descendants survived — two great-granddaughters — living in Atlanta, Georgia.

After his second marriage he moved to Columbus, Georgia, and engaged in the shipping business, being the senior member of the firm of Calhoun & Boss. Supplied boats to the United States for use during the Second Seminole War. In the Mexican War he was captain in a company of Georgia volunteers (June 1846 to May 1847); later lieutenant-colonel, commanding a battalion of Georgia mounted volunteers, disbanded July 1848. — ABEL: *The Official Correspondence of James S. Calhoun*

III

LAGUNA

On the Feast of San José

The close of Mass! Now from the mission gate
Comes forth a pageant, bearing shoulder-high
Their patron Saint, in lace and gilt ornate —
With tapers, bells, and chanting they pass by
To march about the pueblo's old confine —
The criers warn that San Sebastian nears,
To find his throne within a plaza shrine,
To bless the pueblo, soothe its childish fears.

The padre leaves — his ceremony ends;
Now sounds another chant, a Desert cry!
With drum and dance the tribe's old god intends
To make this Christian feast a mockery.
A pagan masque that virtue fails to hide —
Was it for this the old Franciscans died?
— "Ite Missa Est"

My formal introduction to the Pueblo Indians of New Mexico, at Old Laguna, on September 19, 1919, the local fiesta time, was in acute contrast to my meeting with the Hopi and Navajo in the northern Arizona desert eight years before. I say "introduction" because this, the largest of the fiestas, attended by many Pueblo factions and by Navajo and Hopi Indians too, with perhaps a lone and stray Apache not altogether sure of his welcome, enabled me to have something of a formal entrée.

I realized with some pleasure that I should not be entirely removed from the Navajo people, several hundreds of whom, in two widely separated colonies on the public domain, were assigned to the Pueblo Agency at Albuquerque. These were of those Navajo who had never removed to the reservations, and who still occupied and roamed over their old districts in New Mexico, where some of them had been allotted land, following the true course of giving an Indian restricted title to a fragment of desert on which he could not hope to make a living, rather than abandoning or removing him.

The Hopi and Navajo have been imprisoned or protected, as you will, by the sterile barricades of the great desert that white men have penetrated only in little groups as trade with the Indians and the governmental educational plan made necessary. The Pueblo people occupied a quite similar semiarid country, at equally high altitudes, and yet presented a different aspect of civilization. From the rock terraces of Old Laguna one could view sand dunes as menacing as any at Old Walpi of the Hopi, and the valleys were no pictures of agricultural abundance. The geologic formations in many places were as finely picturesque and as diversified as any in the Navajo country. Only a short distance off, at the ancient *penol* of Acoma, one could see rock structures as wild and as weird as those of the northern desert. It was only on going to those pueblos north of Albuquerque, such as Jemez and Cochiti, that one found little colonies within sight and scent of the pines. Acoma, Laguna, and Isleta must view their peaks in the distances — San Mateo, the Ladrones, the Manzanos, having between them long stretches of desert, quite barren spaces, across which the Apaches once raided.

The Pueblo Indians were different in dress, and of course in local customs, from even their close kinsmen the Hopi, who had more than once received them as fugitives and granted them sanctuary for years. Contact with the Plains Indians through tribal trade that once centred in the far-away frontier settlement of Taos, whence came the Utes, the Jicarilla Apaches, the Comanches, and perhaps infrequently the Kiowas and Arapahos, had caused the Pueblo Indians to absorb much of beads and feathers into their ceremonies. And, too, we find that the people of both Taos and Picuris in about 1704 fled to the Plains country, where for several seasons they established themselves in a permanent town, and, in the opinion of Hodge, must have gained an infusion of foreign blood.

One of the Indian features of this Laguna fiesta was a "Comanche dance," in which the war bonnet appeared beside the Southwest mask. While it may not be apparent to the hurried visitor, it grew upon me that each of the Pueblo communities had something of distinction and difference in dress. This was particularly marked in the case of the Isletas, who suggest a people of a distinct tribe. And it seemed to me too that each Pueblo division displayed favorite and predominating colors, the Isletas being devoted to a striking red-and-white scheme, the Lagunas having greens and purples, and the Santo Domingos with much of yellow in their shows.

But the major difference between them and other Southwest Indians was their means of existence. The Lagunas possessed cattle and many sheep, true; and they sold quantities of wool; but the soil was their chief support. These were river people. The Rio Grande, a not bombastic name in these arid provinces, — a great

FIESTA SCENE, LAGUNA
September 19, any year

COMANCHE DANCE, LAGUNA

artery flooding, menacing, and growing shallow again,—formed their Nile; while its tributaries, the Chama, the Jemez, and the San José, lesser streams, often nearly dry, helped serve the Pueblo people. They had harnessed every by-stream, and for many miles owned the great river itself. Along the banks were their fields, and a network of ditches, intakes, and levees — crude, but indefatigable methods of irrigation as rigidly adhered to as the ritualistic planting and unorganized labor of the Hopi.

From the fact that water was not available at all times, from the necessity of seizing it in season, and of protecting the works from damaging floods, had grown the communistic life and customs of the Pueblo tribe. Facing stern necessity, famine leering from the desert all about them, every worker was at the command of the native officials, and in early times subject to severe and perhaps cruel penalties did he evade. Therefore they revered all manifestations of fruition, and had developed or adopted the phallic doctrine that wholly dominated the Hopi. The thing that our tourists, and especially those who eulogize what is termed by them "Indian culture," are pleased to admire as a democratic and equitable form of tribal government among these Pueblo people is actually a barbaric despotism once necessary because of the need for irrigation water. This despotism sprang up to assure the feeding of communities, and amid a primitive people naturally made use of mysticism and a savage mythology, thus immeasurably strengthening the authority of those who found power necessary to existence. The symbol of the Pueblo cacique should not be a kachina mask, a clan emblem, or a stalk of corn — it is primarily a ewer of water. The Hopi could only pray for rain; the Pueblo

had his rainfall in bulk and must needs command it.
The one condition had produced a stolid fanaticism
and fatalists; the other an active cruel despotism and
dictators.

In the early eighties, their whole province — at least
most of the Pueblo grants were touched — had a new
influence thrust through it. The lands of Santo Domingo,
San Felipe, Sandia, Isleta, Laguna, and Acoma were
invaded by the Atlantic and Pacific Railroad, now the
Santa Fe system. The very village of Old Laguna was
pierced directly, so that smoke and cinders from the
locomotives mingled at once with the smoke from hearths.
Trains dragged through this block slowly, because, while
dead Indians are said to be good Indians, they can be
horribly expensive. It enabled the tourist, however, to
see one pueblo and its life without stirring from his car
window — and that was my first view of the Lagunas in
1910. I had no idea that nearly ten years later I should
be solemnly addressing them as Chief.[1]

The coming of the iron horse was the greatest influence
since the entrada of the Conquistadors of the sixteenth
century and the American occupation of the nineteenth.
First appeared surveyors and engineers, next rough
laborers, and from then on a miscellaneous host, ever
increasing. A few individuals permanently remained to
marry with the women of the tribe, and the railroad
to-day brings many whites of different degrees of culture
into daily touch with these Laguna natives. Much of
Indian isolation and retirement vanished in their case.
There was no such effect at any other point, save possibly

---

[1] Sometime after 1910 the railroad line in the vicinity of Old Laguna was straightened, and to-day Santa Fe trains cross Laguna lands without granting more than a glimpse of the old pueblo and its mission in the distance.

at Isleta; and one may say that Laguna is thoroughly Indian at fiesta time only.

And meantime our Government spent sixty-five years (1848-1913) debating whether these brown-skinned people were to be regarded as "Indians" — whether it had any duty imposed on it to impose on them; and Congress delayed ten years more before considering the first steps believed expected of it by the Treaty of Guadalupe Hidalgo. But for the riddle of their legal status, affecting the franchise, affecting control of them as Indians, and affecting their land titles, the story of an Agent's experiences among them would be a repetition of my Hopi book, minus the rattlesnakes.

My predecessor, who was Indian Agent for all the Pueblo Indians,[1] — seventeen living communities and several dead ones, — had seized upon this Laguna holiday as the time and place for an annual Indian fair, to ensnare with its exhibits and premiums and sports the combined interest of all the people. This gave the fiesta a threefold significance: that of a Catholic ceremonial, ritualistic, dignified; a native celebration, part Spanish, part savage; and something in the nature of a county fair. Toy balloons, blue ribbons, and "catch-the-brass-ring," would mix with the *Gloria in Excelsis* and the pounding of Indian drums.

The Pueblo population was above 8000 Indians, and there would gather at least a thousand Navajo; the

[1] While my first commission indicated that I should have charge of all the Pueblo Indians, the jurisdiction was divided into northern and southern districts — the Northern Agency at Santa Fe to have about 1800 Indians, the Southern Agency at Albuquerque to supervise the ten large pueblos south and west of Santa Fe, with public-domain Navajo, a population of about 6800 people holding nearly 800,000 acres of land. The topography of central New Mexico was believed to justify this unequal division. Actually, there should be either one or three agencies, the territory and population of Laguna and Acoma warranting the services of a third Indian Agent.

neighboring Mexican settlements would send in hundreds of their citizens; and as Laguna was so easily accessible by rail and auto from Albuquerque, Gallup, and other points, many of the townspeople would accept this chance for an outing. The council house of the Laguna *principales* would be turned into an exhibition hall for the display of agricultural, household, and school industries; there would be exhibits of blankets, basketry, and especially the pottery for which certain of the pueblos are famed; in the corrals the Indians would hold competitions in their sheep and cattle, and on the abandoned railroad right-of-way would match the speed of their ponies. A "baby show" would engage the attention of matrons and nurses, under the supervision of the Agency physicians. All these things would be of governmental type, including the Agent's duty in the preservation of order, it being "Indian country" and no other official having jurisdiction.

In the public plaza a dance floor had been constructed, and my last contact as an official with my old friends the Hopi came when I found that the band would be composed of Keams Cañon boys, who had learned to play selections from *The Chimes of Normandy* and *The Mikado* at my former school, and now, being men and mechanics, worked in the Santa Fe shops at Winslow. They would also play a game of baseball with the leading Pueblo nine, that of Isleta, to decide ownership in a silver cup donated by citizens of Albuquerque.

The events of the first day began with the celebration of Mass in the old mission of the Franciscans. It was a strange sight that I beheld in that high-ceiled nave, supported by the rude mountain *vigas!* There were no seats or pews; the packed congregation of gayly dressed

THE OLD LAGUNA MISSION
Probably built in 1699

RELIGIOUS PROCESSION

Indians knelt on the floor. The elaborately decked altar was tricked out in native fashion with gilt and silver and lacework and paper flowers; Indians acted as acolytes and Indians made the responses; the sermon was in Spanish, for the native language of the Lagunas is not easily acquired, and surely does not lend itself to an exposition of faith in a foreign creed.

With the close of Mass, the mission bells began a clangor, as they had each year on this fiesta day since about 1710. The congregation issued from the church into that walled space where, as with all pueblo missions, once had been God's Acre, a place now having but one cross, and formed a procession to the plaza, of candle-bearers and bell-ringers, preceded by guards who would stand as sentinels before the shrine of San José. Came the Saint himself, an image borne on the shoulders of four attendants, followed by the padre in his vestments. Then the pueblo *Gobernador*, bearing his staff of office, one of those ebony, silver-mounted, and tasseled canes presented to each pueblo by a patient man named Lincoln in the anxious days of the Civil War; and then a long array of the devout, all reverent and imbued with the solemnity of the occasion, the oldest of the educated ones intoning some Latin chant.

Through the crooked and rutted streets of the old pueblo this march proceeded, so as to circle the plaza before entering it. It was not a long ceremony, and not dissimilar from those one may see in any Spanish-type town on the day of the patron saint. Finally the image was installed in a decorated shrine near the centre of the plaza. I could not help thinking how the early Spanish had retrieved to this purpose the pagan Hopi *kisi*, and its cottonwood boughs. Now shots were fired into the air as the guards assumed their duties on each side of the shrine. The Gobernador, bare of head, and his civic assistants, having made obeisance, took up stations too for appointed periods, and the faithful of the community approached to pay homage to this representation of their Saint, who, for one long day, would bless their plaza with his presence. They brought gifts of many sorts to litter the carpet of the shrine. The candles burned and guttered in the sunlit desert air. And one act of the fiesta had reached its dramatic crisis.

On this particular day a new feature was scheduled. At the far end of the plaza, where the dance floor had been laid, the Hopi band announced a patriotic air and flags were raised. The terraces and house tops filled as I had seen them so many times among the Hopi when the pagan rites of snake worship were enacted. All save the guards left the shrine to hear Agent Lonergan's farewell. With the respectful silence and courteous attention that especially mark the Pueblo Indian in council, they listened. They had suffered Agents before, and have endured them since, to whom they cheerfully would have tied a can. But Philip T. Lonergan had been more than their appointed head — he had been their friend, and had been with them in the front line of their battles. They bore him both respect and affection. There was a deep quiet in the plaza, for this Chief was about to say "Adiós."

Then with a reference to their new Agent, who, having been so long with their Hopi brothers, could be expected the better to understand them, I was introduced, and, in accordance with our traditions as well as theirs, had to make a speech. I am not well trained in the art of making speeches, but somehow I plunged through it, stressing the continued education of their children, and assuring them that a change in headship would not mean that the policies of their former Agent would be forgotten. This one district, Laguna and its outlying towns, had six local day schools. There were nearly six hundred children of school age, and five hundred of them had been enrolled, either at home or in the government industrial and Catholic mission schools of Albuquerque and Santa Fe. There was reason for my counsel. Indians always hope that a new man will remit something, and for weeks my office was crowded each morning with parents petitioning that their offspring be excused. These people possessed records; and they armed themselves with baptismal certificates to prove that their cause was just.[1]

Farewells and compliments being finished, there was a growing murmur in the multitude. The merry-go-round whistle piped, the organ began its grinding measures, the sound of a baseball cracking down a stuffed doll in a booth was heard, the wheels of fortune whirred and raspingly awarded to some lucky one a plaster statuette; hawkers cried their wares, vendors of pottery and mission

---

[1] SCHOOL POPULATION OF THE TEN SOUTHERN PUEBLOS, 1922

Thirteen pueblo day schools	740 pupils
Government boarding schools	490 pupils
Catholic mission boarding schools	428 pupils
Children not in school	283 pupils
Total pupil population	1941

Cost of maintaining thirteen day schools for 740 pupils averaged approximately sixty dollars per pupil.

Cost of Agency administration roughly averaged ten dollars for each individual of the population.

Total disbursements of the Indian Agent, all activities, 1922: $115,235.

The Laguna pueblo had six day schools; Acoma two; and Isleta, San Felipe, Santo Domingo, Cochiti, and Jemez one each. The Agent proposed to build new day schools at Acoma, Santa Ana, and two Laguna districts. These additions have since been constructed. Children shown above as "not in school" included a relatively small number of defectives and a few prevented from enrollment because of early marriage, the larger number being eligibles *without any school facilities*, located principally at Acoma, Santo Domingo, Santa Ana, and Laguna.

grapes in trays made their way through the crowd; and all the varied cries and noises of a mission fair started up as if by signal, and would not cease until very late at night — would continue for some three days in this curious post-town of an ancient king's highway, a place that had received Spanish captains-general, Mexican jefe politicos and gobernadors, stern American soldiers, forces under three foreign flags; that had watched the northern hills for marauding Navajo, and those of the south for Apache raiders; and now, having passed all the stages of rude and physical encounter, was as vigorously contending in American courts of law.

Of color in this crowd there was all that one could ask of Latin America. The local women wore their best mantillas. One could tell those from Acoma and those from Santo Domingo by the pottery they vended — the former bearing intricately ornamented forms of white clay covered with webs of black-and-orange tracings, pieces so fragile that it seemed they would crumble in the hand; the others offering jars and bowls as symmetrical, but deep red and black in color, and having less of ornamentation. When one saw lustrous jet-black vases, shining in the sun as lumps of polished coal, he would recognize them as products of Santa Clara pueblo; and perhaps San Ildefonso would send a few pieces of this same clay, but unglazed save for the design — a polished snake writhing around a shapely bowl. Here a Navajo peddled silver beads, or rings and bracelets, cunningly wrought from Mexican coins; while another of his clan, whose fathers once pillaged Pueblo flocks and were not averse to taking Pueblo scalps, offered blankets made on desert looms. Now the Mexican hombre rode by on his silver-studded saddle, and now the tall-crowned Stetson of a white

Photo. by H. F. Robinson

A GUEST OF THE FIESTA
Navajo of the Canoncito district

cowman lent the one Anglo-American touch to a scene not incongruous with the slopes of the Andes.

Quite the most striking of all the figures would be the Isleta from the Rio Grande. Wearing a flat-topped sombrero, his hair caught in a long knot and bound with a woven red bandage, his blanket worn as a serape, he would stride about. His style in trousers came from Albuquerque shops, and he would wear ornamented boots or shoes rather than mocassins. Nothing unique in this, you may observe. But the glory of the Isleta is his shirt — a pure white garment, having a lacelike front and yoke, the sleeves full as those of a surplice, narrowing toward and caught at the wrists with pipings of red bands. This startling effect of purest white in brilliant sunshine, the whole topped by a singularly handsome and commanding face, marked the Isleta as distinctively apart from and in appearance above the many other types of Indian. You may have a thought at this point, and I hasten to correct it. I have never seen an Isleta in a dirty shirt! Well, if this statement is too broad, considering flood times and ditch work, certainly not at a meeting or fiesta. Their women wore old-fashioned plaid shawls of brightest red — they will have no other — and the buckskin legging of many wrappings. They bore witness, too, that the Navajo *pesh-lakai etcitty*, or silversmith, knew where to market his wares.

Red lemonade, bottled pop, oranges, ice-cream cones, and penny whistles! The merry-go-round's race seemed endless, and its asthmatic organ never faltered through the long hours. Dust fanned up and settled over everything. The police came hurrying with a luckless guest and a stolen saddle. A throaty wrangle with the umpires at the ball game developed into a fight involving three nationalities, and the police settled that, too. Children are the same everywhere; and but for the few who must maintain the dignity of public office, like the Gobernador and his principales, these were all children, and the time fiesta.

Along the crest of a near-by ridge the Navajo camps were strung out, the smoke and odors of cooking rising. A pleasant people now, their raiding days over. Close to twilight, the dark outlines of their tented wagons silhouetted against a scarlet sky and the little flares of their fires vying with the hissing gasoline torches of the booths, they lent the whole scene a dramatic atmosphere,— like night on the Santa Fe Trail in the days of '49,— until one noted the mission bells in their arches, black against the sunset, a mediæval touch, when the pueblo became some castellated town and this throng its merrymakers. Then the strains of lilting Mexican fandangos would be heard, as the orchestra paraded about with mandolins and guitars, a swaying Latin group on its way to the dance floor, where the belles of the villages would match their finery and coquetry with the belles of the pueblos. And the murmur of the crowd as darkness fell, the hoarse cries of ballyhoo men urging one more chance at the wheel, and over all a black and looming hulk — the aged mission leaning to watch this motley throng restlessly moving against its very walls!

Interesting as these scenes were, there had been sights even stranger, and before the shrine of San José. Hardly had the religious features ended, and the padre gone, when the sound of a drum was heard, and garbed in green and purple, masked and decorated with the insignia of old clans, came devotees of a different sort to the plaza.

They paraded to the centre, headed by a little hunchback, a man possessed of unflagging energy and a grace not common among Indians, to begin their chanting and dancing. I have always felt that the padre should not be asked for his opinion of this feature. At one of these fiestas, after the Mass and the plaza ceremony, I met him just within the church door, and stood talking. A great shouting came from the street crossing the church front, and we turned to see what occasioned it. Criers hurried along, calling to everyone, including their spiritual Father and their temporal one, "Go back! Turn away!"

We walked back into the now empty church and continued our conversation while that remnant of barbarism went its way.

"Something of their secrecy, I suppose," was my comment.

The padre gave a rather sad shake of his head. Then I looked about that old temple, with its frieze of phallic designs and emblems where one usually finds only the Stations of the Cross; I noted the curiously decorated altar, and remembered those of the morning service who had knelt and prayed and mixed Saint Francis's religion with their own; and I recalled that the desert was just outside, practically unchanged, its wind and sand, which had buffeted Fray Juan de Padilla and many others who had died for this faith, still remorselessly nibbling at the adobe walls. A job for an afternoon! It had been too large a job for four hundred years.

As Agent, when endeavoring to protect the young people, I found much of Hopi fetishism and many Hopi motifs in Laguna tribal characteristics. And it will require many more years of Masses and services, and many trainloads of children to the government and mission schools, before Laguna, kindly and hospitable and courteous as it is, will be rid of these elements. As for the padre and his predecessors, they were the somewhat helpless vassals of a great system, even as I was; and I realized that neither their system nor mine had found any swifter means to confute these old gods. That the padre could not, by a simple benediction, banish them is not to his discredit. The zealous Protestant missionairies have found themselves equally nonplused.

North of Old Laguna, in the neighborhood of Cebolleta, once an outpost of the Navajo, is now the largest pueblo or village of the Laguna people, that of Paguate;[1] and a modern Catholic mission was built there by the Franciscan Father, Fridolin Schuster, in 1920, and dedicated to the honor of Saint Elizabeth. Thereafter, in 1921 and 1925, this desert pastor built two other churches in the Laguna provinces, one at Encinal and one at Seama, dedicated to the Blessed Virgin and Saint Anne, respectively. There is a chapel in the little community of Mesita.

Father Schuster first served the pueblo of Jemez for three years, visiting Sia and Santa Ana. He went to Laguna in 1913 and served fourteen years among these people, only recently leaving the field for another parish in New Mexico. So far as Indian communities are concerned, his work may rank next to the extended showing made from St. Michaels among the Navajo; with this difference to be considered, that the St. Michaels Fathers have been many, working closely under the influence of the foremost Navajo Indian Agency, which was never an obstruction to their work, and among a people widely different from those of the pueblo stock, whereas this

[1] Pronounced "Pah-what-te."

Father Schuster worked quite alone, among a people who have been torn by dissensions common to the Pueblo tribes.

It may be that the Franciscan discipline discourages pride in one's work, but I have no doubt that Fray Schuster reflects with satisfaction on his having succeeded to the labors of those two pioneer Franciscan friars who left indelible records among the Pueblo Indians — Fray Gerónimo Zarate-Salmeron, who served at both Jemez and Acoma before 1629, and that renowned Apostle of the Acomas, Fray Juan Ramirez, who in that year journeyed on foot from Santa Fe to that hostile people, *solo con su breviario y una cruz!* And it was in this very Laguna parish that the last of the early Franciscans ministered, even after the Mexican decree expelling them as an organization.

Before anyone criticizes the methods of the Franciscans among the Pueblo people, let him reflect on the pagan influences in which they are involved and which root back into dark centuries before Francis of Assisi was born. When it comes to spiritual affairs, and the tendering of one mythology for another, it will be wiser to let the old religion of Saint Francis alone in its long pilgrimage and crusade. Nearly four hundred years ago it planted the first cross in the Southwest deserts, and all too frequently bathed it with its blood. Such sacrifices failed among the Hopi, but its entrenchments at the pueblos, once stormed, have been retaken. To-day its equipment and morale are neither crippled nor wearied. When the Franciscans were expelled by the Mexican Government in one of its periodic fits of political mania, the break of nearly fourscore years wrought havoc in the old parishes of Fray Alonzo de Benavides, who in 1630 boasted of them to his King. The padres returned to many pueblos in 1900, and to Laguna in 1910. It does not take long for these friars, even *solo*, to recover old forts — for a very simple reason: aside from their pleasant, patient sincerity, their religion appeals to the Indian. Colorful, poetic, and dramatic rituals bring red men the quicker to morality than anæmic theories and sad songs. The man who drapes himself in a crimson blanket, and whose silver gewgaws rattle as he strides along, who finds something in the smoke of fires and in sonorous chants, will go to a gilded shrine before he will seek a barren chapel.

Only a short distance from this scene of mission and fiesta, one at times may find things even more mediæval in the *morada* of the Penitentes — a sect that has been described as an offshoot of the Third Order of Franciscans, or the "Tertiaries." There seems to be no good reason for wishing this set of fanatics on the Tertiaries. Salpointe and others denounce these people as being a hybrid-political growth, with no authority or commendation of the Church, and certainly the latter-day prelates have given them no thanks or recognition. But they exist, nevertheless, forming a curious commentary on the state of civilization among the lower-class Mexicans in certain backwaters of New Mexico. They are flagellants. Their spectacles occur in Lent, and particularly during Holy Week, when the meetings in the morada are followed by processions to the place of the cross — first the flagellants, scourging themselves with whips of cacti, then cross-bearers and chanters, accompanied by flute-blowing, chain-rattling, and other mummery to the dismay of the Devil and any others who may be affected by that sort of thing. It has been related that all the details of the Crucifixion have been enacted by them, even to suspend-

LAGUNA

ing some crack-brained devotee from the cross. They are mentioned here simply because of their close proximity to the pueblo of Laguna. They practise also in the country of the northern pueblos. One is tempted to decry the paganism of the Indians, until a vision of the Penitentes gives one pause.

The picture of the Laguna fiesta I have selected because it was my first, and because it is attended by the largest and most diversified crowd. The duplication of this fiesta scene may be found, in different colors and with little changes in local touches, — such as the hobbyhorses at San Felipe that cavort from dance plaza to the church, — at all the seventeen pueblos. Their calendar follows: —

Pueblo	Feast Day	Patron or Feast
San Ildefonso	January 23	San Ildefonso (Saint Ildephonsus)
San Felipe	May 1	San Felipe (Saint Philip)
Sandia	June 12	San Antonio (Saint Anthony)
San Juan	June 24	San Juan Bautista (Saint John the Baptist)
Cochiti	July 14	San Buenaventura (Saint Bonaventure)
Santa Ana	July 26	Santa Ana (Saint Anne)
Santo Domingo	August 4	Santo Domingo (Saint Dominic)
Picuris	August 10	San Lorenzo (Saint Lawrence)
Santa Clara	August 12	Santa Clara (Saint Clare)
Sia	August 15	Asunción de Nuestra Señora (Assumption of the Blessed Virgin)
Isleta	August 28	San Agustin (Saint Augustine)

(At Isleta the fiesta is celebrated on the octave, September 4, sometimes called "San Augustinito Day.")

Pueblo	Feast Day	Patron or Feast
Acoma	September 2	San Estevan (Saint Stephen)
Laguna	September 19	San José (Saint Joseph)
Taos	September 30	San Gerónimo (Saint Jerome)
Nambe	October 4	San Francisco (Saint Francis)
Jemez	November 12	San Diego (Saint James)
Tesuque	(This pueblo has the same patron and date as Jemez.)	

The Pueblo Indians all have other holidays to be celebrated by peculiar customs dating from early Spanish times, and all partaking of that curious admixture of Christianity and what may be termed paganism.

On Palm Sunday the Indians are much concerned to receive the pieces of palm that are blessed and distributed by the priest. In Holy Week they exhibit their reverence at Laguna by having an armed watch at the church, beginning with Maundy Thursday and ending with the night of the Sabbatum Magnum. Very likely this is a distorted idea of commemorating the vigil and guards at the tomb of the crucified Christ, and I have no doubt that the early Franciscans trained them in these simple mystery plays to attract and fix their attention on the feast to be observed and its meaning. At Jemez, this same period is marked by pagan dances, kept secret by rather disagreeable manifestations should any outsider appear on the scene.

All Souls Day (November 2), when the Church remembers the dead, finds Pueblo delegations at their churches keeping vigils begun the preceding night. They toll the bell at intervals and keep themselves awake by playing their "game of the reeds" and "guess the hidden stick."[1] This is not done at Laguna; but in all

---

[1] The paraphernalia consists of an empty room and four hollow reeds, each about seven inches in length, with a small stick to be secreted in these reeds, and a bank of corn for counters. The players divide into two groups, each group having a leader.

LAGUNA

the pueblos, including Laguna, food is placed on graves on the evening of November 1, while on the morning of the feast day women bring offerings of fruit, bread, and grains to the churches. These gifts they bear in baskets on their heads and place them before the altars as offerings to the celebrant of the Mass for the Dead. One padre recalled his experience at Santa Ana: —

A stately heap it was, indeed; corn, wheat, chili, onions, melons, bread, cake, and Indian pies, all thrown together promiscuously. One simple-minded redskin evidently thought that Almighty God would not care for a watermelon, so he ate the melon and threw the rind on the pile as an evidence of good will. After Mass I had the Indians carry the grain to my room; then I told them they could have the rest. Such a scramble! In a very short time the pile had disappeared.

According to the rules of the archdiocese, every family is supposed to pay one dollar and a half for the support of the priest — the so-called *primicia*. As the Indians

---

Group A begins an incantation for good luck, while the leader takes the reeds and the stick, and behind his back inserts the stick in one of them. He then spreads the reeds on the floor before him. Then the luckiest member of Group B is appointed to make a selection. He stalks majestically across the room and squats before the reeds. Amid singing and taunts of the opposition he maintains a perfect Indian calm. He tantalizes everyone present by pretending first to have selected one reed and then another. Perhaps five minutes of this foolery passes, until everyone is filled with an eager expectation. The object is to find the reed containing the stick at the third guess. If the first reed chosen contains it, his party must pay ten grains of corn to Group A; if it is found in the second reed, his party forfeits six points; and if none of his choices procures the stick, his party loses four points. Should he discover the stick at the third choice, the deal changes. Group B then does the shuffling and Group A the choosing. This is repeated until one side has lost all its corn.

Humma-ha, or once upon a time, they would wager their crops, their horses, and even their houses and lands in this game. After working hard all day on the ditches, they would hurry through supper and play this game most of the night. But the days of large wagers and heavy gambling are over. Sometimes they will pledge melons or tobacco, but no more.

The Hopi play a variant of this game with four moccasins and a stone, which requires of the leader considerable sleight of hand when depositing the pill in the shoe.

seldom have money, and then very little of it, they usually pay in grain.

At Christmas the Pueblo Indians hold more extended revels. At midnight on Christmas Eve the Indians dance in their ancient churches, a feature explained by them as an exhibition of their joy and reverence for the newborn Christ-child. These dances *do not* occur in the modern churches, but are held outside them. Such a dance does occur within the old mission at Laguna. Perhaps one may excuse this custom, if in the mood, by recalling a popular legend known as that of the *Jongleur de Notre Dame*.

For three days following Christmas, native dances are held in all the Laguna villages. Final festivities take place on January 6, or the Day of the Three Kings. Then, in all the pueblos of New Mexico with the exception of Laguna, the native governors receive their staves of office in the churches from the padres after Mass. At Laguna they receive these emblems from the sacristan, a custom that grew apparently because Laguna was once without a padre for an extended period.

These staves of office are furniture of the utmost importance, and have been the subject of Court procedure. For quite a time those belonging to the pueblo of San Juan, that ancient place "of the Gentlemen," were in my possession in Albuquerque, held awaiting the decision of the United States Court for the District of New Mexico as to whether or not my predecessor in office should be jailed for having refused to recognize the mandate of a State Court. Having seized these properties of the pueblo, he refused to yield them to a reactionary element upon Court order, and was technically in contempt.

I was extremely careful of these relics. To have

something that Father Abraham had ordered made and personally presented to his red children appealed to my worship of history quite as much as the sword of "Stonewall" Jackson would have appealed to it. And I wondered where I could seek sanctuary should I, by any chance, have lost them.

In addition to the more famous "Lincoln cane," each pueblo has a staff that was presented to it by one of the Mexican presidents. For royal gifts they may cite their bells and old church pictures.

In the ceiling of the Laguna church are the usual carved vigas — huge rafters supporting the adobe roof. The walls of the sanctuary are painted in a sort of arabesque design. Along the side walls is a frieze of native painting, made up of repetitions of a two-color design that is effective and thoroughly pagan. Considering the crude implements of the times, the Communion rail and pillars of the altar are splendid carvings. The pulpit is a curiosity. Above the altar is a picture of the Trinity represented as three individual persons. Below this is a picture of Saint Joseph, their patron; to his right is Saint John Nepomucene and to his left Saint Clare with the Remonstrance. These are old paintings brought from Spain and still preserve their color. There is also a painting of Saint Joseph on buffalo hide. The front of the mensa is covered with a buffalo hide painted in gaudy colors, so tightly stretched that it appears to be a wooden panel. In the ceiling above the altar is another buffalo hide, showing the sun, moon, stars, and the rainbow, emblems of the older native religion.

The Lagunas have a legend to the effect that when the Spanish Governor Cubero visited their infant pueblo in 1699 they asked him for a priest. He told them they should first give some evidences of good faith by beginning the construction of a church. This they did forthwith, and Cubero found a padre for them. This is the nearest approach to fixing the age of the Laguna Mission church. In these modern times the faithful of the Lagunas are worthy of their forefathers. Under the guidance of Father Schuster, they began the construction of churches in the suburban pueblos of the district. The Indians supplied all the common labor gratis, quarried and hauled the rock, built the walls, and freighted free from the railroad stations the materials that their lands did not furnish. The money for lumber, roofing, glass, and fixtures their zealous Father received as donations from those of his white brethren who have Indian missions at heart. In this fashion, three churches stand as testimony to his efforts and the simple faith of the Laguna people.

The whole effect of a Pueblo Indian fiesta that I have pictured is, I believe, one of joyous native simplicity, an ebullition of childish faith and carefree minds. I take no pleasure in closing on an ugly note, and perhaps the sketch would last as long without it. But facts are facts, and multicolored costumes and incense do not palliate the evil effects of illicit beverages. In Washington I had read the reports of agents, missionaries, and others concerning fiestas of the California Mission Indians, when night had fallen, and authority was weak, and the firewater began to appear. With the Pueblo Indians of New Mexico my predecessor had fought through this anxious period. It had not been agreeable work, and was not without its dangers. Midnight, in towns of crooked streets and dark courts, with dancing around central fires to the rhythm of native drums in the hands of half-

INTERIOR OF THE OLD LAGUNA CHURCH
Showing the old pulpit, the altar, and the ancient paintings

intoxicated Indians, may be picturesque, thrilling enough for a novel, even, but rather to be read of than to be personally experienced. The Indian Agent may remain in Albuquerque, occupying himself with the signing of school reports, while these shines are going on; but neither my predecessor nor I believed that native judges and undirected Indian police should be expected to cope with them. Nor are they cured by reading diligently from the Revised Statutes.

There had been a time, too, when liquor was sold openly at Laguna, wherever the vendor could plant his feet on ground not covered by the ancient Spanish title. In 1913, however, the Supreme Court of the United States decided that these people were not free to imbibe, and that the Federal Government was authorized to prohibit such cheer. So, being a timid person who believed in locking the horse in the stable, I would have a fairly strong force of police at these affairs. Some of the men were zealous, and could interpret the regulations in three or more languages, so there was little of halting hesitation. Then there were commissioned employees, both purely American and staunchly Mexican in ancestry. All three grades could be relied on to preserve harmony when discord raised its signal.

I cannot remember a single case of drunkenness among the local Indians, the Lagunas, at this annual fiesta; but when I witnessed the last one at that historic pueblo, in 1921, for two nights the tribal guardhouse was filled with those visitors who exhibited the effects of too much faith in John Barleycorn. The Indian Court, presided over by Judge Pablo next morning, emitted long homilies and few sentences, since most of the offenders were not Indian and could only be dismissed from the Indian lands.

Could we have haled them before some alcalde of the hills, outside the Indian province, and invoked the solemnity of the state law? We could have; but I am writing of rural New Mexico, and it is to laugh.

IV

LAGUNA

The Landed Proprietors

And ye shall measure from without the city on the east side two thousand cubits, and on the south side two thousand cubits, and on the west side two thousand cubits, and on the north side two thousand cubits; and the city shall be in the midst. . . .   — Numbers xxxv. 5

The fact that Acoma — a most populous pueblo, a citadel prominent in warfare and rebellion, which was visited by the earliest of the Franciscans, which had a resident missioner by 1629, and a church no great while after — had in 1782 become a visita of Laguna, as it has ever since been, indicates the swift growth into importance of the younger community.

Perhaps this came about because Laguna, once established, was the better situated as a point from which Spanish orders could be radiated; whereas Acoma, except that it guarded one route to Zuñi, was completely isolated, as it is to-day. Geography and topography determine many of such things. Or it may have been because of the sullen and always inhospitable attitude of the Acoma people that caused missionaries less earnest than the first daring "Apostle" to lose interest. Another reason given is that Acoma, having been credited with 1500 people at the time of the Great Revolt, was decimated by smallpox in 1780–1781, and that ten years later its population was given as 800. But Laguna must have suffered from this same epidemic.

The date of Laguna's founding as a recognized pueblo is July 4, 1699 — nineteen years after the uprising of the Pueblo Indians against the Spanish, and three years after the completion of their reconquest by De Vargas. It is said that fugitive Queres, who had fled from the hostile pueblos of Cienaguilla (extinct), Sia, Cochiti, and Santo Domingo, settled there. But this does not account for the Shoshonian influences that are so prominent in the ritualistic affairs of the people. There is that legend of a Hopi child lost from a caravan proceeding across the Laguna country, when the Sandias were returned from the Second Mesa of Tusayan to the Rio Grande; but it is most likely that the fugitives who settled there were of those who had first fled to the Hopi provinces and who did not return from the Northwest at one time, but drifted back through the years, so that Laguna received a constant infusion of Hopi stock and culture. In 1775, when Fray Escalante went to the Hopi pueblos, he estimated there were 7500 souls, which was undoubtedly the usual double estimate. They may have numbered 4000 (to-day about 2500); but in 1780, when the Spanish Governor Anza visited the Hopi, he found that smallpox had reduced them to less than 800. Anza offered to remove some of these survivors, and about thirty families accepted his offer. Bancroft believes these were settled among the Lagunas at Moquino.

Hodge states that "Kawaika," the native name for Laguna, is identical with that of a one-time village of the Hopi country, the ruins of which were found close to Awatobi; but this does not warrant the identification of these ruins as those of a Queres village.

and Hough all mention this town of Kawaika, once known to the Hopi people.

The Lagunas derive from four linguistic stocks — the Keresan, the Tanoan, the Shoshonian, and the Zuñian. Hodge lists nineteen of their clans, some being extinct, originating in Acoma, Sia, Sandia, San Felipe, and Jemez (of the Pueblo Indians proper), with others important at Zuñi and Oraibi. The study of a people's religious organization and the charting of their vocabulary enable the scientist to determine these things with a fine degree of accuracy. My method was of a coarser nature. One had only to compare the modes and customs of the Lagunas, particularly with respect to marriage, with those of the Hopi, to discover kinship through the sincerest form of flattery. Every trick and argument that the Hopi people had thrust upon me earlier, concerning the mating of their children and the control of offspring, were promptly duplicated at Laguna, with the unfortunate difference that, had I devoted the time necessary to a complete effort at cleansing these affairs, the other nine pueblos, from Acoma to Jemez, would not have seen me at all.

In 1699 it appears that the Captain-General and Gobernador, Don Pedro Rodriguez Cubero, camped at Laguna on his way to the pueblos of the West. Cubero had succeeded to the position of De Vargas, whose application for reappointment and confirmation was either overlooked, or, what is more likely, was intentionally pigeonholed at Mexico City by order of the Viceroy. Cubero spent most of his time in discrediting, lawing, and persecuting his great predecessor. Santa Fe was a long way from Spain, and the route lined with intrigue. For three years the Viceroy prevented a correction of this injustice. But the Spanish are given to fairy-tale rewards and punishments, and in time the King received the protests of De Vargas, and reconfirmed him in the governorship — to take effect after Cubero's term of office had ended.

Life in the meantime had been miserable for the man who had put down the Pueblo rebellion. Actually, when his claims were being acknowledged by his royal master, when he was receiving the public thanks in Spain and was tendered a choice of the titles *marqués* or *conde*, De Vargas was occupying the Santa Fe *cárcel*, where he was confined for nearly three years. Seven years after 1696 the matter was corrected, and De Vargas, who had made his way to Mexico meantime to procure something of vindication, was again en route for the City of the Holy Faith, armed with his new commission and title, and, considering Spanish temperament, no doubt bearing a bitter heart. Cubero evidently thought so. He had no desire to see that martial figure striding across the Santa Fe Plaza toward his audience chamber in the old Palace. Cubero, to use the slang of later days, "beat it while his shoes were good," and, having made his way out of the province without welcoming Nemesis, sought another job in the south.[1]

But in 1699 this Cubero was in charge of the Pueblo provinces, and when he visited the new pueblo of San

---

[1] De Vargas, along with numerous subordinates, was charged by the Cabildo, or corporation of Santa Fe, with peculation. Juan Paez Hurtado, it was alleged, had defrauded the colonists of half the money allotted to them by the Crown. He was accused of collecting $100 each for 38 colonists who never came to New Mexico; of employing individuals to impersonate colonists that he might later collect this fee, subsequently filling their places with negroes; and of receiving the bounty several times over for the one person under different names. Finally, he was charged with having purloined a box containing $7000, and of aiding and abetting the Governor, De Vargas, in oppressive and illegal acts. Bancroft does not declare De Vargas wholly innocent, but states that later the Cabildo retracted its accusations with respect to him, attributing all the blame to his successor in office, Cubero. Juan Paez Hurtado entered New Mexico with the De Vargas expedition of 1693, in charge of colonists, was Lieutenant Governor in De Vargas's second administration, and Acting Governor

José de la Laguna, the plain to the northwest of the village site was named in his honor, and to-day one finds a little Mexican hamlet there bearing his name, in the shadow of San Mateo, "Tsodzil" (mountain tongue), the sacred landmark denoting the southerly limits of the traditional Navajo empire. After this visit, Cubero passed to the abortive skirmish against the Hopi for having destroyed Awatobi (1700) and one of his last official acts was the abandonment of Zuñi. These things mark the high lights of his administration.

Whether or not Laguna dates from 1699, its mission existed nearly one hundred years before San Xavier del Bac, the most notable monument of the Arizona Spanish period, was completed. The Jesuits founded San Xavier as a mission point in 1687, but it was after the revolt of the Indians of "Primeria Alta" (1751), and after the Franciscan succession to the Jesuit missions in the present Arizona area, that San Xavier in the Papago desert was designed. It was of Franciscan construction and completed in 1797. The oldest of the California missions, excluding the Jesuit settlements in Lower California, is that of San Diego, 1769. While Laguna may not boast that it, as a fortified pueblo, obstructed and contended with the Conquistadors of the early sixteenth century, it is of mature age as such things rank in the United States. Before the veterans of the Pueblo Rebellion flocked there, the region "of the Lake" had been settled by their kinsmen — before William Penn had received his charter to Pennsylvania; when La Salle and Father Hennepin were pushing their canoes through the waters of the

---

for one year after the death of De Vargas in 1704, and again in 1717. In 1714 he headed a military expedition against the Apaches on the Colorado River, and in 1724 another such expedition against the Comanches. Apparently he served under five or more Spanish Governors. His name appears on Inscription Rock as late as 1736.

unknown Mississippi; when Charles the Second of England was enacting the last scenes of his merry career.

As a bit of scenery it is worthy of its history. Not all the New Mexican pueblos are distinctive or inviting in their Indian picture. Those of Sandia, Santa Ana, Santo Domingo, Tesuque, San Ildefonso, Santa Clara even, save for an old adobe or a mountain view, are not attractive. But the original pueblo of Old Laguna, now that the Santa Fe has removed its incongruous locomotives and signals, is most picturesque.

It occupies a bony escarpment above the San José River, and all the desert phases may be observed from its doorways. A meagre, drying stream, with eroded banks, protects the town as with a moat. Beyond are huge drifting sand dunes, and desert levels, and half-arid valleys. Like a lofty ship in the distance, San Mateo lifts its blue and snowy sail more than 4000 feet above them, and 11,389 feet above the sea. The huddle of houses resembles a Hopi village, albeit much cleaner. They rise, one row above another, about a central plaza, the whole being on high ground that one approaches over rock ledges forming terraces or steps to the town. Unlike most of the pueblos, their mission of the Franciscans is not on the plaza, but stands one street back from the public centre, and to one side of it, giving the effect of a huge corner buttress.

The lands of Laguna extend west to meet those of Acoma. Until about 1871, except for summer camps, there was only the one crowded pueblo at Laguna. Now there are a number of distant villages under its headship, one of them larger than the parent pueblo. Once the Navajo Indians, who harried the Pueblo Indians until Kit Carson and 1863, pushed the claims of their territory as close as Cebolleta, a point just beyond the northern Laguna lines. Here, in 1749, the Franciscans established a mission with view to converting the Navajo, but the effort proved a failure. Until the American occupation, Cebolleta was considered the Navajo frontier, behind it a vast untracked wilderness that certain of the Navajo still roam over. Cebolleta has been mission point, *presidio*, and far-flung outpost. Very likely this closeness of the old enemy prevented Laguna expansion for years. The removal of the Navajo in 1868 to their western reserves caused the Lagunas to feel safer; and, too, their mission influences, their returned students in later years, and the desire for better planting grounds and grazing, all prompted an exodus from the original site. To-day a colony of their young men is to be found as far west as Winslow, Arizona, where they find employment in the railroad shops. This group has a recognized leader and principales, and, although they own homes and automobiles in another state, and pay income taxes when they cannot get around the privilege, the Indian pueblo still recognizes them, to the end that they contend vigorously in home elections and debates.

In 1922 the government census showed that Laguna's population was 1808 persons, distributed among the several towns as follows: —

Old Laguna	391
Paguate	540
Seama	279
Paraje	181
Mesita	173
Encinal	152
Casa Blanca	92
	1808

The Isleta and Santo Domingo pueblos were next in rank, having 988 and 959 people, respectively. Acoma's population was 900. Taos and Jemez followed with 580 and 561. San Felipe was the only other pueblo to boast a population of more than five hundred persons. From that the towns dwindled down to Sandia and San Ildefonso, nearly gone, having but 92 and 91 people on their records. In that year, the combined population of the Pueblo Indians of New Mexico (ignoring Zuñi, because of its changed political status) was 8205.

The first Protestant missionary in this field came to Laguna in 1851, sent by the Baptist Mission Society. He was authorized by the Government to construct a chapel and a school. The Civil War interrupted the labors of this worker, Samuel C. Gorman, and it is said that little was accomplished until 1871, when Walter G. Marmon arrived as the first government teacher. At that time no member of the tribe could speak English, and only one Indian could read and write Spanish. He had been educated in Mexico, according to the account given by Laguna's local author, Mr. John Gunn.[1]

In 1875, Dr. John Menaul, who was long to be identified with mission work in New Mexico and whose name still endures, came to Laguna as a Presbyterian missionary, and as successor to Mr. Marmon. He established a small printing press, and translated and printed *McGuffey's First Reader* in the Queres language. He spent ten years among these people. His adobe mission, only a short distance from the temple of the Fathers, is

---

[1] Gunn's book, *Schat Chen* (1917), is devoted to the history and folklore of the tribe. I have accepted his dates as to the Protestant influences among the Lagunas. His recital contains ingenious speculations as to the prehistoric antecedents of the Laguna people, and his linguistic proofs are interesting and amusing. The book has a distinct value as a modern record.

now used as the council house of the Pueblo principales, and a modern manse is to be found at another place. This mission has several chapels to-day, and a number of the Lagunas have accepted the Presbyterian faith. With the possible exception of Jemez, Laguna is the only southern pueblo where Protestant missionaries have made the slightest impression.

The Marmon family has been closely identified with the Laguna pueblo. Walter G. Marmon and his brother, Robert, married Indian women. When Walter G. Marmon came as first government teacher, he was joined by George H. Pradt, a government surveyor and a veteran of the Civil War. These two should not be underestimated as influences among the people of Laguna. It is fortunate that they were men of character and vigorous mentality. Had they been of the usual sort who marry with and settle among natives when permitted, a far different effect might have been radiated. Walter and Robert Marmon each served one term as Laguna Governor, and Acoma, too, once had a white man as governor. Local gossip has it that these innovations produced dissensions, to the end that orthodox Indians removed to other pueblos. I know very little of this, and am inclined to credit less; but it is a fact that the Acoma trader who achieved this distinction later expected to control Acoma grazing lands for the benefit of his half-blood family, a view in which he was rudely disturbed. It is my opinion, however, that considering the times, and what might have happened to the Laguna Indians, the advent of Walter G. Marmon and George H. Pradt was beneficial; and I am not moved to say this of the white men I have observed who have settled in this manner with any other tribe. Six other whites later married with the Lagunas, one of them being John M. Gunn, their local historian.

The old adobe mission that now serves as a council house for the Laguna Governor and his principales has sheltered widely different personalities. Officers of the army, such as Generals Sherman and Logan, Carleton and Canby, have used it as quarters; Kit Carson lodged there; and once "Billy the Kid" found it a refuge. Here, too, it is related, General Lew Wallace, when Territorial Governor of New Mexico, worked on his great romance — so that Laguna may vie with Santa Fe in having had its part in the production of a wondrous panorama of desert sands and horsemen and shepherds. Perhaps the somewhat similar stretches of landscape, the dark-skinned people, and the crimson glory of the sunsets, with sheep moving slowly to their corrals, brought Judea nearer to the author as he visioned the days of the Man of Galilee.[1]

Now, at least once each month, the Pueblo headmen gather under its roof to discuss Pueblo affairs, or to consider a momentous letter from their Agent at Albuquerque, or to assimilate if possible some doctrine propounded by the Indian Bureau at Washington. They are not always successful. Many times have I sat on its platform with their Governor, while the long hours droned away, punctuated by questions and discussion; and outside the terraces of the pueblo were bathed in sunshine, and the white fleecy clouds rolled and tumbled through the blue sky that tents Laguna.

This pueblo has a governor, two lieutenant governors,

---

[1] In 1890, Lew Wallace informed the curator of the New Mexico Historical Society that *Ben-Hur* was finished in the old Palace at Santa Fe. The author stated that at the time of his appointment to the Governorship of New Mexico the manuscript was completed down to the sixth book of the volume. The sixth, seventh, and eighth books were written at night in what is known as the "Rito de los Frijoles" room of the

three *fiscals* (each having two *tenientes*, or assistants), and several *mayordomos*. The mayordomos have charge of the irrigation ditches and apportion the water to the people. The village that has neither the governor nor a lieutenant governor, as a resident, has a fiscal, who is the leading officer of that community. In olden times it was the duty of the fiscals to attend the church and the padre on his rounds or visits, but at Laguna this custom has ceased. Some of the other pueblos have officials known as "sheriffs," but their duties would seem to be similar to those of the fiscals.

Where a pueblo continues the ancient and honorable office of *Capitán de Guerra* (captain of war), he ranks next to the governor in importance. Once he commanded the tribe's fighting men, and in these peaceful days acts as Master of the Hunt, and has charge of the tribal dances. Every pueblo maintains the ancient custom of communal hunts, the proceeds of which go to the cacique. Strangely too, this captain of the guard, who was once consecrated to war and bloodshed; now finds himself a sort of deacon to the cacique, since he must make many prayers for the benefit of the people, and pilgrimages to various shrines to invoke the gods for rain. A drought causes him to redouble these efforts, and it is more than likely he would prefer a good healthy war on occasion to vary the stresses of his life. One war captain has been reported as saying that "being a military man in dry seasons is very hard work."

Laguna is distinguished above most other pueblos in another manner, and one that to Indians anywhere is

---

Palace. The author added: "The room has ever since been associated in my mind with the Crucifixion. The retirement, impenetrable to incoming sound, was as profound as a cavern's."

paramount. In 1922 it claimed, not without legal challenge in one quarter (at Paguate), more than 250,000 acres of land, and, except for an occasional trespass by a sheep herder, was in possession of it.

Whenever the affairs of the Pueblo Indians of New Mexico come before committees of Congress, and questions are asked as to their dominions, a general answer is given, — one that has become stereotyped, being easy to remember and to roll most unctuously off the official tongue, — such as that furnished by Commissioner of Indian Affairs Charles H. Burke, when the Bursum Bill and its proponents were receiving their well-deserved public flogging at Washington in 1923. After stating how the United States acquired these people, he continued : —

We found these Indians on these grants, ranging about 17,000 acres, *I think*, in area, a league to the four winds from the front door of the church, and they had lived there for two or three hundred years, and they live there now, but they never have had possession of extensive domains, as many of the other Indians have, *consequently, they have not ceded any land to the Government*.

And, not satisfied with this, Mr. Burke covered more territory, as follows : —

I want to say in connection with what Mr. Meritt mentioned, that therefore every dollar that has been expended for the benefit of the Pueblos has been a gratuity. *They have never rendered any service or given anything to the United States.*

The italics are mine.

Meritt, the Assistant Commissioner of Indian Affairs, had delivered himself earlier of the same astounding statement concerning the parsimony and indifferent greed of the Pueblo Indians, when presenting schedules of

Congressional appropriations and departmental expenditures for the record.

It should be borne in mind that the subject under discussion was "The Pueblo Indians of New Mexico," as they were affected by the provisions of the proposed legislation to clarify and adjust land titles held or claimed by "The Pueblo Indians of New Mexico." With the utmost departmental composure Meritt introduced, as evidence of governmental charity to the Pueblo Indians, thousands upon thousands of dollars expended on the Zuñi Indians, on the San Juan Navajo Indians, on the Jicarilla Apache Indians, and on the Mescalero Apache Indians, all residents of reservations in New Mexico; and, not content with that watering, crossed into Arizona to list gratuities to the Hopi Indians of the Moqui Reserve, and the Hopi Indians of the Western Navajo Reserve. Only two of these classes were divisions of the *Pueblo stock*, even. Or, to picture it another way, moneys expended for bridges that a Pueblo Indian proper would never likely see, much less cross; for hospitals that he would never enter; for dams and ditches whose waters he could not enjoy; for schools that would educate pupils not of his getting.

Meritt showed in a neat bureauistic tabulation that in the course of fifteen years, ending November 1922, the Indian Service had expended, for irrigation and water service alone benefiting *pueblo-type* Indians in Arizona and New Mexico, the huge sum of $1,176,146; and to achieve this staggering total for the record he included every dollar that had been spent on Zuñi and Hopi water problems, probably including the cost of the Zuñi Dam. The Zuñi and Hopi expenditures totaled $856,390, thus leaving to *the Pueblo Indians of New Mexico* — that is, the persons who were asking for something — but $319,756 in fifteen years. And the combined Zuñi and Hopi populations totaled less than 4500 individuals, whereas for 1922 the Annual Report gave the Pueblo population as 8344.

Zuñi is 116 miles from the westernmost Pueblo railroad station, and 340 miles from Taos; the Hopi First Mesa is 265 miles from the nearest village of the Pueblo Indians of New Mexico, and 480 miles from Taos. Let us doubt that there could be a drought at Washington when it rained yesterday at Louisville.

One of the vital questions before the Committee was the necessity for assuring to the Pueblo Indians of New Mexico (seventeen communities) modern methods of irrigation and a sufficiency of irrigation water from the Rio Grande system — not from the Rio Zuñi, nor the Oraibi Wash, nor the Grand Cañon of the Colorado. Using round numbers, this $319,756 had been expended in fifteen years as follows: —

For the drilling of wells on various pueblos	$89,000
For irrigation projects at Laguna	69,000
For irrigation projects at Cochiti	35,000
For irrigation projects at San Ildefonso	29,000
For irrigation projects at Sia	16,000
For irrigation projects at Santa Clara	15,000
For irrigation projects at San Juan	11,000
	$264,000

This left to the remaining eleven pueblos not named, in fifteen years, $55,000, or roughly $5000 each, a yearly average of $333.33 each — about enough per pueblo to build footbridges across their community ditches. And pueblo wells have nothing to do with the irrigation of agricultural land, not to mention the fact that the expenditure of funds did not always produce water in the wells. Last, but not least, most of the Laguna appropriations had the potent word "reimbursable" tagged to them by the thrifty Congress. "Reimbursable" means that the Indians will somehow, sometime, repay from some sort of revenue the moneys *advanced as a loan*.

Meritt set up these figures to refute the statements that little had been done by the Government to assure the Pueblo livelihood, which depended on irrigation and their just share of the Rio Grande waters; and the committees swallowed this statement without gulping.

Actually, during 1922 alone, expenditures for the Pueblo Indians of New Mexico for all purposes (administration, education, irrigation, legal counsel, salaries, district medical service, sanatoria, hospital emergencies, rents and routine-service fees, transportation, supplies, upkeep of equipment, repair of buildings, repair of bridges across the Rio Grande, pay of Indian police, and so forth) had been large enough in all conscience — $408,761, without combing the world for extras. Indeed, the rigid economy preached by the Indian Bureau at Washington, until the nation had staggered back to normality, would have warranted cutting this down a trifle, if possible. As an instance — in 1922 two of the officials handling Pueblo Indian appropriations disbursed nearly $3000 to the relief of Albert Bacon Fall, a charity that Meritt failed to note for the record.

"They have never rendered any service or given anything to the United States."

Let us get a sharp focus on this expression of official policy. Is it to be construed that titles to land acquire more or less of validity in proportion to the amount of taxes paid or services rendered by the claimant to the United States? Is the United States a government that, before yielding justice, must be tipped like a waiter?

What services could the Pueblo Indians of New Mexico have rendered the United States? When James S. Calhoun reported concerning the alarming disloyalty of native citizens and the terror inspired by hostile Indians on the frontier, did he include the Pueblo Indians in this category? When Sibley marched his forces up the Rio Grande in 1862, taking Albuquerque and Santa Fe and threatening Fort Union, — seizing as well the little garrison at Cubero on the borders of Laguna, — was it a service that the Pueblo Indians remained loyal? When Union officers, and, for that matter, Confederate officers too, found it difficult to operate in New Mexico because of hostile Indians, was it a service that the Pueblo Indians were the enemies of those hostiles? Colonel E. R. S. Canby, in charge of the military zone, was forced to raise money for the payment of troops. There is a story that the Abeita family of Isleta actually financed Union forces during this anxious period, and were never reimbursed. If this story is true, was it a service? The Governor of Colorado in 1861 wrote to Colonel Canby: "The Indian populations west of Arkansas have united with the rebel war to the amount of 64,500." Was it a service that Canby did not have to garrison the Indian pueblos of New Mexico? Where were their sympathies during the War with Spain? In the late unpleasantness, when we gratefully accepted their pittances and did not reject their sons, did they render service? They were not citizens, remember, and could have acted as indifferent, dissatisfied wards.

LAGUNA

You see, I am not sure about these things, a long residence in the desert and remote places having somewhat dulled my perceptions. I merely ask the questions.

What services to these United States did ever the Apache, the Navajo, or the Sioux render? Were they not hostiles as long as there remained a chance for their success in the field? Were they not first fought off, and then, through treaty moneys and gratuities, bought off? Have we ceased paying the bills? Is it possible that the Pueblo Indians of New Mexico are less deserving than these?

But from another angle one may argue that the Pueblo Indians were unreasonable in their application for the interest of Congress after seventy-five years of neglect; and that they should not have viewed the Bursum Bill with alarm and distrust, because, being safe from the terror of allotment in severalty, and resultant land appraisals and land sales, they could not offer anything to attract such collectors of real estate as exist in South Dakota. They may be issued "certificates of competency," but the certificates do not carry with them patents in fee, and thus do not permit them to dispose of land. "They have not ceded any land to the Government" because, whatever their fancied grievances, they have never been wholly at the mercy of Congress and its appointees.

And as for the "17,000 acres, I think," it would be idle, perhaps impudent, to advise the coachers of the Indian Bureau to consult diligently its own not inconsiderable library. Perhaps Salmeron and Benavides, along with other ancient chronicles, are not to be found there; perhaps Bancroft, Bandelier, Davis, Prince, Lummis, and Twitchell are absent; but the library should produce

Hodge and Fewkes, Mindeleff and Winship, in neatly bound, green-covered volumes. And all are to be located in the Congressional Library, which stands in Washington to the eastward of the National Capitol, a large ornate building of which the cost was $6,347,000. The *New York World Almanac* says: "The collection is now the largest in the Western Hemisphere. It comprises over 3,420,000 printed books and pamphlets." In fact, although of small literary merit, the long array of reports from the Indian Agents for the Pueblo Indians, beginning with Calhoun's, should shed some light on this matter — a subject, it would seem, that an Indian Commissioner should be aware of.

This stereotyped answer at once classifies the Pueblo Indians as "small potatoes," and certainly limits them in a Congressman's mind to a meagre holding of less than a township of land each — not so much as one South Dakota land speculator may hold of lands sold for the best interests of the Sioux, under laws designed by a certain Congressman who sought to improve them before he began to father them.

Hodge mentions the original grant to the Lagunas as comprising 125,225 acres, but he undoubtedly included in this estimate their "purchased lands." Whatever area the Lagunas were permitted by the Spanish to hold and enjoy, it was confirmed to them and patented by the United States Government as 17,361 and a fraction acres. But long before the American occupation they had acquired by purchase from Spanish or Mexican holders several large areas, and twice presidents of the United States had granted them the use and occupancy of additional tracts (Executive Order reservations). The total of this one pueblo's holdings in land is far different from 17,000 acres, as will be seen from the following table. Fractional acres have been dropped for the sake of clarity.

	ACRES
Original Spanish grant, as confirmed by patent	17,361
The "Paguate Purchase"	75,406
The "El Rito," "Gigante," and "San Juan" purchases	25,233
Executive Order, July 1, 1910 (Taft)	29,665
Executive Order, March 21, 1917 (Wilson)	117,214
Total acres	264,879

For a number of years the Paguate Purchase tract was in litigation with respect to its actual boundaries, the matter having gone to the Supreme Court of the United States finally, but without disturbing the original decree of the Valencia County Court adverse to the Indians. By the Supreme Court's ruling of June 1, 1926, the Lagunas lost probably one fifth of this old holding. It is not likely that the Indians would have lost anything had governmental political appointees been alert. No appeal was taken by the Pueblo Special Counsel from the decision of the State Court, to bring the matter into the purview of the United States District Court for New Mexico. And thus the final decision was in accordance with the rules.[1]

[1] The Paguate "purchase" tract of the Indians was alleged to be in conflict with the Cebolleta grant owned by Mexican-type citizens. Each of these grants had been confirmed by the same Congress in 1868. The Paguate survey was made in 1877 and the Cebolleta survey in 1881. The south line of the Cebolleta grant and the north line of the Paguate Purchase were surveyed *by the Government* as the same. There was no overlap shown.

Owing to continued trespass, it was necessary to quiet title to the Paguate tract, and Francis C. Wilson brought such suit in 1910. The Cebolleta owners pleaded in their defense that the boundary established by the government survey was incorrect; that the true boundary was a mile and a half south of that line — thus claiming an area of that width within the Indian holding. The issues were litigated on the theory

The pueblo of Laguna is unique among the pueblos also in having a recorded title to all of the lands it claims, and the Commission now established for the clarification of pueblo land titles will find it comparatively easy to adjust the affairs of this pueblo.

The pueblos of Sia, Tesuque, Nambe, San Ildefonso, San Juan, Picuris, and Taos are to be found in the 17,000-acre class. Cochiti, Santa Ana, and Sandia have each more than 24,000 acres, while San Felipe and Jemez, adding their Executive Order reservations, have 34,767 and 42,359 acres respectively. The five largest pueblos hold, in grants, purchases, and Executive Order areas, as follows: —

	ACRES
Laguna, now about	250,000
Isleta, approximately	174,000
Acoma	95,792
Santo Domingo	92,398
Santa Clara	49,369

---

that the Cebolletas had title to that tract under adverse possession under their original grant. In August 1914, the Valencia County Court decided against the Indians, thus arrogating to itself the right to revise and define a Federal survey.

Before any final decree had been entered, Wilson filed a motion for a rehearing, setting up among other points that the Court had no jurisdiction to shift an official survey of the Government. This motion for rehearing was before the Court when Wilson resigned his position as Special Counsel for the Pueblo Indians, he having accepted the nomination of the Progressive Republicans to run for Congress. His resignation was accepted by the Indian Bureau on September 17, and one Jacob H. Crist was appointed to succeed him as Special Counsel.

On September 28 the final decree of the Court was entered, when, for the first time, it was possible to take an appeal. The appeal should have been filed within one year. Crist did not take an appeal, although petitioned and urged to do so.

Thereafter Wilson was engaged as private counsel by the Laguna Indians, and sought to get this case into the Federal District Court on the theory that a Federal question was involved — that the decision of the Valencia County Court was void for want of jurisdiction and because the basis of its adverse finding operated to change the boundary of a Federal survey and to establish in its place a boundary claimed by oral testimony only. Wilson could not prevail on the District Court to accept his view that a Federal question was involved, nor was he successful in the Supreme Court of the United States later.

Before the Bursum Bill was proposed, the reports of Indian Agents showed to the Indian Bureau:—

	POPULATION	ACRES
Northern Pueblos (7)	1,766	150,086
Southern Pueblos (10)	6,439	781,092
	8,205	931,178

This is, roughly, 1450 square miles of territory. Limiting the seventeen pueblos to 17,000 acres each gives a total of 289,000 acres, less than one third of the area they actually held by one title or another, the validity of these titles not being, for the most part then, and in a lesser degree to-day, under dispute. But it should be borne in mind that the pueblo areas *susceptible of irrigation* are relatively small, and at some pueblos, notably San Juan, were largely in the possession of squatters or persons holding under doubtful titles.

Nor is this all. Let us examine the evidence as to other lands, not cited to the Congressional committees, that the Pueblo people once held. Acoma long ago lost a considerable and valuable strip of its western lands through the schemes of unscrupulous white men, aided by testifying traitors of their own who were bribed not to distinguish carefully between two important springs. The land may not be recovered to them. The rules prevent any resuscitation of justice.

Isleta was more fortunate. This pueblo claimed for years, and was finally awarded by departmental decision, all the land between its surveyed east line and the "backbone" or crest ridge of the Manzanos Mountains, subject, of course, to white mining claims and white homestead patents filed during the period of departmental lassitude. The actual bounding of the original grant was plain, but for a generation the Isletas had no title to their mountain slopes, with timber and water and mineral, because a surveyor had decided that "the foothills" represented "the backbone" of a huge mountain range, and, following this easy solution of a tough job in walking, ran their east line in the foothills. But for the fact that, thanks to President Roosevelt, this area fell within the limits of a National Forest Reserve, and was somewhat protected from entry and settlement, the Isletas would have lost not only the surface, and water, and timber, but whatever of valuable ores may yet be found in this believed rich mineral section.

The old pueblo of Pecos had a Spanish grant; but in 1820 its population had dwindled to fifty-eight persons, and about eighteen years later there were but seventeen survivors. This remnant, following their Indian impulses, left the grant lands to reside with their kinsmen, the Jemez Indians in the San Diego Cañon country, where Agustin Pecos, the last of them, died on July 20, 1916. Sometime in that period between 1876 and 1913, the first being the date of the Supreme Court's "Joseph Decision," and the last being the date of the Supreme Court's "Sandoval Decision," which reversed the Joseph Decision so far as Pueblo citizenship, Federal guardianship, and Pueblo Indian ability to alienate lands were concerned, the pueblo of Pecos *was sold for state taxes!* No effort to my knowledge has ever been made by the Government to recover it, if indeed such an effort could possibly succeed. This famous area, once the welcoming landmark to Gregg and those who hurried over the last stretches of the Santa Fe Trail, has now been legally acquired by the proprietor of a "dude" ranch. Thus the proud old pueblo of Pecos, or of Cicuye, as you will, which Vetancurt described as possessing "a fine church with six towers dedicated to Neustra Señora de los Ángeles de Porciúncula," which once could muster five hundred warriors boasting that "no one has been able to conquer them," becomes a legend like the Quivira frontier, and passes from tax lists to mortgage files, down through lawyers and real-estaters, to its present picturesque Lord of the Manor. *Sic transit gloria mundi!*

Fourteen hundred and fifty square miles of land in central New Mexico is enough to arouse cupidity — an area much larger than the land surface of the State of Rhode Island. However arid and seemingly worthless it appears in places, it is actually valuable and most necessary to the present and future needs of these Indian people. They cannot be dismissed. They must exist. Their state of being is a fact; their condition was ameliorated once if not justified by the laws of Spanish kings, who, when necessary, had time to decree as petty things for them as the extent of pasture lands and the proper limitations for pueblo swine. Witnesseth: —

. . . And in regard to the pasture lands, it is my will and order, that there shall not only be separated from the settlements and Indian places the thousand varas[1] mentioned in the said ordenance of 26th May, 1567, but even a hundred varas more, and that these one thousand one hundred varas shall be measured from the last house of the settlement or place and not from the Church; and if it should seem to my Viceroys of New Spain that the pasture lands are at greater distances than within the said one thousand one hundred varas, it shall be declared as soon as this dispatch is received or is made known,

---

[1] Vara — Spanish yard = 33.1 inches, or 2.759 feet
League — 5000 varas = 2.636 English miles
Land league — 4428 acres
Pueblo land grant — 4 square leagues = 17.712 acres

that in relation to all the above, I give to my Royal Court of Mexico power and authority to order to be done and executed whatever may be necessary without limitation whatever, enjoining them as I now do, that they shall seek by all possible means improvement in the treatment and preservation of the Indians. . . .

And whatever of this may be executed, a general and particular account shall be given to me on all occasions, because I desire to be informed of whatever may be done for the benefit of the Indians.

I, THE KING

Done in Madrid, *4th June* 1687
 By command of the King, our Master
  D. Antonio Ortiz de Otitalora
Sealed with four rubrics

When, in 1919, I succeeded to the responsibilities of Agent Lonergan, a long battle between the state and the Federal authorities was nearing its close — or, as one might describe it, the zero hour for the state's last desperate assault. This mêlée, with the Pueblo Indians enacting the parts of ignorant audience and valuable prize, had been in steady progress since the ratification of the Treaty of Guadalupe Hidalgo (1848), marking the close of the Mexican War and the proposing of the Pueblo riddle. But, during the years, forces of intelligence had been acquired in their cause. Mr. Justice Colin Neblett, of the United States Court for the District of New Mexico, Mr. Summers Burkhart, the United States Attorney for New Mexico, Judge Richard H. Hanna and Mr. Francis C. Wilson (both of whom had served as Special Pueblo Counsel), were foremost among those who aided the Agents and enabled them to accomplish something with the pueblo problems. From 1911 to 1922 the Pueblo Indians had a dozen seasons of protection, and guidance, and progress — not without local turmoils, but without great material losses. In that period they had to suffer but three Agents, and for the greater part of the time had but one. Since June 30, 1922, they have rejoiced in nine different directors at their two Agencies, and will no doubt testify that variety is the spice of life.

Having managed to elude other menacing legislations in the guise of "citizenship bills," and having once neared Congress with a measure that would have guaranteed to them the same Federal administration as other Indians without affecting their titles to land, they were suddenly confronted with the Bursum Bill. They had found a new friend in the person of the Secretary of the Interior. He hailed from New Mexico; he knew their conditions; he had long had his eye on them. He acquiesced in the curing of their land diseases by the application of a splendid document. To doubt the wisdom or justice of this new charter was dangerous, if not seditious. It had been pruned and whereas-ed by some of the keenest legal minds of New Mexico, who were invited by him to exhibit their skill.

Under the new administration, a new Special Counsel for the Pueblo Indians took office, and could not be expected to antagonize those who had befriended him. The two Indian Agents were soon removed to other fields, and two successors, imported directly from the land-sale country of South Dakota, were installed as mufflers. The United States District Attorney resigned as the Wilson Administration passed into history. The Pueblo provinces resembled a gloomy race track, filled with tipsters and jockeys, but without judges; the favorite drugged, and New Mexico's staunch mud-horse, paying 100 to 1 in the well-oiled machines, touted to win in a canter.

But an unreasoning public arose from its lethargy, fell upon the Bursum Bill, and dismembered it. The public printer has in stock the reports of hearings before a subcommittee of the Committee on Public Lands and Surveys of the United States Senate, 67th Congress, 4th session (January 1923), and hearings before the Committee on Indian Affairs of the House, same Congress and session (February 1923), concerning bills proposed as substitutes for the mangled and discredited Bursum Bill.

These two documents, comprising 695 pages of fact, and some little fiction in schedules, will be found very instructive. There are places where the pages become graphic. The reader may then assure himself that Ralph Emerson Twitchell was an historian before accepting his position as Special Assistant to the Attorney-General; that Francis C. Wilson was an advocate without sentimentality or spleen; and that others had no fish to fry. They said so themselves. One will receive the astounding information that Congress has never denied justice to the aborigines — or, at any rate, not in the time of the Chairman; and one will observe to what lengths the files of the Indian Bureau are used in a pinch, and what parts of them are not produced in a dilemma. These reports close with a splendid picture — that of the Secretary, surrounded by his satellites, anxiously, even courageously, defending the purity and integrity of public officials, a tableau that somehow brings to mind a once famous painting by Munkacsy.

V

THE MAN IN THE GOLDEN HELMET

> Courtiers abandoned lands and fees to reap a thousand-
> fold;
> From Cadiz and the Pyrenees came men who wanted gold —
> And turquoise blue, and pale sapphires, raw silver for their
> bowls;
> The loot of conquest! while the friars were covetous of souls.
> — "The Bells of Cochiti"

From the very beginning of Pueblo things, as we know of them, two influences were dominant — religious fervor and political intrigue. The first was represented by Fray Marcos de Niza, and the friars of Saint Francis; the second by Mendoza, the Viceroy of New Spain, and his protégé, Don Francisco Vasquez de Coronado.

On April 14, 1528, a Spanish expedition under Narváez was on the coast of Florida, and in the following November a small boat bearing members of this ill-fated company was wrecked somewhere on the Gulf Coast. Three white men and a negro slave survived. These were Cabeza de Vaca, Dorantes, Maldonada, and the negro Estevan. They started on an amazing pilgrimage westward in the hope of reaching Spanish settlements. Eight years later these undaunted four entered San Miguel de Culiacan, April 1, 1536. Compared to this, Peary's dash to the Pole was but an episode. In July 1536, the four men reached the City of Mexico, and were received by the Viceroy, and by Hernando Cortes himself.

The arrival of the Cabeza de Vaca party caused a sensation. Mendoza purchased the slave from Dorantes, and later selected Fray Marcos de Niza to explore the northern empire these survivors had traversed. The negro was to accompany the friar.

Fray Marcos was, therefore, the first white man to see the frontier of the Pueblo provinces, and Cibola, which is Zuñi. Different writers have spent much time in considering whether or not Cabeza de Vaca saw any of the Pueblo towns. Bancroft is convinced that he did not, although he says it can never be quite definitely proved that his route of wandering did not cut off the southeastern corner of what is now New Mexico. Bandelier states that the theory is without foundation, and is at pains to prove his contention. Others use their skill in identifying flora, fauna, and geographic evidences given in Cabeza's narrative to show that this party may have touched the southernmost edge of the Pueblo civilization. But the consensus of history is to the effect that the Franciscan, Fray Marcos, deserves this honor.

In 1538, Fray Juan de la Asunción and another friar were sent on a mission of exploration north of New Galicia-Sinaloa. Bandelier believes that these two reached the lower Gila River, and perhaps the lower course of the Colorado; and thus, two Franciscans probably discovered and traveled through what is now southern (that is, the line Tucson to Yuma), Arizona, one year earlier than the year of de Niza's adventure on the trail of the Pueblo Indians.

Fray Marcos was born in the city of Niza, then included in the Duchy of Savoy. Beyond the place of his birth, nothing is known of this prelate prior to his appearance in the New World, in 1531, on the island of Santo

Domingo, and the following year in Peru. After several years in Peru and Quito, he came to Mexico. His first work in New Spain seems to have been as a missionary at Jalisco. The accuracy of his writings concerning the Indians of Peru and Quito was attacked by Cortes; but Cortes demonstrated generally that he was jealous of anyone who sought distinction in those fields he claimed as his own. His prestige was waning. At any rate, the Provincial of the Franciscans, in 1539, issued to Fray Marcos a certification of character and knowledge, including cosmography and navigation along with theology. Bancroft's idea of de Niza is thus expressed: —

> ... an imaginative and credulous man, full of faith in northern wonders, zealous for spiritual conquest in a new field, fearful that the great enterprise might be abandoned; hence the general *couleur de rose* of his statements; hence perhaps a few close approximations to falsehood; but there is no good reason to doubt that he really crossed Sonora and Arizona to the region of the Zuñi.

In short, Fray Marcos was for several centuries branded as a splendid liar because Coronado's findings did not check out with his anticipations in riches. And Bancroft and others accepted this valuation of him. Bandelier states that for over three hundred years Fray Marcos was the most slandered man in history. After his Pueblo reconnaissance, he was elected Provincial of the Seraphic Order in New Spain, retired to Jalapa in 1558, and died in the City of Mexico.

Coronado was born in Salamanca, and married a cousin by blood of Charles V. Her father had been Royal Treasurer of New Spain. Coronado received as a marriage gift a very large estate from his mother-in-law, and also one confirmed by royal grant. He came to New Spain with Mendoza, the Viceroy, in 1535. We find him in 1537 quelling a revolt in the mines of Amatapeque, and in 1538 he appears as a legally recognized citizen of Mexico, where he was a witness to the recognition of the royal order giving Hernando de Soto the right to explore and conquer Florida. In 1539, Coronado became Governor of New Galicia. Here he was engaged officially when Fray Marcos de Niza started on his journey to Cibola. Coronado accompanied the friar as far as Culiacan, the most northern settlement of the Spanish (founded 1531), and when Fray Marcos returned to recite the adventures that earned for him a long reputation as a Munchausen, Coronado accompanied him to the City of Mexico and his interview with the Viceroy.

A second expedition was then planned by Mendoza, for the purpose of conquering the Pueblo provinces, and Coronado was placed in command of it with the title of Captain-General. Coronado had been preferred over Cortes, and thus we reach the first of the New Mexican Conquistadors, his army of two hundred and fifty to three hundred "gentlemen on horseback," and upward of eight hundred Indian allies. The whites of this expedition were mostly soldiers of fortune, among them the sons of many noblemen, the employment of whom the Viceroy had found a problem. Here was a chance to occupy them. It is recorded that only two or three of them had ever been settled residents of New Spain. Compostella, on the Pacific Coast south of Culiacan, was fixed as their place of rendezvous and point of departure. Pedro de Castaneda de Nacera, the historian of the expedition, gives the names of the principal officers, and they should interest the tourist pathfinders of the present: —

THE MAN IN THE GOLDEN HELMET 89

Standard-bearer, Don Pedro de Tovar; Master at arms, Lope de Samaniego; Chief of artillery, Hernando de Alvarado; Commander of infantry, Pablo de Melgoza; Captains, Don Tristan de Arellano, Don Pedro de Guevara, Don Garcia Lopez de Cardenas, Don Rodrigo Maldonado, Diego Lopez, Diego Gutierrez.

Castaneda mentions a number of illustrious names among the other gentlemen "on this the most brilliant company ever collected in the Indies to go in search of new lands."

On February 23, 1540, this army of eager adventurers started. The footmen were armed with crossbows and arquebusses, some having sword and shield, wearing iron helmets or vizored headpieces of tough bull hide; the Indian allies painted for protection and armed with the bow and club. There were more than a thousand of these natives and servants, red and black men, to lead the spare horses of the cavaliers, to drive pack animals with the baggage, to herd the droves of cattle and sheep. There were more than a thousand horses in the train, besides the mules loaded with camp equipment and a half dozen *pedreros* or swivel-guns. It was eighty leagues to Culiacan by the route they took, and the army arrived there before Easter — March 28, 1540.

At the same time the Viceroy outfitted and projected another expedition, by water, that of Hernando de Alarcón, who proceeded up the Gulf of California to the Rio Colorado of the West, it being expected that Coronado would follow the coast. But Coronado's route swung eastward, and Alarcón returned.

After many days of discouraging marching through a barren country, tried by thirst and wearied by sun and sand, during which time Coronado divided his forces and pressed on ahead with a majority of the fighting men, he came within sight of the first city of Cibola (Hawaikuh) a place of about two hundred houses, located fifteen miles southwest of the present Zuñi pueblo. If this were the treasury of loot the army had visioned, then Fray Marcos must have lied. Castaneda relates: " Such were the curses that some hurled at Fray Marcos that I pray God may protect him from them." Different dates have been conjectured for this arrival on the frontier of the Pueblo Indians, and the capture of the Zuñi stronghold. Hodge says that Coronado reached Hawaikuh July 17, 1540.

But miserable and unworthy as the place appeared, it required a sharp and rather desperate fight to reduce it. Many of Coronado's men had arrived weakened from the long march. Hawaikuh was a walled city, demanding an assault with ladders and the taking of a gate. Defense was made from above. The Captain-General himself had a rough experience:—

They knocked me down to the ground twice with countless great stones which they threw from above, and if I had not been protected by the very good headpiece I wore, I think the outcome would have been bad for me. They picked me up from the ground with two small wounds in my face, and an arrow in my foot, and with many bruises on my arms and legs, and in this condition I retired from battle very weak. . . . They all directed their attack against me because my armor was gilded and glittered. . . .

After the defeat of the Zuñi, and the occupation of their pueblos, Coronado dispatched Don Pedro de Tovar to ascertain what the province of Tusayan (the cities of the Hopi) promised; and the intrepid friar Juan de Padilla accompanied this party. Later he dispatched Don Garcia

THE SANDIA MOUNTAIN
Near the site of ancient Puaray

Photo. by H. F. Robinson

TAOS PUEBLO
of San Geronimo

THE MAN IN THE GOLDEN HELMET

Lopez de Cardenas to investigate the stories of a great cañon in the west and the upper Rio Colorado. Then Coronado received a deputation of natives from Cicuye (Pecos), and forwarded Hernando de Alvarado ahead of his main column to seek that place. Alvarado's division passed by Acoma, reached Tiguex, and went on to Pecos. Coronado, taking another route, reached a group of pueblos that Bandelier and others believe to have been south of the present Isleta, on the Rio Grande, and from thence he followed the river northward to the Tiguex province.

Puaray was the winter quarters of the army, but not before a battle had been fought, growing out of Alvarado's treachery to the natives of Pecos, which caused the whole province to rise against him. This first betrayal, followed by others, culminated in Cardenas's order to burn alive two hundred captives, for which he was imprisoned later in Spain. But the error had been made, and thereafter Coronado reaped misfortune.

Tiguex[1] was the central province of the Tihua Pueblo Indians, now represented by those of Isleta, Sandia, Picuris, and Taos. In the time of Coronado, and for many years afterward, Puaray (located very close to the present town of Bernalillo, sixteen miles north of Albuquerque) must have been its most important pueblo, since all the early explorers and missionaries were at once attracted to it. The Tihua were separated into three groups: those of Taos and Picuris in the far north; those of the Tiguex province proper, which extended from north of Bernalillo south to the borders of the Piro, near old La Joya, Isleta being to-day the centre of this line; and a third group, situated on the eastern slopes of the

[1] Pronounced "Teewesh," the plural of Tiwan or Tihuan.

Manzanos Mountains in the pueblos of Chilili, Quarai, Tajique, and others now unknown. It would appear that the name "Tiguex," as used by modern writers, embraces the pueblos of the Rio Grande bank only; but it would seem from Castaneda's description of the province that the pueblos of the Manzanos strip and pueblos west of the Isleta-Bernalillo line were included. This would place settlements, now unknown, on the Puerco, and has confused some writers, even Bancroft. Quite likely there were Puerco pueblos, and probably these marked the original habitat of the Trias (Sia), and not the present location of Sia on the Jemez River.

Having reduced Puaray, Coronado marched to the buffalo plains and the Quivira adventure. On his return, the Captain-General suffered a fall from his horse in a race, the animal's hoof striking his head, and this most serious accident had been foretold long ago in Spain. His indisposition was accompanied by premonitions of death, and visions, all gloomy. His soldiers became restless, and petitioned for a return to Mexico. They had found no riches, nor any country that promised estates. Moreover, there had been desertions. The whole business spelled failure from the standpoint of a Conquistador — a drab picture when compared with the glories of Cortes. So in April 1542, Coronado gave orders for the homeward march.

The Franciscans were of sterner stuff. Three of the religious remained behind with several servants and Indians. Fray Juan de Padilla turned his face resolutely toward the Quivira country, where he was to meet his death and grace a legend; Fray Juan de la Cruz remained at Tiguex to be killed in November of 1542; and a lay brother, Luis Descalona, went back to Pecos and was never heard from again. Thus the entrada of the Conquistador, and the entrada of the Franciscan — the one a blurred memory along the Rio Grande, the other still active in the field.

There is no doubt but that, when Coronado's depleted column passed the last of the pueblos, before striking into the lone, inhospitable desert, he sighed that his once grand vision had simmered to these miserable mud hovels that had yielded nothing but forays and blows. He little thought, as he looked back to see the last of them, that these strange people would make up his whole fame; that they would engage the attention of nations for centuries after his death in obscurity; that they would form part of a war's loot and have a distinct place in treaties; and then, for nearly a century, present themselves to courts as a vexing riddle; that they would arouse the cupidity of padrones and peons lower than themselves, and finally, after having suffered neglect, derision, and exploitation, without striking a blow would gather to their simple cause a host of friends and counselors, jurists and legislators, most of whom had never seen their adobe walls. Coronado no doubt despised them as a driveling show, as indeed to him they were, as to-day in some respects they are. But whatever the Conquistador thought of the Pueblo Indians, these savages formed a people; and a people will maintain their historic entity when the greatest of conquerors and the lowest of padrones have disappeared.

As for the Pueblo Indians who watched Coronado's column over the horizon, they no doubt held councils in the kivas that night and arranged dances to celebrate their relief, and during the next few weeks received messengers and sent forth others, weary scouts who trailed that column into the south. Was this the last of these strange visitors? Save for a few of the Mexican Indians whom the Zuñi persuaded, one way or another, to remain behind, and save for those three courageous friars, it would be the last of them for the better part of a lifetime. Soon the three friars had gone to their rewards, and the Pueblo Indians would see no more of white men for forty years.[1]

In these forty years the Spanish settlements gradually moved north. The frontier crept from New Galicia to the southern portion of what is now Chihuahua, where the Spaniards worked mines in the vicinity of Jimenez. The Franciscans had not forgotten, however, the sacrifice of Juan de Padilla, and it is said that a few of them, alone, penetrated the northern country, to Tiguex and Pecos. The record of them is but rumor: but the next definite footprint is that of a Franciscan, one Agustin Rodriguez, a friar stationed on the frontier. In 1580 he applied to the Viceroy for permission to explore the Pueblo country. The King had ordered that no such privilege should be granted, but the Viceroy organized a volunteer escort, notwithstanding the royal command, and the Provincial of the Franciscans gave his permission. Bancroft says that the escort consisted of but eight or nine soldiers under one Chamuscado. With Fray Rodriguez went two other friars, Francisco Lopez and Juan de Santa Maria.[2]

---

[1] 1563-1565, Francisco de Ibarra made exploration north of the Spanish settlements, and on his return boasted that he had discovered "a New Mexico." This may have been the first application of the name. Bancroft says there appears to be no grounds for more than the vaguest conjecture as to what region was actually explored by Ibarra.

[2] According to Torquemada, Fray Francisco Lopez, an Andalusian, was the superior of the three friars; Fray Juan de Santa Maria was a Catalan; and Agustin Rodriguez was a lay friar, a native of Niebla, Spain.

They set out from San Bartolome, June 6, 1581, and it appears that they journeyed directly up the Rio Grande to Tiguex. After making various explorations, going eastward to the salt lakes and the plains, and being prevented from visiting Zuñi because of snows, the soldiers returned to the Spanish settlements, leaving the friars among the natives. Chamuscado arrived with his men at San Bartolome, but he died on the way to Mexico City where he was to make his report. The testimony of two soldiers, Bustamante and Gallegos, was taken before the Viceroy. According to the statement of Barrundo, another of the soldiers, three Indian servants had remained at Tiguex with the missionaries. One of these Indians later returned to San Bartolome bringing news that one of the priests had been slain, at which time the three servants had escaped believing that all the friars had suffered the same fate. One of the servants was killed during their flight south, but the third was discovered in the mines of Zacatecas, and confirmed the story of the first.

The martyrdom of these three missionaries revived interest in the Pueblo provinces, and Antonio de Espejo tendered his services to the Franciscans as one willing to lead and finance an expedition, if someone in authority would authorize it. They accepted his offer, and a license and commission were procured from the Governor of Cuarto Cienegas. With a very small force, — less than twenty soldier volunteers, — Espejo achieved to himself a distinguished place in the roster of those who first entered this Indian empire; for he managed to visit all the points of interest, including Acoma, where he was entertained by a solemn dance; Zuñi, the Hopi pueblos, going even beyond them to somewhere in the neighborhood of Bill Williams Mountain north of Prescott, Arizona; thence returning and going eastward to Pecos, to follow the Rio Pecos to the buffalo plains; thence visiting the Jumanos, and reaching San Bartolome again in September 1583. At Zuñi he had found three of those Mexican Indians, left behind Coronado's column over forty years before, who had almost forgotten their native tongue.

In a little more than ten months, and without losing a man or engaging in conflict with the Indians, Espejo had covered these extraordinary marches. It should be remembered, though, that Espejo was not ferreting out treasure or making huge demands on the natives for the feeding of an army. He was no Conquistador. His was an expedition for the purpose of acquiring information for the Franciscans. Coincident with his return and report there were several projects brought to the attention of the authorities by those who wished to enter the north; and Espejo himself proposed to the King directly for authority to colonize the Pueblo country, offering to expend 100,000 ducats in the venture and to give bond for the faithful performance of his contract. Had he received this permission, he would have graduated into a Conquistador; but nothing came of these proposals.

The next entrada was made in 1590 by Gaspar Castano de Sosa, who was Lieutenant-Governor of Nuevo Leon. He did not consult anyone for his authority, but proceeded to Pecos, where he had a battle with the natives. It is believed that he reached Taos, which he did not enter, and returned south because of severe weather and snows. He visited the Galisteo, Queres, and Tiguex divisions, thence down the Rio Grande to meet a force of Spanish that he thought would prove reënforcements. Instead of welcoming de Sosa as a highly successful explorer, entitled to the palm, this force arrested him, placed him in chains, and returned him to Mexico. Then, between 1594 and 1596, the Bonilla-Humana expedition enlarged the scope of its original orders to pacify the actual frontier, and sought Coronado's Quivira. This expedition was attacked by an army of Indians, and there were but three survivors, one of whom, a Mexican-Indian deserter, told the story in 1598 to Don Juan de Oñate, in the presence of his poet-historian, Villagra.

The most important act in the Spanish cycle of the great New Mexican drama now follows, and this Don Juan de Oñate is its star. For Oñate conquered New Mexico and the Pueblo Indians, established the Franciscan missions, and colonized the country. He entered it in January 1598, with a well-equipped army of four hundred men, one hundred and thirty of whom brought their families. Many influential Spaniards helped to promote this expedition, and it contained among its company the sons of Juan Salvidar, who, sixty years before, had been a captain under Coronado. Bancroft gives a long list of these first settlers in New Mexico, and their names are common in the state to-day.

Don Juan de Oñate was a man of wealth and ambition, the son of an officer under Nuno de Guzman, who resided at Zacatecas. His wife's grandfather had been one of that town's founders, and owned mines there. Oñate entered into an agreement with the Crown for "the discovery, pacification, and settlement of the provinces of New Mexico, which are in New Spain," and he was to bear the entire burden of the expense.

Between 1598 and 1608 he ruled as Governor and

Captain-General. It is possible that he remained in New Mexico much longer, certainly until the arrival of his successor in 1609; but Vetancurt says that in 1608 the King assumed the support of both garrisons and missions. Like Coronado, Oñate would seem to have died in obscurity.

VI

CHAUFFEURS AND COLONISTS

> In years to come some savant that a Salamanca builds
> May trace my crumbling record on a cliff the sunset gilds;
> To wonder if I died there in the lonesome long ago —
> And simple ones will think my name was *Anno Domino*.
> Most men at arms drift to one end — they make an arrow stay,
> And leave their names to taverns on the future King's Highway;
> But I 've a sweeter rendezvous, and I would fare amain
> To my enchanted castles in the purple hills of Spain!
> — "A Santa Fe Siesta'

THE events of the Year of Our Lord, 1598, that time of Oñate's entrada, are recorded shadows on a vast vague background. Some things in New Mexico were very different then; and to-day, if one marches about in the Pueblo provinces, there will be experiences sufficient to offer amusing contrasts. In the natural order of things everyone has to suffer an entrada. Therefore I remember mine. It was of little historical importance, but it sufficed.

In 1916, three years before I gave my receipt for the Pueblo Agency cash, property, and grief, it was my fortune to journey down from the Holy City in company with several desert officials. One of these was an old Washington chum, who, after directing for a time the activities of the Service for the Suppression of the Liquor Traffic among Indians, grew tired of raids and battles, and sought peace and relaxation as an Indian Agent, first at the Pueblo Agency at Santa Fe, and next, among the San Juan Navajo. At the time mentioned, Harold Coggeshall was "Nahtahni" at the "Shiprock Agency," and, as he proposed to travel there by motor from Albuquerque, he invited me to accompany him as far as Gallup, whence I would take my own car to the Hopi or Tusayan provinces. As a comparison with the movements of the Conquistadors, trudging along in armor and bull-hide boots, this may seem ridiculous, and especially when one visions a huge seven-passenger car, its mighty engine purring smoothly, that stood at an Albuquerque curbing. No Conquistador ever had a thing like that to sweeten his marches. I hasten to assure you that it was not a government machine. It belonged to an Indian trader.

We started one morning from Albuquerque, and by noon had reached the pueblo of Laguna. Here Coggeshall proposed that we forage for a meal, but the trader said that by twilight we should see the lights of Gallup and refill bunkers in another of those excellent Harvey hotels. So we did not even replenish the drinking-water canteen, but purred onward, across crude and seemingly shaky pueblo bridges, through the frontier town of Cubero (once a garrison post), past Acomita, and then McCarty's Station, the last settlement of the Acomas, close to the western boundary of the Pueblo country.

The monotony of the journey was relieved by Coggeshall's reciting his adventures among the Pueblo people of the north, and indeed the tale was moving enough. He had fought all creation, including the Indian Bureau and its inspecting officials, in his efforts to protect the Indians of his jurisdiction. In this he had been staunchly assisted by the Special Pueblo Counsel, Mr. Francis C. Wilson, of Santa Fe. They had faced bitter hostility; but as Coggeshall's training had been that of a fullback during a period of Amherst's glory on the field, he never knew when he was licked; and it would seem too that Wilson's character contained Irish as well as legal elements. The futility of his experiences had somewhat embittered Coggeshall, and he apparently meditated plans of revenge that involved several degrees of Pueblo torture. Recalling his influence at Washington, I suggested: —

"Why not secure to yourself the job of Commissioner, and then . . ."

"I would rather be God for five minutes!" retorted Goggeshall, grimly.

And we purred onward. The homemade bridges carried us safely across the meagre gutter of the San José, but eventually we came to a ford. Now one is justified in sneering contemptuously at the Rio San José, when he has bridges, even those suspicious spans of Indian construction; but one is never warranted in deriding a Southwest stream at a ford.

Said the trader: —

"We crossed this all right coming down."

That had been several days before. I had lived five years in the Hopi country, and I urged upon him that one should get out, remove clothing, and wade the crossing to learn definitely whether or not it possessed a bottom. This would have consumed several minutes, and I was used to it. I even volunteered for the service.

"We crossed it all right coming down," repeated the trader. "This engine would pull out the San Mateos. Here goes!"

The car roared down the slope and took the water like an ocean-going tugboat. The Rio San José at that point was not more than forty feet wide. The car ploughed bravely across it, but it also burrowed downward, and the water came up over the floor, and the engine coughed desperately, and the car *did not* climb out of the Rio San José. It managed to place its front wheels on the far slope, but the rear ones became discouraged and churned hopelessly.

We did not sit there idle, and reminiscences were forgotten. We all disrobed to plunge into the Rio San José, carrying desert brush and a few pieces of old plank left from some other tragedy. With these we sought to corduroy the bank. All efforts failed of success. Came three o'clock, came four o'clock . . . came a Mexican don with a wood wagon, driving a miserable span of desert-fed bronchos. He was enticed by the showing of several pesos, hard silver, to lend the assistance of his Arabians. He possessed a length of chain, and I crawled down into the Rio San José to make this fast to the front axle of the twentieth-century behemoth. Then I assumed charge of affairs, because I was experienced in the herding of cars through Hopi washes. I knew that the Mexican could never inspire that team in an event of this kind. It would require a sudden explosion of nervous energy, vigorous action with a whip, and violent Anglo-Saxon language. The Mexican had the whip.

The car was eased back into the stream to enable a bit of a start. Coggeshall, the fullback, with the aid of the Mexican, was to crush in the rear of the car once it started, and the trader was to buck his engine coincident with the explosion I would generate behind that team. At a given signal, all and everything moved in harmony.

For once a desert team surged into the collars lustily, and with that peculiar half-swinging motion that drags things, the engine roared madly, the hidalgo fell into the mud, and Coggeshall exerted as much of strength and vitality as had once carried him across goal lines. We proceeded forward grandly, until about halfway up the sloping bank, when all the motive power collapsed. The car eased itself again, groaning against the brakes, into the Rio San José, and rested. It was discouraging.

Because, if you know anything about desert teams, you will know this — they make such an effort, even when handled by a master, but once. After that they smooch together, heads hanging, flanks trembling, fit only for the crows.

Night would soon sweep down on us, still in the Rio San José, and the air began to cool. It was no place in which to be at that hour, according to our schedule. Moreover, we had nothing to eat, and by this time had consumed all the water of the canteen. Good judgment did not invite one to drink of the Rio. And for several hours we had worked. Then the Mexican reminded us that he would like to wend his weary way homeward. I disapproved of this, pointing out that he had not as yet completed his contract, and that the eight-hour day was not to be invoked in such an emergency as this. He demurred, and said he wanted to go home. I became morose and seated myself on his wagon's tongue, thus preventing his harnessing the team. A battle was imminent, when Coggeshall reminded me of the horrors of an alcalde's court, toward which he said confidently I was headed. So the Spanish contingent departed.

Now came still evening on, and we were, if you remember, right there in the Rio San José. The sunset was a superb scarlet-and-gold effect, followed by great banks of deepening purple clouds that smothered San Mateo's highest peak into the night. But we paid little attention to this demonstration of desert loveliness. We recited no litanies, and if a Franciscan had come along we would surely have put him to work.

"How far is it to the nearest American team, with vestments of real leather harness, including a block and fall?" I asked them, for my companions knew that locality and I did not.

"Moving from here in a northerly direction," explained Coggeshall, "until one strikes the Santa Fe *camino*, thence moving westward along its timbers for about seven miles, one approaches the town of Grants. A seasoned traveler, light on his feet, might do it by ten o'clock or even midnight."

"Sooner than that," I said, thinking of a Hopi's pace.

"He will have to walk ballast and crossties," lamented Coggeshall.

"No trails?"

"The railroad or nothing," he said, gloomily.

We decided that two walkers, thus furnishing each other company, would lighten the journey by discourse and accomplish the feat quicker than one lone sulky messenger; so we flipped a coin, and the trader and I lost. Coggeshall would remain with the car, which had tufted cushions and several blankets.

"Fetch me something to eat," he called out as we departed.

I shall never forget that walk to Grants. The Santa Fe main line is superbly ballasted with stone pieces, each having an average of five sharp edges, and I wore canvas shoes. And whoever first arranged the design of crossties simply considered a decorative effect without thought of practical pedestrianism. After walking, slipping, and stumbling between twenty and thirty miles, we were convinced that we had passed Grants in the dark. When about to give up hope, we perceived a sullen glowing red eye in the thick blackness.

"That's Grants," said my companion.

Two hours later, when we had traversed at least ten more weary miles, we staggered into a little railroad station and drank the well dry. Then we aroused the local trader from his slumbers, and he very kindly assured us that he would lend every assistance, providing we would wait for daylight. We agreed that Coggeshall would have retired long since and should not be disturbed; so we rolled into bed. Shortly before dawn a cook prepared for us a splendid breakfast, and arranged choice viands in a container for the one at the lonely bivouac. A boiler of steaming coffee accompanied it. The trader provided a lusty team, a genuine wagon, and a block and fall. It was one of those beautiful desert mornings, and we arrived at the Rio San José only a little after sunrise. Coggeshall was awaiting us, an expression of keen expectancy on his face.

"Here's breakfast, Cogge, old scout!" we called cheerily. "You fall to, while we snake out that omnibus. . . ."

"Did you bring me any water?" asked Coggeshall, sourly.

So help us! We hadn't. . . .

I knew when to say nothing with a complete verbosity. Coggeshall did not upbraid the trader, but I was an old friend. It is friendship that bears the burdens of these distressing matters.

Then we quickly snatched the car out on to the bank, and in a few minutes were again purring along smoothly toward Gallup, a station that we reached without further misadventure. In those days, for motoring across the desert, there was nothing like a sturdy American team, and a block and fall.

As for Don Juan de Oñate, he suffered no such troubles. On April 30, 1598, his splendidly equipped army had reached the Rio Grande and proceeded up the west bank. The historians mention a number of incidents in connection with this march, and remain utterly blind to one of vital importance. Bandelier has realized the significance of Gaspar de Villagra. He says: "New Mexico alone may point to a poem as the original authority of its early annals." But even Bandelier overlooked the possibilities in Captain Marcus Farfan de los Godos, the first playwright of the Southwest and perhaps the father of American drama. On the night of April 30, 1598, somewhere in the vicinity of the present city of El Paso, the army witnessed Farfan's "original comedy." There was no doubt plenty of standing room in that immense auditorium on the banks of the Rio Grande, and it is quite likely that a claque of coyotes and the ghostly cacti furnished all necessary incidental atmosphere. We have no record whether the play enjoyed anything of a run, or, if a failure, where the scenery was stored. Another original comedy, *The Merchant of Venice*, was then having its first performances in London, engaging the attention of those who preferred the smell of a flambeau at a play to thirsty struggles in desert wastes. Who knows but that a dangerous rival was lost in this Spanish Farfan? A most versatile fellow, and perhaps jealous of Villagra the poet, who, equally versatile, could turn from the manufacture of couplets to the pursuit of horse thieves, a hunt lasting months, to hang them out of hand when apprehended, thus introducing that gentle custom to the Southwest. Farfan, when not inditing scenes and curtains, would make long journeys to the mines west of Tusayan, and he took a leading part in the great battle of Acoma. Talented and redoubtable figures! Let us not abandon hope. Farfan's prompt-book may yet be found, probably as a palimpsest, and I would suggest a search for it among the papers of Don Miguel Nemecio Silva de Peralta de la Cordoba y Garcia de Carillo de la Falces, since he has given evidence of a morbid interest in old Spanish chronicles. This is a believed joke that may trip some curious tourist. The self-created nobleman mentioned perpetrated the greatest fraud of the Southwest.

Through the indifference of Spanish bureaucrats, America lost in this period a figure that did rival Shakespeare. We find an obscure gentleman of Spain, in 1587, going to Seville, seeking employment as a provisioner to the Armada, and so anxious to make good in his position that he was excommunicated later for his excessive zeal in collecting wheat at Ecija. In 1590 this same man presented a petition to the King, applying for any one of four posts then vacant in the American colonies. His petition was endorsed briefly: "Let him look for something nearer home." Oñate could have used these talents, for his men were always foraging and not always with success. So the fellow went on patiently laboring in Spain, becoming poorer and poorer until, when Oñate was making his army ready for the northern adventure, the able provisioner and public drudge had failed to balance his accounts, and was in jail at Seville, where he busied himself with a pen, and produced a romance that he described as "just what might be begotten in a jail." Thus America lost *Don Quixote de La Mancha*. What if Cervantes had secured one of those four posts in the colonies! Who were the officials that denied us this glory? Alas! The biographer and the historian would appear to have neglected them.

Oñate reached Puaray of the Tiguex province in the latter part of June; and here, like Espejo in 1583, he was assigned to the principal room of the village guest house, where he could contemplate a mural decoration depicting the martyrdom of those three lonely friars, Rodriguez, Lopez, and Santa Maria. The actual site of Puaray has been the subject of much discussion, with Bandelier, as usual, clarifying the case. The Rio Grande, augmented by the waters of the Jemez, here sweeps very close to the lone and abruptly towering Sandia Mountain. The present town of Bernalillo (founded 1695) indicates the neighborhood of ancient Puaray. Why search to-day for the very foundations? Rio Grande, ever restless, has had many beds. One can stand in a Bernalillo lane, or, if one must have Pueblo atmosphere, in the suburb of Santa Ana close by, and vision Friar Juan de Santa Maria going toward those gaunt and barren Sandias on his way to El Paso del Norte, actually to end all his pilgrimages at San Pablo.

On July 4, 1598, Oñate was encamped at Gipuy, on the banks of the Arroyo de Galisteo, somewhere in the locality of the present pueblo of Santo Domingo. Bandelier says this point is more than a mile east of the present railroad station of Domingo, New Mexico, a trader station on the automobile highway to Santa Fe. A little beyond Domingo Station a bridge crosses the Galisteo. Domingo marks the first contact the Santa Fe Railway makes with the present Pueblo Indian country. Thereafter, it has its right of way through the communal lands of six of the pueblos: Santo Domingo, San Felipe, Sandia, Isleta, Laguna, and Acoma, in the order given westward, touching also the purchased *ranchitos* of the Santa Anas, close to Bernalillo, and does not leave the ancient Pueblo Indian stage until beyond McCarty's Station, where is the last village of the Acomas, a distance of 125 miles. The trains pass very close to the pueblo of Santo Domingo and its huge mission, a town containing perhaps the most stubborn and contentious of the present Pueblo divisions. The Santo Domingos have been cheerfully in the forepart of many wars. They have leaped to battle in any Pueblo cause, worthy or not. They are the Irish of the Pueblos. I know. I have had the unpleasant job of telling them where to alight, and trust I may be pardoned for recording that they got off at exactly that point. And, too, I have fought for them, being accused once of having taken up arms against the sovereign state of New Mexico, and receiving as my reward, shared with Judge Richard H. Hanna, of Albuquerque, the unusual experience of having a Santo Domingo dance performed in my honor. I doubt that Oñate could boast as much. And after many adventures in old Santo Domingo, I managed to enroll them as friends, even to aged Julian Lebato, whose reed basket serves to catch my manuscript as I write.

Not only does Santo Domingo picture a hectic history of revolt and torture and murder in the past, but one would think, on examining its census of to-day, that Oñate's column had settled there permanently. We find Olguins, and Aguilars, and Penas in profusion, the heads of Indian households. Bancroft's list of the first settlers of New Mexico is largely repeated. A curious sight to see one Ponce de Leon Aguilar bent over a rock in the sun, patiently grinding and polishing bits of turquoise he has procured, somehow or other, from the Cerrillos mines district, once the treasure-trove of his ancestors, and, of course, now owned by white men; or to have some Herrera, half-dressed and not too sanitary, protest, perhaps with a few piratical oaths, your entering the mission compound, especially should you pack one of those devil-boxes for picture making, a thing as full of mischief as an ancient arquebus. Should you have a letter from the *Superintendente de los Indios*, it may help in time of stress; but do not count too much on this credential — not unless you are confident of the Superintendente's personal and local rating. More than one such official, including myself, has been menaced there, as were the less successful of the Conquistadors. Coggeshall exchanged blows to build the government day school, and I sadly suspect that others, not without cause, were ousted ignominiously.

From Santo Domingo, Oñate proceeded to the establishment of the first capital at San Gabriel, close to the present pueblo of San Juan above Santa Fe, when the hospitality of the natives gained them the distinction of being called "of the Gentlemen." The building of the first permanent church was begun in August, and on September 8, the Feast of the Nativity of the Blessed Virgin, this chapel was dedicated in honor of San Juan Bautista. Fray Alonzo Martinez, the commissary, most likely celebrated the first High Mass in New Mexico on this day. Certainly the ceremonies were as full of ritualistic splendor as the dramatic Spanish could contrive, in order to impress the multitude of curious natives that assembled.

On the following day, September 9, 1598, occurred the most important event in the early annals of New Mexico. With so large a body of Indians present, the Captain-General took the opportunity to explain the purpose of the expedition; Fray Martinez then assigned the seven friars to their mission districts. It was the beginning of the permanent work of the Franciscans in this field, work which in less than twenty-five years would reach the astounding proportions described by Benavides, and in seventy-five years would command the admiration of all commentators.

This division of the Pueblo provinces into mission parishes was like all such beginnings of empire. It was like the assignment to Calhoun of the immense territory of which he was put in charge by his ignorant superiors in 1849. A vague, practically unknown area was designated for each of the religious pioneers. Bancroft's list is interesting as indicating the very large number of pueblos existing at that time, according to the early chronicles, in contrast with the few that remain to-day. His list probably presents duplications, but even considering this possibility of error, our seventeen living pueblos were once surrounded by scores of others; although, as Mindeleff has cautioned, they may not all have been occupied at one time.

The seven original parishes were, briefly, as follows:—

To Fray Francisco de Miguel
   Province of the Pecos; seven pueblos of the eastern Cienega; the Vaquero or wild tribes of the eastern frontier; the pueblos of the "gran salina"; probably forty towns in all,

of which there remain only the ruins of Pecos, Galisteo, Abo, and what has been styled "the Gran Quivira" district (not to be confused with Coronado's frontier Quivira), with various nameless heaps.

To Fray Juan Claros

Province of the Tihuas. Probably this friar had whatever of native civilization there was along the Rio Grande, from Tiguex southerly to the locations of the Piro. Isleta and Sandia are the present-day monuments of this division, once estimated as having more than sixty pueblos.

To Fray Juan de Rosas

Province of the Queres. Early records include with these people the now extinct Tanos division and omit Sia. Otherwise the records make it plain that the Queres towns of to-day — Cochiti, Santo Domingo, San Felipe, and Santa Ana — are located in the immediate neighborhood of their ancient sites. Laguna, a comparatively modern construction, is an exception. Acoma, on account of its isolation, was grouped with the pueblos of the west.

To Fray Cristobal de Salazar

Province of the Tewa: Of the many pueblos named, there still exist those of San Juan, Santa Clara, San Ildefonso, Nambe, Tesuque, and Pojoaque (this last no longer Indian).

To Fray Francisco de Zamora

Province of the Picuries: together with the Apaches north and west of the Sierra Nevada, the pueblo of Taos, and the villages of the upper Rio Grande.

To Fray Alonzo de Lugo

Province of the Jemez: and the Apaches (that is, Apaches de Navajo) of that region. Bancroft expresses his lack of confidence in the number of Jemez pueblos, and lists nine only. Bandelier lists eighteen, but Hodge shows that Bandelier's list may easily contain nine duplications.

To Fray Andres Corchado
Province of the Trias (now accepted as the Sia). This was the western parish, including Acoma, the Zuñi, and even the Hopi of Arizona. It is suspected that Trias was not the present Sia, close to Jemez. Bancroft tries to reduce the distance between the present Sia and Acoma by suggesting that Acoma may have been situated at a point farther north, on the Puerco. It would seem more likely, considering the physical aspects of Acoma, that there was a Trias province centring on the Puerco, the towns of which have entirely disappeared. Zuñi should be considered the western frontier of this parish, since the remoteness of the Hopi would demand another distinct division.

The giant task that these few priests faced in this lonely, inhospitable land, is graphically expressed by Bandelier:—

Though the Pueblo Indians accepted the new faith voluntarily, and to a certain extent adopted it from their own peculiar standpoint, they expected material benefits from a creed that promised to give them spiritual advantages. In their conception, religion is but a rule of conduct controlling man while alive, and on strict compliance with which his success in this world depends. In short, the Pueblos looked on Christianity as upon another kind of magic, superior to the one which they practised themselves; and they expected from the new creed greater protection from their enemies, more abundant crops, less wind and more rain, than their own magic performance procured.

Having arranged a capital, and the establishment of religion for the conquered people, Oñate set forth on further explorations. Late in October he started for the pueblos of the west, reaching Acoma on the twenty-seventh, where he narrowly escaped being killed, for, while the pueblo submitted, a hostile cacique sought to entice the Captain-General into one of the kivas to put him to death. Oñate was wary of such invitations, and thus escaped being butchered.

He went on to the Zuñi pueblos, arriving there about the middle of November. Here he found the crosses that had been erected by Coronado, fifty-eight years before, and, like Espejo, met some of the Mexican Indians who had been Coronado's allies. Oñate then visited the Hopi towns. From the Tusayan province he dispatched Farfan and Quesada in search of mines, said to have been located about thirty leagues to the west. And from this camp among the Hopi, he ordered Juan Salvidar by messenger to march westward and join him with thirty additional men. The advance of this contingent brought on the first battle at Acoma.

When Salvidar reached Acoma with his relatively small force, the natives again tendered their hospitality. The soldiers ascended the mesa, their suspicions lulled into a feeling of security. They separated to different parts of the pueblo to procure needed supplies. Quite likely their foraging was rude and discourteous, for suddenly they were set upon by the warriors. Five of the Spaniards leaped from the mesa's brink to escape their assailants, and it is recorded that four of them survived the effects of this fall. I could not swallow this statement, did I not know of an incident at the First Mesa of the Hopi that parallels it. A small boy pitched from the edge of that mesa and was found below, severely bruised and shaken, but having no serious injury. Now Acoma, at the particular place of the Spanish leap, may have been buttressed and mattressed by centuries of offal and débris, as was the First Mesa. These Spaniards surely did not drop the full three hundred and fifty-seven feet, which is the official height of the mesa.

THE ACOMA MESA
The pueblo may be seen on the crest

AN ACOMA BLOCK

In the fight eleven of the soldiers lost their lives, including their leader, Juan Salvidar, together with two servants. Four others of the party were wounded. This was December 4, 1598.

The distressing news reached San Gabriel in due time, and word of it was dispatched to the Captain-General. He spent a night in prayer before returning to his little capital at San Juan. There he assembled the friars to learn their views as to the prosecution of *a just war;* and their answer, when considered in all its details, comprised a very able decision in the matter, and one that did not hamper him. Oñate preferred to have something of ecclesiastical sanction for the campaign that he purposed to carry forward relentlessly. It would enable him to fend off sentimental criticism later, and we may be sure that distant Spain had its coterie of sentimentalists. He selected the most courageous of his captains, among them Farfan and Villagra, and placed them in command of Don Vicente Salvidar, brother of the slain leader. This party consisted of seventy men. It is evident that they intended to wreak vengeance on the hostile pueblo of Acoma, and while the idea of slaughter is not pleasant, one cannot but admire the courage of only seventy men coldly and calmly considering it.

All the early chronicles emphasize the strength of Acoma as a fortress, but most of the writers grossly overestimated its garrison. To-day, Acoma has 900 people. In 1680, Vetancurt gave it 1500. Benavides in 1630 had estimated 2000 inhabitants for Acoma, and Oñate placed their number at 3000. It is probable that Acoma never had a larger population than that given by Vetancurt, which would enable the assembling of between 300 and 400 combatants; and surely, considering their defenses, this was force enough to hold the place against seventy Spaniards.

The ascent of the Acoma mesa to-day presents no alarming difficulties to the visitor, but it would not be selected for an assault against odds. Castaneda, historian of the Coronado expedition, thus described it: —

There was a broad stairway for about two hundred steps, then a stretch of about one hundred narrower steps, and at the top they had to go up about three times as high as a man by means of holes in the rock, in which they put the points of their feet, holding on at the same time by their hands. There was a wall of large and small stones at the top, which they could roll down without showing themselves, so that no army could possibly be strong enough to capture the village.

Therefore, the last phase of the ascent was up the face of a sheer cliff. Consider this problem in the dim light of dawn, that year of 1599, with hundreds of savages above one, armed with their deadly bows, having boulders in plenty, stone axes, boiling water even, and immediately the task becomes a trifle hazardous, if not dangerous.

These Spaniards may have seemed a bit childish when proposing some grand scheme to a distant King, or when enacting an original comedy on the desolate banks of the Rio Grande; but once before a place like Acoma, seventy against three hundred (not counting the Amazons), they explain fully the martial glory of Spain.

Vicente Salvidar's force reached the scene on January 21, 1599. It was greeted with jeers of defiance and showers of arrows. That night he divided his men, sending twelve under Villagra to ascend the rock at one side, at a point distant from the regular trail along which the main body would make a feigned attack. It would seem that Villagra's twelve made their ascent in the night, to arrive, if at all, about dawn; and that they succeeded and had commenced a diversion about noon of the next day. The accounts differ. The feigned attack of the larger party then became an assault in earnest. By the morning of the twenty-third, the whole force of Spaniards had gained a footing on the summit.

A terrible hand-to-hand struggle began. After having driven the Indians from the edge of the mesa, the Spaniards had to assault and take the town; and to quote Lummis: "A pueblo is a fortress in itself, and Salvidar had to storm Acoma, house by house, room by room."

One of the pedreros had been dragged along somehow, and slowly it began to batter the adobe walls. Then the houses of the pueblo took fire, or were fired, and to the excitement of battle were added the horrors of flame and smoke. This desperate fight lasted until noon of January twenty-fourth, or nearly three days. Many of the Indian warriors sprang from the cliffs rather than yield to the Spanish, and by the time the few remaining leaders sued for mercy, about 900 of the Acomas had been slain or smothered in the burning houses, if we estimate its population at 1500, since only 600 survived the battle. All the Spaniards were wounded in more or less degree, but only one man had been killed outright. The pueblo and its great store of supplies in grain had been destroyed, most of its able-bodied men were dead, and Salvidar came away with eighty girls as captives. Acoma, the stronghold in the sky, had fallen. The effect of this upon other hostiles must have been most salutary. To them, it was beyond precedent, beyond the imagination, for they all had feared the Acomas and did not doubt the impregnability of Acoma. Fifty years would pass before the Pueblo Indians would again become bold enough to organize a revolt against these strange and terrible white men out of the south.

This presents a picture of the ruthless Conquistador, and the pacifist may comment on it at length. But the Conquistador could advance much testimony in his defense. Advancing, not overburdened with supplies or gear of war, and with relatively few fighting men, into a country that, except in the trackless mountains, possessed little game; that presented heartbreaking distances and barren waterless stretches, and that had all the appearances of a hostile and teeming population of natives, the Conquistador was not without his headaches. He had no reserves, no line of communication with a base of supplies, and, if he did not conquer his commissariat, his army would starve. One cannot be a Conquistador with an emaciated army. At Hawaikuh, Coronado's musketeers had arrived so weak and feeble that they could scarcely stand. Unlike other military captains, conducting campaigns that, compared to his, were rather swift raids, the Conquistador could permit no straggling. His weary and sick and wounded must be carried with him. On him too was the responsibility for the safety of hundreds of noncombatants. He dared not leave hostile towns, undefeated and exultant, in his rear. Once having entered this empire of the savages, every vestige of final success and self-preservation depended on his crushing every opposing force.

He had more to support than this. There would be a day of reckoning with his superiors, who could do nothing to assist, but who expected a heaping share in the ultimate glory and profits — first, the Viceroy, who was wearing out an anxious chair in the capital; and

CHAUFFEURS AND COLONISTS

second, those powerful patrons who had helped to finance this expedition. Beyond them were the swivel chairs and ferret hutches of Spain, and a covetous King, supported by his law courts and prisons. More than one aspiring Conquistador had been welcomed home in chains, disgraced, vilified by those who had cheered his departure. Personally, he had gambled every penny of his possessions and his official standing in the venture, and perhaps expected something besides embroidered glory as a reimbursement. Often, too, as in the case of Coronado, there was that "pretty wife" awaiting his return, to preen herself, perhaps at Court, in the bloody feathers of his conquest. Thus, dogging the footsteps of any Conquistador, were the spectres of Defeat, Disgrace, Debt. His only hopes were in the prospect of final Success, Glory, Fortune.

Under similar circumstances, any captain would have had to exercise the same bitter, unrelenting, cold-hearted methods. This was War, in a vast unknown country, supplies and reënforcements being hundreds of leagues away. Unless a courier carried the ringing news of success, some half-mad fugitive might struggle across the desert to report the utter extermination of his column.

But, chants the commentator, Espejo did not find it necessary to be ruthless in his venture of 1583. Quite true. And Espejo was not a Conquistador. He did not plan to hold and colonize many provinces. He did not have a grumbling army to feed. He was the first tourist.

With the fall of Acoma, Villagra's poetic account ceases. He promised the King that he would continue it, but very likely this stirring event appealed to him as the best curtain; for after Acoma, while Oñate made extended explorations, they were without grand dramatic scenes.

"El Morro" holds the record of his return, April 16, 1605, from "the discovery of the south sea," that time when he followed the Colorado River to its mouth.

Oñate was Governor for ten years, the term of his contract. It has been assumed from most meagre data that he founded Santa Fe; but this is now disputed. Undoubtedly he proposed to change the seat of government from San Gabriel, and planned "the Villa," but documentary evidence indicates strongly that the actual work of founding Santa Fe fell to his successor, Don Pedro de Peralta, not earlier than the autumn of 1609.[1]

[1] While the record is incomplete, especially between 1608 and 1621, the list of known Spanish Governors and Acting Governors at Santa Fe numbers 55 in 224 years (Oñate, 1598, to Melgares, 1822). Don Facundo Melgares, who headed a remarkable military expedition to the Plains region in 1806, and who was the officer to take Zebulon M. Pike as a prisoner to Mexico in 1807, was acting as Governor *ad interim* when Iturbide's revolution ended Spanish rule in New Mexico.

VII

A MYSTERY AT ACOMA

> "How many miles to Acoma?"
> The eager tourist said;
> "Can we get there by candlelight,
> And find a bath and bed?
> We saw a poster on the cars,
> Of sand and desert pools,
> With women bearing water jars
> And children far from schools;
> It brought a thought of foreign lands,
> Algiers and old Cathay;
> And when we get to Acoma
> What will the people say?"
> — "*An Indian Agent's Lullaby*"

THE Indian Agency at Albuquerque was in a quiet street, the sleepy aisle of which was lined with tall Lombardy poplars. The busy centre of town was a number of blocks away. The Agency grounds were shaded by old wide-branching trees. A hedge of lilacs masked the rough fence at one side, and dahlias and cannas and silken flapping poppies bloomed in its prim beds and around the base of a tall white flagpole. Japanese morning-glories climbed riotously over the colonial pillars and screens of the upper floor, and nearly always the water pipes were throwing their silvery sprays into the warm air. An old-fashioned place, more like a home than a busy office of the Government. The lawn surrounding its bay windows and verandas was a deep-piled velvet carpet. The untiring efforts of Andres Moya kept the garden as trim as an old woman's quilt.

The reason for this rhapsody is to prepare for a sharp contrast. The Pueblo Indian Agency was the last place where, on arising in the morning and enjoying the sight and perfume of that garden, one would expect to drift downstairs to face a murder. Nevertheless, such grim and ugly things do worm their way into the often monotonous work of an Indian Agent. He may conduct his Agency skillfully, and beautify its surroundings, if he is that kind of man; he may have the confidence of a large part of his Indian charges, and rejoice that they obey him without murmur; and he may go to his lunch and arrive from his dinner, and indite reports, and gamble with the next year's Annual Estimate, and attend meetings of the Rotary Club, all proving him as uninteresting a fellow as the insurance agent down the block or the baggage-handler who meets No. 9. But once in a while he comes suddenly, and with no desire for the experience, on a sure-enough murder.

I concede that the insurance agent hunts down, sells, and adjusts insurance policies, a very honorable and creditable piece of business; and that he must at times face tragedy and perhaps peculiar doings; that the baggage-handler swings trunks, and there have been trunk mysteries. Some day he may stumble across one. But when either do, the matter is reported to the proper authorities, and that day's dinner at home is spoiled by recitals of the affair. The Indian Agent, however, has no such refuge. With Indians, he is the proper authority. Talking about his murder will relieve him of none of the responsibility. And his opportunities for encountering it, in murder's grimmest aspects, are a bit more probable, for his lines of communication reach out from that pleasant garden and the mission effects that he hopes, with the cunning of Andres Moya, to ensnare, into the desert, north and south, along the great troughs of the Jemez, the San José, the Rio Grande; and these lines end in curious sixteenth-century villages, isolated, remote, some of them quite beyond the pale. One could still stumble across evidences of witchcraft, and credos are supplemented by sorceries and the booming incantations of drums.

There are Indian Agents who view pestilence and the rising mortuary reports, defiance of authority, persecution of innocent tribesmen, the prostitution of those who should be in school, and murders even, with the same equanimity with which they regard a cattle trespass or the onslaught of some lawyers bent on undermining a title. All these unfortunate things are sent by God, and to be endured with a shrinking and wholesome humility. Indeed, left to itself, the Indian country anywhere will contrive to run itself, after its own sixteenth-century fashion. Therefore, why should an Agency physician worry his Agency chief about trachoma, or syphilis, or murder, for that matter? And why should the Agent, in his turn, worry himself or Washington? Trachoma has been known since the days of the ancient Egyptians, and it embarrassed Napoleon in Egypt. Syphilis must have troubled Moses, or he would not have laid commands on all Israel. And as for murder — there is the episode of Cain.

But those two fellows from the distant desert were most persistent. They were a district resident employee, grotesquely styled by the Indian Service as "a farmer," and the government physician from that station. And they had become so imbued with their fantastic, Nick

Carter idea, that they had dropped everything else to attend to it, motoring all the way in from the district of Acoma, ninety-odd miles, to report in person, believing that letters required too much of literary strain and loss of time. I listened to the details of their suspicions, and asked questions, which produced other suspicions and additional grimnesses, not to say suggested horrors, all the while admiring their engaging fancies, and wishing that they had let me alone to complete the Annual Report, a document of extraordinary importance in the annals of this nation.

Then I told them to have their car fixed (always an incident when pueblo employees came to the Big Town) and to await further orders. The details of this murder were not pleasing or quieting. Perhaps those two dust-covered fellows were not altogether such fools as they had at first blush seemed. The evidence being considered in its proper order, and under the glass of a little imagination, it was possible that someone had been murdered. The disquieting part of the affair was that no one — certainly not the supposed victim, nor his mother, nor his wife, nor his tribesmen — was worrying about it other than those two suddenly energetic employees who, unfortunately, had begun to worry me about it.

There was this much of which one could be fairly sure: A man had left his home and disappeared for some days, and no one had sought him. Then, quite suddenly, and in rather a strange manner and place, his body had been found. Thereafter his body had been hurriedly removed to the old penol of Acoma and buried with all the rites and pomp associated with the Acoma tribe. This man had lived at no great distance from the farmer's station, but no concern had been displayed at his prolonged

A MYSTERY AT ACOMA

absence from home, and after the discovery of him no outcry of distress or great grief had been in evidence. This was entirely contrary to the behavior of the average Pueblo household. As for the removal of the body for burial at Old Acoma, they were all carried there when they died in the suburban communities of Acomita and McCarty's, the rural districts of the Acomas. These two Indian settlements are on the Rio San José, within sight of the Santa Fe trains, west of Laguna. The Acomas have their irrigated fields along that stream. The penol of Old Acoma, sometimes called "The City in the Sky," is twenty miles to the south. Few white persons go there save a priest, an Agency employee, the Agent when he feels like it, and an occasional tourist who comes away with a camera filled with impressions, a mind full of theories, and a wallet lacking several dollars. Sometimes the tourist complains to the Agent at Albuquerque that he was ill treated, not to say gouged, on this visit, and the Agent makes some remarks to illustrate his sympathy and the impossibility of entirely reconstructing a primitive people in four hundred years.

The government physician was located in the Laguna districts, and visited the country of the Acomas once each week, unless called by telephone to some urgent case. That was another point. Among the Pueblo Indians it is common to call a physician in an emergency, indeed to demand one hastily, at midnight even, on the slightest provocation, such as a common stomach ache, for instance, as many worthy doctors have bitterly complained to me. In this case, it remained for the farmer to report the death to the physician.

Indian Service doctors are instructed to report promptly all births and deaths, that the census may be posted accurately, and to support their reports with birth and death certificates, on forms furnished, exactly as in the case of other medical officers. The certificate of death is supposed to show the cause of death, in the judgment of the physician, who should act as a coroner unless the Agent is present. The cause of death may not always be diagnosed accurately, but the physician may shrewdly guess, and does. And the doctor should view the body of the deceased. Among such Indians as the Navajo nomads, who bury their dead in haste and burn the camp, this is not always possible. In fact, it is seldom achieved. But with the pueblo type, who have permanent domiciles and established burial grounds, and many of whom are, superficially at least, Christians, and who have been within the zone of civilization for several centuries, we expect other conduct.

The physician had inquired into the disposition made of the body, and on learning that it had been removed to Old Acoma, he and the farmer departed for that enchanted place. They "flivvered" the twenty miles southerly, and toiled up the winding rocky stairway to the mesa summit. They were not long in locating the house of grief. The man had been the only son of his mother, who lived permanently at Old Acoma, and she had demanded his body for appropriate burial from her house. Rumor had it that this man had not been appreciated by his wife's people, and that no love was lost between the two houses because of this lack of affection. Among the pueblo-type people, the Capulets and Montagues are often aggrieved by the treatment of their sons rather than their daughters. Rachel is not nearly so important to the scheme of things as is Jacob. I have related all this concerning the Hopi; and sufficient to say here that Jacob, after marriage, becomes a bond servant in the house of his wife, is often dominated by her more aggressive people, has few rights that he may call his own, and, should they take an actual dislike to him, his days in the land may be made surprisingly disagreeable. In such cases, the mother of the boy laments exceedingly that his virtues are not appreciated. And it was so in this case. The mother remarked bitterly that her son had suffered everything at the hands of those despicable people, whose girl was no better than she should be, and now he was dead. These were harsh words.

So the physician went into the home expecting to be allowed to view the body. Judge his surprise on being told that he could not see it. The mother flatly refused him entrance to the room of mourning. Then followed one of those irritating conferences with the members of an obstinate and grief-stricken Indian family. The physician had no means of enforcing his wishes. Farmers are seldom, and physicians never, commissioned officers having authority to regulate anything. When rebuffed, they report to the Agent, the only official within the Indian country who may issue orders without first consulting everyone else. And if they had been authorized, the subordinates would have hesitated to act without the knowledge of the Agent. Two men, unaccompanied by police, will do well to step softly at a time like this, so as not to antagonize thoroughly a native population at a place so far removed. The Agent may go there, and risk his neck if he chooses; but farmers and physicians are not paid for that sort of work.

The threat of reporting such occurrences to the Agent, however, usually enables the subordinate to gain his ends, always providing that the thing to be achieved is reasonable and explained in detail. When this card was played, the mother consented to permit the doctor to view the body; but he was not permitted to examine it. He saw a body, prepared for burial, swathed in robes and coverings; and that was all he saw. There was something about the whole affair that inclined the physician to believe the man had not died from either pellagra or arteriosclerosis.

Returning to the settlement of Acomita, more inquiries were made by the farmer and the doctor. They located the youth who had found the body, and heard what he had to say about it.

The village of Acomita occupies a shelf on the south bank of the San José River, a sloping mesa side rising gradually behind it. The railway main line runs along the north bank, and immediately beyond it rises a rugged mesa. The valley is narrow at this point, the north mesa rounding and projecting into it. In a distant cleft of this north mesa, which was itself within sight of the man's home, the body had been discovered. The man had been rabbit hunting, had shot a number of rabbits, and when returning homeward at dusk, or perhaps after dark, had fallen into this crevice, thus meeting his death.

Very good. A robust healthy man of thirty years may go rabbit hunting, and may start to cross a rugged mesa on his way home; and his return may have been delayed until after dark; and he may have slipped and pitched to his death at the foot of a precipice, of which there are many thousands in the Southwest and some of them in the Pueblo provinces. But it is not likely, especially when you consider that this mesa was to him familiar ground, within sight of his home, and that the crevice at this point was not five feet across, *and not more than six feet in depth.*

The body had been found in a recumbent position, on its right side, and not in a heap. The man must have gone down sideways, and that would have meant bruises and scratches, certainly; perhaps a broken arm, probably broken ribs, and possibly a lacerated skull; but not death. The man could have been stunned by such a fall, occurring in the dark, but on his regaining consciousness, even if handicapped by a broken arm and fractured ribs, he could and would have struggled home. Of course men have been killed in such slight falls, but not often, and it is not to be expected.

And then a returned student of the Acomita community, one who had received a good English education, and who had drifted away from much of the old Acoma style of life and thinking, remarked to the farmer that "those people spent one whole night quarreling among themselves" just prior to the husband's disappearance; and another Indian, who worked at a distant store, had seen an altercation between the eldest of the brothers and the deceased on the day following this quarrel. It had not been a fight in white man's fashion, but the meeting had not been a cordial one. It appeared that the reason for the argument had been that the husband returned home too frequently from the sheep camp. Under their system he should have gone to the sheep camp and remained there indefinitely, devoting himself to their fortunes, and thus proving himself a good husband.

These things were disturbing, and justified suspicion, but were scarcely strong enough of themselves to warrant a murder charge. There was one action that could be taken at once, and perhaps should be taken; but it would cause a storm of grievance and protest. Nor was it a pleasant thing to consider, but it was one of those things that fall within an Indian Agent's field of duty. There was a body. At least there had been one. The deceased had been absent from his home about four days when his body was discovered, and the funeral affairs had occupied several days more, and the going to and fro of the employees had consumed more time. Now quite likely this body had been interred in the old graveyard at the Acoma Mission, although there had been no Christian service. The Acomas retain very peculiar ideas concerning their mission church. Occasionally the priest has to inform them vigorously that it is the property of the Catholic Church, the title resting in the Archbishop of the diocese; and on occasion the Agent himself has had to demand the church keys, once accompanying his request with the promise that he would apply a foot to the person of the sacristan who debated the necessity for showing the sacred precincts to official guests. The Acomas do not report deaths, nor seek a priest to officiate at burials, the fact being that Christianity is revived once each year, at fiesta time. Their regular religious services are held in a chapel at Acomita. There is no assurance that if a padre visited the old peñol daily, or had his residence there, the natives would be any farther removed from their desert gods.

Now, assuming that this body had been interred in the old graveyard, I could have it disinterred promptly, and the physician could view it at his leisure, if he cared to be slow about it. It would be better to have the opinions of two physicians, and I had five of them to call on for such service. And it would be just as well to have the testimony of a physician of long service among Indians, one whose statements would not be disputed by some clerk of the Indian Bureau. The chief Agency physician, residing in Albuquerque, was the very man for this unwelcome task. Dr. A. M. Wigglesworth for many years had been identified with the Navajo health work at Fort Defiance, and was now serving the Pueblo people. Also, again considering the remote situation of Old Acoma, and the contentious spirit of some of its leading citizens, it might be just as well to have along a squad of Indian police. We should need gravediggers, anyway.

The following morning saw a party off for Old Acoma. In addition to the two physicians, there was one Juan Chavez, from the San Felipe pueblo, a dependable deputy-special officer, and the redoubtable Louis Abeita, Chief of Indian Police. Other policemen could be picked up at Laguna. In cases of this kind, native police of the district to be invaded should not be included. Local sympathy is not good ballast. In justice to the records of Juan Chavez and Louis Abeita, however, their sympathies could be easily stifled. In point of faithful, intelligent service as officers, these two were superior to all the other desert policemen I have observed. When anything broke on the Pueblo Indian horizon, they were both respected and feared by the guilty. Any group of Indians could talk most United States marshals into hesitation, for a marshal usually proceeds on the assumption that Indians are interesting children and most easily managed through buying them soda crackers at a neighboring store. Neither Louis Abeita nor Juan Chavez held any such deluded theories. One was an Indian, and the other had lived among the Pueblo Indians for many years. They were pleasant and calm enough in demeanor, and filled with Spanish courtesy up to a certain point. They never bribed Indians into acknowledging their authority. And this much was certain with respect to either of them — given a warrant or an order to apprehend, arrest, and deliver to the Agent any culprit, and one of two things could be expected: either the accused would be delivered, not always in good order and condition; or else Juan Chavez or Louis Abeita would be dead.

To-day, they are both sleeping soundly on the Rio Grande, each having faithfully followed through to the end of his last commission. The rise of the river, the fiesta's gayety, the rumor of trouble at a distant pueblo, no longer concern them. Whatever little vagaries of habit or idiosyncracies of character marked them in life, — however foolish they may have seemed at times, — each was a colorful figure and a faithful servant; and I am happy that no petty criticisms or dissensions marred the many days of our association.

To reach Old Acoma by the auto route, one must pass through the pueblo of Isleta; and at Isleta we were greeted by one whose importance in this case was not at once developed. This was the Indian Governor of Acoma, eighty miles from his home and place of official residence. Now Acomas do not visit Isleta frequently, and an Acoma having business with the Indian Agency, or in Albuquerque, would have continued by train to that point. Why stop at Isleta? He was very curious to know our destination, and even though he did not learn it in so many words, nothing prevented his guessing it. In one of the autos sat the Acoma farmer and the Acoma physician, and in another auto sat two policemen. We were all known to him. I am firmly of the opinion that he had posted himself on the Isleta highroad to learn whether or not the official delegation from Acoma would persuade the Agent to institute an investigation. Having discovered that the delegation had succeeded, he boarded an afternoon train at the Isleta station to arrive on the ground ahead of our party. That night he was busy using the local telephone line, speaking to various people in his own language, as was reported later. The result was that all the Acoma Indians joined the "know-nothing" party. Even the returned student, who had given some little information concerning the family quarrel, would now be chary of further disclosures, since life could be made miserable for her if she testified in a public hearing, and might be made unsafe.

Of course, you will think this an exaggeration. It is the popular impression that such things ceased when Gerónimo was taken to Fort Sill. Well, you are entitled to any idea you may wish to indulge concerning the Indians, including the Pueblo Indians of New Mexico, because I am sure you have them, and will favor your own brand anyway. But as an Indian Agent, I am afraid you would occasionally find yourself in hot water — No! not because of public accounts, or the comprehension of circular orders from Washington, but simply because of underestimating the curious wiles of Indians. As for myself, I never claimed to understand them.

Just what pressure the Governor of Acoma brought to bear on his people, I can only surmise; but an Indian governor can bring plenty of pressure to bear when he feels in the mood. And I make the statement that, when an Indian of the pueblo type (this including the Hopi and the Zuñi) knows nothing, he knows it with a thoroughness and a mental vacuity that is profound. One might as well question a stone wall. He is aware that the compelling methods of the third degree may not be used against him. The separating of witnesses, and keeping them separated; repeated questioning; the sitting for hours and putting the same query in half a hundred forms, avail nothing. They are practically nerveless. Under stress of some abrupt happening, like a distressing accident or an unprovoked assault, they may exhibit hysteria, and their mourning grief can be beyond description; but once facing a white man in authority, who wishes to inform himself of something that may cause their tribe embarrassment, their indifference is sublime. They can plead imperfect understanding, although they have the advantage of three languages to his one, and he may be handicapped through interpretation. "Counciling," or "talk," has been their fine art for centuries. Therefore it is best to get tangible and physical evidence promptly, because conviction will be on that evidence or not at all.

My error was in not arresting the Acoma Governor and keeping him from his people until the investigation was concluded. This will fill the minds of the elect with misgivings, as an undemocratic and high-handed procedure; but it should have been done. It would have prevented his influencing that evasive thing spoken of and described elsewhere as "Internal Affairs" — that is, the manners, customs, and usages of the people.

The huge adobe mission of old Acoma stands at the edge of the mesa, dominating a corner of it, and probably so placed for purposes of defense. This church stands at some distance from the pueblo proper, and one approaches it across levels of rock, the mesa floor. Before the church is the graveyard within a wall. It is like a terrace or parade ground before some mediæval stronghold, the doors and belfry towers of the mission commanding it. The south and east walls of this terrace are built on the very edge of the cliff, their balustrade being of rocks set on end, and from them one can look down into the depths below. The edge of the mesa at this point slopes away irregularly, and the walls on these two sides are much deeper than the north or floor wall. The three form a huge box, and Acoma tradition has it that the earth filling it was packed up from the plain below, that God's acre might be within the shadow of their sacred mission — a bit of labor that consumed forty years. The Indians say that ten years were spent in the construction of the church and its convento.

The dimensions of the Acoma Mission are striking. It is about one hundred and fifty feet in length and thirty-two feet wide, inside measurement. The nave is about forty feet in height. The adobe walls are at least ten feet in thickness at the lower courses. The vigas of the church roof are logs about forty feet in length and fourteen inches square. These timbers must have been cut in the mountains, distant more than thirty miles, where snow-capped San Mateo looms. The Indian tradition is that these logs were packed by companies of men, and that from the time they were cut until they reached Acoma, they were not permitted to touch the ground.

The original patron saint of Acoma appears to have been Saint Joseph, afterward changed to Saint Stephen. This was Saint Stephen the protomartyr, but by some mistake the feast is celebrated on the second day of September, actually the feast of Saint Stephen the King. Acoma has an old chalice of hammered silver dating from the early Spanish days, and its chief treasure is the picture of Saint Joseph, said to have been presented by Charles II to Fray Juan Ramirez, who brought it to Acoma soon after 1629. This is the painting that nearly caused a war between Acoma and Laguna in 1847, its ownership being finally decided by the courts.

On the occasion of the investigation, however, our little expedition was not occupied with these historic details. Arriving at the churchyard, well-winded from the climb, and loaded with shovels and other equipment, we discovered two things coincidently. Both were significant. One was a newly made grave, and the other was the Acoma Governor standing beside it as a solitary mourner. He demanded to know our business. I told him that it was my intention to exhume the body. He wished to know why, and I told him that it was necessary that the physicians might examine it, the government medical officer having been denied that right by the family before burial.

"You cannot do this thing," he declared.

Notwithstanding the fact that I had been informed of his actions on the previous evening, I still had no wish to treat him disrespectfully. The *opéra bouffe* that has grown up around these native pueblo officials never did appeal to me, but up to a certain point it had to be recognized for reasons of diplomacy; and, to be plain about it, to avoid furnishing ammunition to those zealous friends of the Indian who every now and then arise to chant about liberty, democracy, and freedom, and who, when on the ground, would seem to enjoy making obeisance to an unlettered native. An Indian Agent should be prepared to report, when necessary, two things: first, that he treated everyone courteously; and second, that he carried out the regulations. With how much inflexibility an Indian Agent carries out the regulations, and the interpretations that may be placed on some of them, depends on himself. Opéra bouffe, in the theatre, is very amusing; but in real life it soon becomes boring.

"I know the law," the Acoma Governor insisted. "You cannot open a grave and disturb the dead without

On the occasion of the investigation, however, our little expedition was not occupied with these historic details. Arriving at the churchyard, well-winded from the climb, and loaded with shovels and other equipment, we discovered two things coincidently. Both were significant. One was a newly made grave, and the other was the Acoma Governor standing beside it as a solitary mourner. He demanded to know our business. I told him that it was my intention to exhume the body. He wished to know why, and I told him that it was necessary that the physicians might examine it, the government medical officer having been denied that right by the family before burial.

"You cannot do this thing," he declared.

Notwithstanding the fact that I had been informed of his actions on the previous evening, I still had no wish to treat him disrespectfully. The *opéra bouffe* that has grown up around these native pueblo officials never did appeal to me, but up to a certain point it had to be recognized for reasons of diplomacy; and, to be plain about it, to avoid furnishing ammunition to those zealous friends of the Indian who every now and then arise to chant about liberty, democracy, and freedom, and who, when on the ground, would seem to enjoy making obeisance to an unlettered native. An Indian Agent should be prepared to report, when necessary, two things: first, that he treated everyone courteously; and second, that he carried out the regulations. With how much inflexibility an Indian Agent carries out the regulations, and the interpretations that may be placed on some of them, depends on himself. Opéra bouffe, in the theatre, is very amusing; but in real life it soon becomes boring.

"I know the law," the Acoma Governor insisted. "You cannot open a grave and disturb the dead without permission from the family or the Governor, and you should have a permit from the authorities. I have been to a lawyer in Albuquerque, and he told me so. You can be arrested for coming here, and you will be taken to court if you do this thing."

I do not doubt that he had been to a lawyer in Albuquerque, and had received this advice. But he had not been to his Special Counsel. Notwithstanding that the Congress of the United States employed at a considerable salary a most distinguished gentleman of the bench and bar to advise them, they seldom ran to him with their complaints. They sought other and unofficial attorneys, a large number of whom seemed utterly incapable of grasping the fact that the Federal Government, having been advised by the Supreme Court of its duty to exercise a fostering care over these Indian people, would proceed to do so without consulting all the petty ordinances of the villages, towns, and cities in New Mexico. It was costing the taxpayers nearly one half million dollars annually to foster the Pueblo Indians of New Mexico, without the assistance of unauthorized lawyers, peons, Penitentes, and back-county J. P.'s who could not speak English.

So I explained patiently to the Indian Governor, who had been reared in this atmosphere, the necessity for complying with the medical rules of the Government.

"You must get a permit," he persisted.

"In that case, I would have to return to the Agency and issue such permit to myself; and if it proved to be illegal, then I would have to arrest and prosecute myself. Now there, like a good fellow, go over and rest yourself in the shade of the church. I intend to open this grave, to-day. When we came through Isleta pueblo, you were waiting outside the jail, and should you interfere now, I will provide a place for you there, inside the jail, and for thirty days. I don't want to do it, but I have had to face a lot of unpleasant things."

"You cannot arrest the Governor of a pueblo," he said.

"That will be demonstrated shortly, unless you stand out of the way."

"I am here to see everything that you do, because I mean to take you into court for this outrage!"

"I have no objection to your seeing; but you can see just as nicely from that place I have pointed out. Now get into it, or the policemen will put you under arrest."

Then the Governor retired, sat on his haunches, and chewed his gums. The shovel men began to work. This part of the task had little of interest in it. Nothing short of murder, and a most distressing murder at that, would ever bring me to such an affair again. There have been critics kind enough to remark on my powers of description; but those powers, such as they may be, will be very moderately exercised in this part of the narrative.

The shovel men worked steadily, and finally the body was brought to the top of the ground. The physicians had provided themselves with rubber gloves, and with alcohol for the frequent sterilization of their hands. They began the examination of the body. At this juncture, the last two shovel men behaved in a manner exciting my pity. They had inclined themselves at a dangerous angle over the mission parapet, and they were not admiring the scenery. They had reached that stage where they were afraid that they would n't die. So I procured a graduate from the bag of the chief physician, loaded it with spring water from a canteen, injected therein a stiff portion of 198 per cent pure alcohol, and administered first aid to those shovel men. But before doing this I threw all my Liquor Service commissions into the valley below.

The unfortunate who had been dragged from his last resting place presented evidence of the fullest, in the judgment of the doctors, to warrant a charge of murder against somebody. He had been struck at the base of the brain with a heavy blunt instrument, very likely an iron bar, for his skull was in a sad state, and his left arm was broken in two places. He had sought to shield his head, perhaps, from an assailant approaching him from behind. His abdomen was a mass of bruises. The physician who had been denied a look at the body before burial had not then seen the man's face. We all saw it now. It was not a reassuring sight, for he had died in a fearful, desperate sort of struggle.

For those who may have an interest in Indian burial customs, I will say that this body presented unique decorations after their fashion. Symbolical designs covered the face of the dead and his silken shirt, executed with great skill in different colors. His final wrappings had been blankets. And in the grave with him had been placed every conceivable thing that a traveler to distant parts might require — packages of food, utensils, and weapons. One of the last things thrown out was *a box of safety matches*. Paint and the arrow survived, but the days of flints were over.

Once the physicians were sure of their findings, all these materials were returned to the grave, with the body rewrapped in its blankets. Disagreeable as the work was, it was performed to the best of our ability. While we had the Indian Governor as a watcher during all this, he was not joined by any of his people. This was another proof that most of the Acoma people had known or suspected the manner of death; for had the man died naturally, the members of his family would have surely appeared to protest the opening of his grave. But they remained away, and the picturesque pueblo of Acoma might have been a town under a spell, so deserted it seemed, so indifferent to this culmination of a tragedy.

With some feelings of relief, we then departed to Acomita. The boy who had discovered the body piloted us to the place in the rugged mesa where he had found it. The fissure was the beginning of a watercourse in the rocks that, as it neared the mesa edge, widened and became very ragged and deep. Where the body had been found, the sides and edges of the rocks were waterworn, and at that place the crevice was not wide — one could easily jump across it — and it was not more than six feet in depth. The body had rested on a quite level floor, the bunch of rabbits with it; but the light rifle the man had carried, or was supposed to have carried, had been found *balanced* on the edge of this crevice. He had not been struck with the rifle, as its perfect condition showed, and the nice balancing of it seemed entirely too well contrived.

It was our common judgment that no man of his age and physical condition could have suffered those terrible injuries through so slight a fall. The footing was of rock, all about the fissure, with no sand or small growth for some distance, so that there was nothing to display a footprint. Then Louis Abeita pointed to the far side of the cleft. There was a grim thing that challenged attention. It was a trifle larger than a ten-cent piece, an evil wafer that had become encrusted and blackened as it dried in the sunshine. There was something shocking about it. It did not affect Louis in that way, though.

"Looks like," he commented, sardonically, "he was

coming home with rabbits, and fell into the hole, and hit himself such a knock that his blood jumped up to the top again."

"Look around, Louis. They may have struggled somewhere close by."

"No!" he replied, confidently. "The man was brought here. Remember those bruises on his stomach? He was carried, across a saddle. Wait here, and don't anyone go moving beyond this rock ledge. I'll look for tracks."

The physicians did not agree with this theory concerning the bruises on the man's body, stating that such marks must have been received before death.

"Maybe he wasn't dead — then," said Louis. He went north on the rock ledge and began milling. After about ten minutes he called for me to come. He pointed to another rocky surface, and there was another viscous spot of blood. He had crossed a sandy space to reach this point, and I asked: —

"Did you find any traces in the sand?"

"They kept to the rocks," he said. "You'll find no tracks in sand wherever there is a rock ledge handy; but we'll find these blood spots until we come to where the horse stopped."

Ahead he went again, and soon called. I found him kneeling close to a clump of desert growth.

"They came this far with the horse — tied him — see the hoofprints? Right here he stepped around a little — shied; and see there! They ought to have wrapped that fellow up better."

A little film of sand thinly covered this rock surface. I could see no hoofprints until the expert pointed out faint disturbances of the sand where the forepart of a pony's feet had left little segments. Midway between these marks of the front and hind feet were several drops of blood.

"That happened when they got him off the saddle, and the pony shied — stepped around. A horse don't like a dead man."

"Can you pick up and follow that horse's trail?"

"I am not sure of doing it," he said. "There has been a rain since, and that has gummed up the adobe sections."

"And this trail is leading away from the village," I said.

"They made a big circle," explained Louis, sweeping his arm around to the northeast of the mesa. "I think myself that they started from somewhere close to the village, but they would have made a big circle. The trail will lead down the far side of this 'mesa."

"Well, you see if you can follow it; and watch out for a heavy bar, or a coupling-pin. They may have thrown it away in the brush, and we will not be likely to find it at any other place."

Louis Abeita grinned.

"I have been thinking of that," he told me, "and the bar, or whatever it was, is in the San José quicksand."

Our party took the shorter trail back to the village, and Louis started off to circle the mesa. Sometime later he joined us, but had little to report. The horse trail, at all places very indistinct, had vanished far back in the rocks. He had picked up another horse trail on his return, but could not be sure that it was the same horse. On the regular mesa paths or trails, rain had obliterated everything. He thought that he had identified similar hoof-prints in an old corral, but there was nothing certain that a particular horse had been used to carry the gruesome burden over that mesa. We held a little conference,

Louis wished to know whether or not I suspected anyone.

"Considering the quarrel in the family circle, lasting all one night, and the threatening of the man afterward by his brother-in-law, — that time when he was expected to be with the sheep, — and other rumors indicating that the man's home life was unhappy, they — those brothers-in-law — may have had a final row with him, and killed him. But I cannot figure out a sufficient motive for a murder."

Louis partially agreed. He gave his theory.

"You do not know Indians. They wanted to be rid of him. The man was poor, came of a poor family. The marriage had not brought them anything but his labor, and he had grown tired of working for them like a slave. He didn't get along well with the wife. That's village talk. And once he was out of the way, she could marry somebody else. Now how about going down to their house, and searching it?"

"For what? They would not be so foolish as to leave a weapon about. It might show bloodstains, bits of hair, or something. And you can't expect anyone of them to confess."

"Let's go looking for a saddle," said Louis. "It's the last thing an Indian will get rid of. Costs money, a saddle."

So that afternoon we went to the house of the wife who should have been disconsolate, to find her sullen and resentful of visitors. The brothers were not about. It was explained that we wished to look through their quarters. There was nothing in the house other than simple furnishings, such as most Indians of this type possess.

"How many corn houses have you?" Louis asked the woman.

They had several, and the doors were locked as usual, and as usual the keys were in the possession of someone who was absent.

"It will be easy enough to break in the doors," said Louis, a thing he would have done had he been alone. But I sent him after the custodian of the keys, and when he returned he escorted a prisoner. It proved to be one of the brothers. The keys having been produced by him, the corn houses were opened, and Louis began a search through the thousand and one things that agricultural and stock people collect. At first it appeared that he would discover nothing of importance, but finally he dragged down from an upper corner, under the rafters, a mass of wrappings, and came into the sunlight with a saddle, a very good one, quite new. The yellow leather of the pommel and skirts was discolored, a spattering of reddish stains that seemed to answer all his suspicions.

"Here!" called Louis, catching the brother in his grip and pulling him forward. "Whose saddle?"

"Mine," replied the man.

"What's this? These spots?"

"Blood," said the Indian, stolidly.

"How did blood get all over your saddle?"

"Fourth of July! There was a chicken-pull."

Once again the thing went up into the thin air. There had been Fourth of July celebrations in the near-by towns, and such merrymaking usually embraced the business of fighting on horseback for a chicken — one that had first been buried to the neck in the ground. Riders seek to tear the unfortunate pullet from its ground trap, riding at full speed and bending down from their saddles; and when one does succeed in this feat, he is immediately beset by all the other horsemen, who endeavor to take the fowl away from him. A mêlée occurs, and in it the successful one usually belabors all about him with the prize. Naturally, this involves damage to the chicken, and the crowd of riders finds itself besmeared with blood and feathers. It was soon determined that this brother had attended such a festive affair. The fact that he had carefully wrapped up and packed away the saddle meant nothing more than that he wished to preserve it from dust and discoloration.

"Where do you keep your horses?" asked Louis.

"They are out on the mesa."

"Don't you keep a horse in that old rock corral across the river?"

"No," said the Indian, "no horse there."

"But you had a horse there, some time ago."

"No."

"We'll go over and see his tracks," promised the policeman.

Again we crossed the stream, and brought up at an old corral on the mesa side. Louis halted everyone at the pole gate, and going inside began at the outer rim of it and gradually milled to the centre. He stopped and said:—

"Here's the tracks of that horse."

Coming out of the corral, he said to the prisoner:—

"Take off your shoes."

The man did not hasten himself about this, so Louis bent down and tugged at the laces. He carried the shoes back into the corral and very carefully placed them in two footprints. He called me to come. The shoes fitted the prints perfectly, and certain heel markings were plainly discernible in the dried mud. The heels of the man's shoes corresponded with these markings.

"The horse was kept in this corral," said Louis to me, afterward. "And he did go in there to get the horse, at some time, and for some job. That's all I know about it."

But you cannot convict an Indian in a white man's court on that sort of evidence, especially when you are his Agent and bound to give him every benefit of the doubt. I had saved several Indians from murder trials, and once I had pressed a case about which there could be no question. And I had been called everything from a bloodhound to a Judas. No! one must have more than heeltaps and indefinite hoofprints.

There was still a possibility that someone of the community would give testimony that, in connection with these findings, might help to prove something. Notice was served on a score of people to assemble that night at the schoolhouse. Those who did not arrive promptly were brought by the police. They were kept separated from each other, questioned, and then dismissed without coming into touch with those still waiting. Until close to midnight I strained what of ingenuity I possessed in cross-examination, and developed nothing. Whatever they may have known, suspected, or dreamed about the matter, all idea of it had vanished. I have always thought that the returned student knew more than she had told at first; but it was necessary to protect her from publicity, for those in remote pueblos who know and tell too much invite disagreeable experiences, and I still believe Acoma no exception to this possibility.

There was to be a final thrill. At the close of the hearing, the oil lights of the schoolhouse were extinguished. Outside it was very black, and, coming at once from the glare of the lamps, it was confusing. Close at hand there sounded a perfect fusillade of shots, and it seemed that they had been directed toward the schoolhouse door. Then a light was seen, dancing about, far up on the sloping side of the mesa. It was Louis with his flashlight, and he was still firing. On coming from the house he had espied a suspicious shadow at a pile of wood close to the window of the room in which I had questioned the Indians. The sash of that window had not been fully closed, nor had the blind been drawn all the way down. Someone, fully interested in the proceedings, had crept up to hear what he could. Louis had called on this uninvited guest to halt and explain himself. He had not obeyed this command, and therefore the automatic's barking.

"He will run until he crosses the border," said Louis.

When we returned to Albuquerque, the two brothers and the widow accompanied us, and were lodged in the Isleta jail to await the opinion of the District Attorney. He was not impressed with my evidence, and indeed I had not expected him to be. I offered to have an analysis of the bloodstains on the saddle made, but he did not encourage me.

"I can hold those people in the jail for some time," I suggested, "and they may talk —"

"Is that likely?" he asked.

"— among themselves. The Isleta jail is a very tiresome place."

This was another idea traceable to Louis Abeita. When not on active duty, he was the warden. According to his plan, then, he escorted imaginary prisoners into the jail at different times, to cells adjoining the one in which the suspected men were locked, and when the doors closed it would be Louis himself in the cell next door, to remain the night, listening. He learned nothing, for the prisoners said nothing, and in a short time they were returned to Acomita; and that was the end of our man hunt.

In justice to a great many people who live in that pueblo, and who perhaps have never committed a serious wrong in their lives, I do not offer this experience as evidence of an all-embracing atmosphere. There are many amiable and well-meaning people among the nine hundred Acomas. But they exhibit very poor judgment in the selection of their native officials, as many travelers can testify. Through demanding fees, and by acting in a threatening manner toward visitors, they have more than once brought themselves to unpleasant notice. An unsavory experience affects a whole neighborhood. Despite the fact that Old Acoma has the most wonderful setting of all the Indian pueblos, I could summon little interest in the old penol. I have never been able entirely to efface the picture of that post-mortem in its ancient churchyard. Not all the beauty of San Mateo in the distance, the Enchanted Mesa across the valley, the garden of the grotesque rocks, "El camino del Padre," nothing could remove its gruesome memory.

VIII

CHRISTMAS REVELS

> I too have known the solemn calm
> Of Holy Week and litanies;
> The faith in Cross and blessed palm
> On simple hearths the padre sees;
>   The blessing that the guests receive,
>   The Christ-child fires on Christmas Eve.
>   — "El Palacio"

THERE are many kinds of Christmas celebrations. I recall some lonely ones in the far northern deserts of Arizona, with snow, to be sure, and bitter temperatures at night, and the mails a week delayed, and titbits spoiling in transit, and some of us feeling that we were "richer by one mocking Christmas past." And there are several kinds of Christmas seasons in New Mexico. The crooked streets of old Santa Fe hold fanciful little fires on Christmas Eve, and children sing around them, and in many homes the windows show lighted candles. Christmas among the Pueblo Indians is best described by a Franciscan. If there are no Old English carols in this chapter, such as we are familiar with, then be it remembered that the institution of the "crib" in Catholic churches is said to have been originated by Saint Francis of Assisi himself, to inculcate the doctrine of the Incarnation; and we find at San Felipe a curiously interesting variation of the idea that, for some good reason all their own, perhaps, too, inspired by Saint Francis, the Franciscans have not demolished.

"On the afternoon of December 24 I left Pena Blanca to celebrate midnight Mass at the pueblo of San Felipe, fourteen miles away. I went through the pueblo of Santo Domingo, where I noticed that not all the preparations for the morrow had been completed. Dense clouds of smoke could be seen curling from the semiglobular ovens, a sign that baking was still in progress. Throughout the year they are often obliged to skimp, but on this feast there must be an abundance of bread, even *guayave* (a thin, paperlike Indian bread), or at least *biscoches* (a confection), must be served.

"Half a dozen elderly Indians, apparently city fathers, their weather-beaten faces carefully wrapped in woollen blankets, walked, silent and dignified, from house to house, to announce to each one the approaching salvation of the world. The leader of this embassy carried three or four feathers in his hand, which, had they had the color, might well have been mistaken for palm branches.

"I called at the house of the sacristan, for in previous years he had accompanied me on this nightly tour. But as he was not at home, I made the journey alone. I did not need a guide. Since the Government has built a bridge across the treacherous Rio Grande at San Felipe, it is not necessary to ford it any more.

"It was rather late when I reached the pueblo. The fiscal, or churchwarden, had already expressed his anxiety lest something had detained the padre. Presently the old cracked church bell announced to all in the pueblo that the *tontoech* was already in their midst. Supper was soon over. It was relished pretty well, for hunger is the best sauce. After the Indians had rolled a few cigarettes and smoked them, I proposed to retire. On the way to the church building, where a small room serves as my

THE MISSION OF SAN FELIPE

Note the phallic horses, pagan symbols which the padres have failed to eradicate

sleeping place, we passed a house, from which wailing sounds told of someone in great distress. We entered and beheld a pitiful sight, not in keeping with Christmas joy, a picture of human misery. In the corner on the floor lay a woman, wheezing and groaning, her face covered with festering sores. Apparently she was in danger, and I hastened to perform my duty. As the patient spoke Spanish but imperfectly, and no English whatsoever, I prepared her for the sacrament with the aid of an interpreter as well as circumstances allowed. After administering Extreme Unction, I spoke a few words of consolation and encouragement, and left her quiet and resigned.

"In the sacristy I explained to the fiscal where the hands of my watch would be when it was time to wake me. At two o'clock there came a rap at the door, and then the brazen-tongued bell sought to arouse the sleepers. The fiscal, accompanied by his aides, and beating a drum, led the way through the village. It is their custom to have *pregoneros* go from house to house to gather the congregation. The ringing of the church bell is of no consequence.

"I entered the church where I found the altar tastefully decorated. Before it the Indians had erected a hut of cedar twigs covered with a roof of straw. Tufts of cotton gave it a wintry appearance, and, as it was bitterly cold, it seemed the more real. One by one, the Indians dropped in. *Festina lente*. Wrapped in their blankets they squatted on the floor. Of course it could not be expected that all would be present. The dancers must prepare themselves to dance before the crib immediately after the Mass; but to do both — attend Mass and then dance — impossible.

"I began Mass about three o'clock. During it all was quiet except for the flute players who can faithfully imitate song birds. At the sermon, delivered in Spanish, I employed an interpreter.

"After the Mass an Indian woman took the statue of the Infant from the crib and placed it on her knee. A little boy stood beside her. Now all present passed before her, making their acts of homage and offering pieces of bread, which would prove a good supply for the sacristan even though seven unfruitful years should set in.

"After this came the dancers, their heads decorated with feathers interwoven with many colored ribbons; from their loins hung coyote and wildcat skins; beaded strings quavered on their wrists; tiny bells tinkled at their ankles; their hands held dried hollowed gourds in which small stones rattled at every motion.

"Entering the church in single file, they were followed by the choir and the drummer who carried a huge *tombe*. They take their places in two rows, the tombe is beaten, the choir begins to chant, and the dance is in full swing. Their faces betray no emotion, for the dance is a sort of prayer with the Indians. Only the first dance is performed in the church, the others being given in the plaza, and they are kept up for four days at Christmas time.

"It was now high time for me to be off to the pueblo of Santo Domingo. I took leave of my parishioners and mounted my faithful broncho, held in readiness at the church door. It was indeed a beautiful night, the vast expanse of the heavens studded with countless sparkling emeralds like so many lights on an immense Christmas tree. And the full-faced moon looked tranquilly upon the earth. "Silent Night, Sacred Night!" Then a passenger train of the railroad whizzed by close to me, and my Indian pony became somewhat excited. Even on Christmas night the world knew no rest. Travelers were en route. I thought of my own travels, and that last meeting with my own people. . . . Lost in my reveries, the time slipped away quickly; the distance of about nine miles had been covered, and I was at Santo Domingo. Just then the cock began to crow. Very appropriate, for the *Missa del gallo* was now about to be celebrated.

"At 5:30 A.M. I entered the mission sacristy, where about a dozen Indians, who had been watching through the night, were lying at full length around the hearth. Their eyes were heavy, but I knew an excellent means to revive them. I threw some candy among them, and they were all on their feet, crying: 'Christmas! Christmas!'

"The fire was stirred and tobacco passed around, for *haame* is indispensable, and if tontoech should forget it, they would not hesitate to call his attention to it. The warmth of the fire soon restored my stiffened limbs, and, seeing a pallet and a thick Navajo blanket, I tried to rest for a few minutes; but the beat of a drum reached my ear, interrupted by the discordant notes of the false trumpet and the shrill sound of the pipe. The Indians of Santo Domingo are very much like children, and noise is an essential feature of every celebration. The greater the din, the greater the solemnity.

"I prepared for my second Mass. The Indians were clothed very sparingly despite the cold, but painted all the more gaudily. The good sacristan assisted as well or as poorly as he knew how. Holding a book before him, generally upside down, and ceremoniously moving his lips, he presented an imposing figure. At any rate, he contributes his share to the solemnity by adding to the din. Thus at every genuflection he rings the bell, and on feast days at the elevation of the Host, the altar bell, the church bell, the drum, trumpet, and pipe unite in grandest discord. Such demeanor in church may seem undignified and even desecrating to civilized whites, but who can tell but that many a native, thus giving expression to his joy and intention to honor God, may stand higher in God's estimation than the educated white man?

"At the sermon I noticed a rather large attendance. The fiscal had engaged a guard to stand at the door, lest anyone should leave too soon, and several times during Mass I heard the audible challenge: 'Heizonarshro?' (Whither?)

"After Mass the whole congregation chanted the *Ave Maria* in Spanish, and the Doxology, sung with might and main. Then a few children were baptised in the sacristy, and my day's work here was finished. The sun was quite high when I took leave of these parishioners, and my pony soon carried me to Domingo, a mile away, where I was to say my third Mass at the Mexican mission."

Thus Christmas, 1912.

Christmas Eve in the little city of Albuquerque presented in miniature the street crowds, and the shopping at the last minute for gifts, and the wish to send a score of very expensive presents, and the final compromise on a Christmas card — the usual thing that animated every street of shops from Fifth Avenue to Market Street. The thing always appealed to me, and I indulged myself in it to the farthest extent of an anæmic purse. There was nothing calling me to any one of the ten Indian reservations of my jurisdiction; but a little before the holiday season someone, whose conscience troubled him, and who had the purity of the yuletide at heart, had ventured to

CHRISTMAS REVELS

suggest to me that, at some of the missions, the birthday of the Redeemer was not observed as it should be. Indeed, it was insinuated that at most of these pueblos of the native Americans a midnight Mass was celebrated, and that the goings on were in the nature of barbarism, not to say scandalous. I had not then read Father Jerome Hesse's simple and very beautiful account of Christmas at San Felipe.

Since I had been raised in the atmosphere of the Holy Roman Catholic Church, I felt that my informant must be mistaken. I had played at ball with the Christian Brothers in the cloisters of a beautiful old church, but we had never played in the sanctuary. And certain of my relatives were in seminaries, studying for ordination, and certain others were in convents; while a lot more of them were destined to become black sheep like myself. Therefore, the sacristies and sanctuaries of the Church, that to many of the laity are mysterious places, and to those outside the pale, places of mummery and image-worship, were to me familiar ground. And, being thus informed, I felt that I should set forth to investigate just what sort of bedevilment occurred at midnight Mass in the old mission church at Laguna, seventy-five miles from Albuquerque. Had I read Father Hesse's account, I should not have ventured forth into the keen December wind that was blowing across the desert.

There was one employee with me, another lonely soul at Christmas, and together we occupied the generous front portion of a Ford car. That was where the trouble began. In winter, in the desert, one may expect trouble from any sort of conveyance. As this car was practically new, we had not packed it full of spare parts. The trouble began to develop when we had reached a point about forty miles from Albuquerque. It was a gray afternoon, with a sullen sun setting in the west, half obscured by snow-bearing clouds. And there had been snow the night before, a covering that we had not expected, for the streets of the town had received none of it. As one goes from Albuquerque to Laguna there is a constant rise across broad mesa lands, and weather conditions may be very different. Much of the snow had melted in the road, and the car required more and more of gasoline energy to plough through the mass of stuff some call adobe, others red clay, and all agree on as "the plaster of grief." The water in the radiator boiled and boiled, and of course boiled away. The water from the reserve canteen was contributed as long as it lasted, but there is an end to everything. Now and then a roadside pool enabled us to refill the canteen. The sun sank lower and lower, and finally dropped out of sight behind the mesas. And as we climbed higher, it grew colder, with a bitter piercing cold, and the snow had ceased melting, and there were no more roadside pools. We looked anxiously into the distance for the welcoming sight of Mesita and its well, for the car had developed alarming symptoms; it grew very warm and tired, and promised to quit working altogether unless furnished with water constantly. With a black night coming on, and the possibility that the road would grow worse as we neared the pueblo, our chances for arriving in the mood for a midnight Mass evaporated like the water in the radiator.

About six miles from Laguna there is a long winding hill road ascending a mesa. It was then like all Indian mesa roads — washed in places where surface water had drained across it, lined with boulders, and possessing the invariable sharp ascent at the very top. Needless to say that such a hillside under snow is slippery. And in justice to the Ford car, one should admit that it always bravely assaults nine tenths of such a hill. During this nine tenths of the anxious journey it works itself into a desperate condition, quite like a sprinter in the last five yards of the hundred, when the pace has been under ten seconds flat. On at least three thousand occasions I have piloted Ford cars up such hills, starting in a mild frame of mind, the engine working coolly, to arrive worried at the last ten yards of it with the water boiling, the engine gasping asthmatically, the wheels churning mud and gravel, and I listening for that death rattle which, unless a miracle occurred, would begin five yards from the brow of the hill. And in this case it did. Worse than that! There came a swishing fountainlike burst of boiling water from immediately behind the radiator, covering the windshield with a rusty liquid, the engine groaned and died, the car began to glide backward against the emergency brake, and my companion leaped to find a rock with which to chock the wheels. We examined things to find that the rubber radiator connection had served its time, and we had no other.

"This is a fine way to attend midnight Mass," we agreed, in language that completely matched the occasion.

And there we were. We endeavored to make repairs with electric tape, and several times managed to convince ourselves that the machine, if gently backed down the hill, and given a Chinaman's chance again, would ascend the mesa, an extra three-horse power being exerted behind it by my companion. Several attempts were made. In each case the car responded bravely, and the pusher demonstrated extraordinary powers, but it was a forlorn hope. In each case the momentum of attack dribbled away and expired at that same five-yard post. By this time the water was "all," as the saying is, and the night growing colder. Neither of us relished the thought of a six-mile walk into the pueblo, through snow and its underfooting of slimy adobe mud, but there is such a thing as knowing when one is defeated. There are times when this knowledge becomes a virtue. With the utmost docility the car allowed itself to be eased down into the ditch, so as not to block the road, and with long sighs we shouldered our greatcoats and handbags, and started.

That is why I never observed the goings-on at midnight Mass in a Franciscan mission of the Pueblo country, and why I am willing to take Father Jerome Hesse's word for it. We arrived at the government station very late that Christmas Eve, and were thankful to find beds, after having partially scraped away two inches of adobe mud from our knees downward. We did not sit up to catch Saint Nicholas.

I slept until late in the morning of Christmas Day, and then was aroused by a messenger who stated that the telegraph operator at the railroad station had been queried as to my probable whereabouts. The telephone line was not working at its best, and I sent the messenger to the station to collect the good news. It was just possible, I thought, that Washington had wired me a promotion, or that some good friend had died and left me a legacy. At the very least, it would be one of those Christmas messages, decorated with holly and berries, and wishing one a Joyful Christmas and a Happy and Prosperous New Year. Exactly!

But the telegrams were from the United States District Attorney at Albuquerque and the Special Counsel for the Pueblo Indians of New Mexico. Each of the gentlemen seemed concerned about recent incidents at the

CHRISTMAS REVELS

pueblo of Santo Domingo, and anxious to pass the glad tidings to the proper official, to wit: the Indian Agent for the Pueblo Indians of New Mexico in general and the Santo Domingo Pueblo Indians in particular. Their information ran along after this fashion:—

OPERATOR. Inform Superintendent Crane at Laguna that Santo Domingo Indians have fired on State Mounted Police. Governor Larrazolo demands that steps be taken to avoid bloodshed. Word from Domingo indicates that Indians have police surrounded and fighting may begin at any moment. Employees report firing in the pueblo.

CRANE, superintendent. Go at once to Santo Domingo and prevent massacre of State Mounted Police. Have informed Governor that action may be taken by Indian Agent only.

Now the Indian Agent who received this choice bit of yuletide festivity was exactly one hundred and fifteen miles from the scene of the expected massacre. His automobile, allowed him by a generous Government devoted to the Ford car, was in the ditch several miles off. The brace of cars available at this government station had been in service for many days, and were in poor condition for a century run through snow, mud, and other climatic handicaps. The Santa Fe Railway was only two miles distant, its station being a regular stop for trains, and in a case like this any train could be flagged; but one must first have a train. The schedule showed that no train should be expected, moving in an easterly direction, before seven o'clock that night, and all indications pointed to the possibility that the train would be late. It was during that period of reconstruction after the War when the Santa Fe had not altogether recovered its reputation for promptness.

The time of filing of the telegrams indicated that several hours had elapsed since the news had reached Albuquerque, and on Christmas Day that town is very quiet. I therefore concluded philosophically that, if the State Mounted Police were to suffer martyrdom at the pueblo of Santo Domingo, the event was now a thing of the past. It had occurred, probably according to schedule. It was a condition and not a theory.

I had two other thoughts:—

1. Who and what were the State Mounted Police, and, if so, why?
2. What had they been up to on Federal ground?

To begin with, I had never heard of the State Mounted Police; but as the United States Attorney stated that such an organization existed, and was in danger of its life, this must be accepted as fact. If such an organization had gone into the pueblo to enforce a state order or regulation, it was there illegally, and, it would appear from the evidence, such as it was, had bitten off a trifle more than it could masticate. The population of Santo Domingo was between 900 and 1000 persons, and when thoroughly enraged the pueblo could summon at least 200 able-bodied fighting men, who would be well armed, and who had on several occasions protested vehemently the instructions of their own Agents. Only a short time before, these villagers had been haled into the Federal Court and admonished that, unless strict obedience was paid by them to the counsels of their appointed Agent, prison sentences would be their portion; *and*, they had been told in the plainest language by the Big Judge that they were to obey no one else. Evidently they had taken him at his word, literally; and the unfortunate

SANTO DOMINGO
A pueblo of many courts and streets

THE MISSION OF SANTO DOMINGO
Rebuilt after the flood of 1886

State Mounted Police were the victims. I did not find these thoughts entertaining.

The train was very late, and it proceeded slowly, and I arrived in Albuquerque close to midnight. Efforts to communicate with officials at this hour, and on Christmas night, developed little. Apparently the State Mounted Police had few friends, or else the general run of their acquaintance had lost nothing valuable in the vicinity of Santo Domingo; because I heard of no relief expeditions having been dispatched to their rescue. The general run of mankind is not anxious to start a war on Christmas Day, and, it seemed, had left those who did begin one to their unhappy fate. So far as I was concerned, since I had had nothing to do with the affair, I felt that I could be properly sorrowful over a massacre, but I was determined to be very diligent in an investigation to discover on what grounds these Santo Domingo people had been disturbed and their holiday season desecrated. I chartered a seven-passenger automobile from the garage that served me whenever the economical trinket of the Agency was indisposed. I insisted on having a large car, for the reason that it might be required as an ambulance or substitute for the mortician's ornate carryall.

I could have reached the pueblo by two o'clock in the morning, but it seemed to me better judgment to await the dawn. Solo measures had been tried by the disciples of Saint Francis ages ago, to the end that a large number of them were butchered. No! if the State Mounted Police had rushed in and found an old-time welcome, such as Governor Perez had experienced among these very people, — that time when they carried his head in triumph to the Santa Fe suburbs, and as cheerfully tortured and murdered his Secretary of State, — the thing was deplorable indeed, and to be deprecated, but further sacrifices seemed foolish. And too, as Governor Larrazolo had dispatched these men from Santa Fe on an errand that was plainly none of his official business, why not permit His Excellency to duplicate the performance of his predecessor, Perez, and see how it worked out? Should there be any criticism of my courage in this matter, on the part of persons ensconced in Chicago or New York, for instance, then I hereby grant such critics my full permission to invade the pueblo of Santo Domingo at the hour of two or three A.M. in any season. I will not insist that they go immediately following a massacre; but I will grant them any peaceful morning for the visit, in the summer time should they feel that winter imposes undue hardships. As for myself, I felt that daylight would be best, especially for the identification of bodies, the arranging of them in rows and recumbent positions, to await the coroner and the politicians who would rush in to make capital of the event.

Quite early in the day my car approached the pueblo of Santo Domingo. The village looked as usual. Smoke was even issuing from the chimneys of houses, indicating that early risers were preparing breakfast. Thus, I thought, the stolid Indian goes about his three meals per day, if lucky and prosperous, unmindful of tragedies in his dooryard. But there were no indications of mobs in the streets, nor did I perceive any evidences of a battlefield. For a few brief moments it looked as though someone had perpetrated a hoax. Then a watcher stepped forth from the council house and signaled us to approach. He said that the Governor and elders were awaiting me. When I entered the council house I found all the principal men of the village assembled.

CHRISTMAS REVELS

They sat in rows about the walls, and they looked very grave. Occasionally a young man would light a long wand at the hearth, and, pivoting himself, extend its fiery end about the circle so that those who smoked could light their cigarettes without moving. Close to the Pueblo Governor, and at some distance from the door, sat a gentleman of another race. He introduced himself to me as Colonel Montoya, and, whether he knew it or not, I sensed that Colonel Montoya was a prisoner. Like Zebulon M. Pike in Santa Fe some years before, he was being treated with every courtesy, but he was not likely to get away intact.

The Colonel was a depressed and very much abused man, as he explained. He had approached this pueblo early on Christmas morning, armed with a "blanket" search warrant issued by somebody or other, his business being promptly to discover evidence of cattle rustling. His advances had been scorned by the Pueblo Governor, who had refused to recognize his official document — in fact, it appeared that in later proceedings this sacred document had been torn into pieces and flung into his official face. The sovereign power of the state of New Mexico having been flaunted, Colonel Montoya had departed to communicate with his superiors by telephone, and, it would appear, had received further peremptory instructions, for he busied himself in assembling such a posse as would, by numbers and determination, overawe the savage. In the meantime, the Governor had assembled the Pueblo principales, including his Captain of War. When the posse of between twenty and thirty men, heavily armed, arrived, the Colonel posted sentries around the town so that no one could escape.

The Pueblo Governor then called a truce. He

explained to the commanding officer that he, the Governor, and his people, the Santo Domingos, were Indians of the Pueblo tribe, and not citizens of the state of New Mexico; that the grant lands formed their separate untaxed country under Federal protection; that an Agent — an "Ah-hin-te" no less — had been appointed for them by the Great White Father who lived in the pueblo of Washington; and that when recently he had defied this Agent, numbers of soldiers had appeared and dragged him to the Court, where the Big Judge had instructed him and his headmen in no uncertain terms. Therefore, he, the Pueblo Governor, who had been told by Washington that he must obey this Agent, and no other, could not concede the right of Colonel Montoya to search his pueblo. It was possible that somebody, in the circumstances, would go to jail, as the Big Judge had said, and the Pueblo Governor had no longing to find himself in that embarrassing position. He invited the Colonel to use the telephone at Domingo Station, to communicate with Albuquerque, after which the Agent would come and settle the whole discussion.

But, on the other hand, when a man is given a commission by the Governor of the state, and some other official has given him a blanket warrant to search a whole town, and he has procured a posse of brave *compadres* who are at his heels, it is not likely that he will deign to consult, communicate with (by telephone or otherwise), or abide by the counsels of a mere Indian Agent, a person entirely without standing in the politics of the county. All this was the attitude of the Colonel before being made a prisoner.

The Pueblo Governor's earnest protests were unavailing. He was thrust aside, told to attend to his ceremonies, and forthwith the minions of the law proceeded to the search of homes. It is likely that even then no resistance would have occurred had not two guilty Indians, from among a half-dozen who had rustled cattle, made a dash for the Rio Grande, their intention being to destroy pieces of hide bearing brands. To get to the river they had to pass the guard line, and without slackening speed they passed it. They were called on to halt in their rapid progress, but, as I have explained in other writings, few Indians halt until knocked down. Good judgment should have dictated the following of those Indians, and, if not their arrest, at least their identification as suspiciously acting persons. But not so. This was a military affair, sanctioned by high officials, and to be carried out according to the rules. When a guard halts a man, and he does not heed, there is but one thing to do according to civilized warfare — fire on him. Promptly then, the guards of the line fired in the direction of the two disappearing Indians.

Immediately all bets were off, and a foul claimed.

Colonel Montoya gave me a heart-rending description of what happened immediately after the shots were heard. The pueblo of Santo Domingo seemed to have been riven by an earthquake. It heaved. An orderly and dignified military expedition found itself balanced precariously on the crumbling edges of a volcano.

"They swarmed out of the houses like bees," he said; "and they were armed with everything from a butcher knife to a Winchester rifle. There were hundreds of them, and they were angry, and for some reason or other they acted as if we had done something to them. My men retreated together at once, and, back to back, we made for that little rise close to the church, where they surrounded us. It was a howling mob of Indians. That was when the search warrant was torn up and flung into my face. The Governor and a boy who had been to school saved us. They pleaded for no bloodshed. If it had n't been for that English-speaking boy, we would n't have lasted three minutes. And they milled around us. . . ."

The Indians sat silent during this narrative. A Peublo Indian, once in council assembled, can be most volubly silent in Spanish, English, Queres, and several intermediate dialects. And they watched my face to see how I would receive this astounding report on their behavior. Even a Santo Domingo can be filled with courtesy, but in this case it was a cold-blooded courtesy that has fought a war, concluded a surrender, holds the commanding officer as hostage, and wants to know the extent of reparations.

Here was a pretty situation, if not a delicate one. In view of their instructions given in the Federal Court, the Indians were clearly in the right. To censure them for their resistance would mean the creation of doubt, hesitation, and suspicion. To censure the captive would mean the approval of a near-massacre. Actually, it was the Indian Agent on trial before a people who had been told to look to him for adjustment of all their troubles.

Of course, one could have sidestepped the dilemma by affecting to take the matter under long-drawn consideration, by promising to refer it to Washington, thus easing it off into infinity. But what might happen the next time? The next time several Mexican-type citizens of this fair land, whose votes were needed in county elections, might be crucified before a scholar of the Santa Fe Indian School could appear on the scene and plead for a change of venue.

And look you! I had shown a most determined spirit

in punishing the past offenses of Santo Domingo. I had refused to concede their tribal and religious desire for complete secrecy and isolation; I had refused to approve the old method of leasing their lands; I had policed their fiesta and denied those concessions that involved gambling; I had searched their pueblo for pupils when they tried to evade the school regulations; and I had had a number of them indicted and haled to court charged with the maltreatment of a Pueblo woman, as will be described later. And now the old offender had possessed himself, for once, of the lawful end of the whip. Notwithstanding the stir that would be made throughout the political precincts of New Mexico, it occurred to me that Santo Domingo had some rights, and had suffered enough, and should not only be defended in this matter, but somehow commended, if that were possible without thanking them for a riot.

"What authority had you for entering this pueblo to make a search by force of arms?" I asked their unwilling but official guest.

"The authority of my search warrant, and, when it was refused, the instructions given me from Santa Fe."

"But there is no official of the state who has authority to issue a warrant affecting these people. They are Indians, and — "

"The state of New Mexico cannot punish thieves?" he cried.

"The state of New Mexico has no authority over the pueblo of Santo Domingo. The Indians, on their communal lands, are not subject to the laws of the state, but to Federal law only."

The Santo Domingos were following this colloquy intently, for several of them understood simple English, and their Governor, wrapped in all his Indian dignity, sat back like the Rock of Gibraltar, as if determined to learn at last whether or not justice would ever be meted out to Santo Domingo. "No man can serve two masters," was his creed.

"Did not the Indian Governor inform you that these things would have an adjustment through the Agency at Albuquerque?"

"He wanted me to telephone to Albuquerque for the Agent; but I had my instructions from Santa Fe."

"And you came very close to joining the angels."

Of course, I was not perfectly sure of his ultimate destination, but it is always best to place a milder construction on these things.

"You should see, Colonel, that from the very beginning of the affair you were in the wrong; and while I cannot approve of a massacre, still your men fired on these people, and I am not reprimanding them for defending themselves against you. Nor will I seek to have them punished for resisting you. Now I am perfectly aware that you will not accept this decision from me. No one in New Mexico ever does, except the Indians; but I will take you in my car to Albuquerque, where their Special Counsel, Judge Hanna, will so inform you; or for that matter, the United States Attorney will instruct you; and if they aren't sufficient, then we will ask Judge Neblett, of the Federal Court for the District of New Mexico, to set your mind at ease."

"I have no superior officers in Albuquerque," said the Colonel. "I take my instructions from Santa Fe."

"You mean from the Governor of the state?"

"There is the Governor, and the Adjutant-General; and we have an Attorney-General, too."

"Well, I do not receive instructions from those gentlemen, although I try to respect them when it is possible. However, I shall not mind going to Santa Fe, taking with me the Pueblo Governor and all necessary witnesses. I shall telephone to Albuquerque to have Federal counsel join us in Santa Fe. There we will arrange a meeting with those officials of the state; and when we are all assembled, I hope to convince the state officials for New Mexico, including you, that through reading a little law they may hereafter manage to mind their own business, and thus avoid the possibility of massacres."

Then into the seven-passenger car climbed the Pueblo Governor, and his fiscals, and his witnesses, along with Colonel Montoya, the hostage, and we wended to the ancient city of Santa Fe. The Special Counsel for the Indians arrived by train.

At that time the Agency for the northern pueblos had not been established at Santa Fe, being located at Española, on the Santa Clara Pueblo grant. It was not feasible to request that state officials meet with Federal officials in the public street; but there were the law offices of Mr. Francis C. Wilson, who once had been the Special Counsel for the Pueblo Indians. It may not be pleasing to old-line officials at Washington, but the fact remains that little arises in Pueblo Indian affairs without someone consulting this Mr. Wilson. He has been a Pueblo champion for many years, first as their counsel, when he prepared the "Sandoval" case; afterward as private counsel handling the Paguate land case, and still later their advocate when he proceeded thoroughly to disarticulate the Bursum Bill.

Various officials of the state were invited to attend this informal discussion. There was no disposition on the part of the Federal officials to debate the matter, but it was believed that if the state could be coaxed to assimilate a little charitable education the Government at Washington, through its appointed agents, could then peacefully proceed with the Indian problem, irritating as it was, and perplexing as it often proved.

The only state official to attend this meeting was the Attorney-General, and he first heard the almost tearful recital of Colonel Montoya, who, now in the city of his superiors, waxed eloquent. He stressed the point that these Indians were constantly "preying on his people" by willfully slaughtering their cattle; and that *his people* had no other means of redress than to procure fantastic search warrants and advance on the pueblo to gather evidence on which to base a plea for justice.

Actually, the reverse had been the case for years. The Santo Domingo Indians had been the prey of Montoya's people, beginning in early Spanish times, when their choice lands and their exterminated pueblos had been granted as prizes to successful captains and greedy colonists; and in Mexican days, when the Indian was too poor to buy a hearing and to ransom justice to himself; and, to be perfectly fair, in our own times, through the negligence and political "boot-strapping" of the officials of the United States Government at Washington. The Agents in New Mexico had been as helpless as the Santo Domingo Indians themselves.

The Attorney-General for the state could not understand, or affected not to understand, that the Pueblo Indians were wholly under Federal control. That was the attitude of practically all New Mexico. They were thoroughly informed as to the effect of the Joseph Decision of 1876; it would appear that they had memorized parts of it; but they could remain studiously blind to the Sandoval Decision of 1913. When it was forced on their attention, they would contemptuously refer to it as "a liquor case." It often seemed to me that but six persons in all New Mexico at this time had considered the "Sandoval" case, and but six persons evidenced any disposition toward obeying its ruling. These were the Federal Judge, the United States District Attorney, the Special Counsel for the Pueblo Indians, their former counsel, Mr. Wilson, and the two Indian Agents. The Indians themselves were ignorant of any and all decisions, and should not suffer this criticism. But the remainder of New Mexico, literate or illiterate, man in the street or man at the Bar, seemed to have hypnotized themselves into the belief that a decision of the United States Supreme Court in 1876 was paramount and beyond question, inasmuch as it played the game for them; whereas a decision of the same high tribunal in 1913, reversing the former one, could be ignored with impunity, and would be ignored because it completely blocked the game for them.

Discussion at this meeting proceeded very smoothly under the expert guidance of Judge Richard H. Hanna, who, having been of the state Supreme Bench, and in 1917 its Chief Justice, could scarcely be sneered down. Or, in other words, the New Mexican attitude toward Indian Agents and Indians, whoever they might be, could not be donned with Judge Hanna. The advice of Mr. Wilson, gratuitously injected into the argument, was bluntly to the effect that if the state's officials would be good enough to restrain themselves from interfering with the Indian Agent, his authorities, duties, and wards, he believed that the Indian Agent could manage successfully to attend to Indian Pueblo affairs.

But the pride of the state was involved. It could not be disguised that a regularly deputized posse of state minions, headed by a commissioned officer, had been ignominiously surrounded, disarmed, threatened, badgered, bullied, and what not, by the savage and unrestrained inhabitants of Santo Domingo. The newspapers were full of it under double-column heads. Something must be contrived to punish severely these descendants of those who had beheaded the Mexican Governor, Perez, in 1837, and tortured his officials, else no man's life or property would be safe hereafter. Facing this array of legal talent, the Indians said nothing, and their Agent very earnestly said but little, and that little to this peculiarly undiplomatic effect: —

If you will arrange to notify and keep the officials of the state — that is, the game wardens, sheriffs, deputy sheriffs, bailiffs, county constables, and the justices of the peace; in short, every official staggering under a tin badge — away from these peaceful Pueblo Indians, I will guarantee to have them behave themselves, as they usually do; or, in case of their failure, I will have them punished in accord with the Federal laws enacted for the benefit and control of Indians.

But I said nothing about punishing them for having scared Montoya out of three shades of sunburn.

In order that everything should be carried out with full respect to formality, it was necessary for the accomplished Judge Hanna and the distinguished Attorney-General for the state, accompanied by the Indian Agent, to wait upon the hidalgo of the hills who had started the proceedings through the issuance of that mockery of a search warrant, the legal gentlemen expecting to convince him that he had caught a bear that must be adjudicated by the Federal Court.

Anyone unable to imagine a travesty on the dignity of the sacred law should attend a formal session of a J. P. court in the back counties of New Mexico. We repaired to the little Mexican town of Pena Blanca, that stood directly on the north line of the Santo Domingo pueblo, where some people were unkind enough to venture that, if the pueblo lines were accurately determined, they might be found running through the hamlet's streets. There was the spectacle of a magistrate in these United States who could not speak English, and who held his court in a former saloon, surrounded by an array of mangy pool tables, the while near-beer and soft drinks were dispensed over the old bar. This strikes me as sufficient. The outraged dignity of this Justice was mollified by his being given to understand that specific persons among the Indians, charged with having illegally butchered cattle, would be presented to the Federal Court. No warrants had been issued for specific persons. In fact, the persons guilty of this cattle rustling were not known to any of the officials — hence the blanket search warrant, that a whole town might be brought under the guns to procure evidence on which to prosecute someone.

After this, Judge Hanna and I crossed the Rio Grande and entered the pueblo of Santo Domingo, meaning to counsel the Indians against any further outbreaks, whether of a yuletide nature or not. The entire population assembled and dutifully accepted the admonitions of the Judge, and immediately thereafter assured us that there were no hard feelings. And just to show their gratitude for having been supported, they would put on a dance in our honor, which was done, forthwith. In other words, the keys of the city! Seats were arranged for us at the Governor's house on the main plaza, and a hundred or more gaily decorated Domingos issued from the kivas, clad in all their barbaric finery, and performed most effectively. The war was over, and this was a substitute for an old-time victory dance — without scalps, though. And it was too bad, from a dramatic standpoint, that Montoya had preserved his hair.

Now if you think that we two officials should have been the better occupied in hastening to our respective offices, — the Judge to dictating the involved verbiage of suits to quiet title, and I to the calculation of the values of washtubs, — you may be technically correct. A pagan dance is scarcely the place in which to find a thirty-third-degree Scottish Rite Mason and a pillar of the Catholic Church. But we knew our Indians, and we did not scorn their courtesies. We sat in the December sunlight, and with the utmost gravity observed all the eccentric convolutions of that Indian dance, being not only protectors of the poor, but desert diplomats.

Let each be accused of his own childishness, and measured by his own stick. At another kiva — that of the state capitol at Santa Fe — learned legislators were memorializing Congress that action be taken against the Santo Domingos in general, and the United States Indian Agent in particular, for *having taken up arms against the duly constituted authorities of the sovereign state of New Mexico*, an unctuous petition that I read later when in Washington.

But there remained the dregs of expediency to be digested. Said the United States District Attorney to me: —

"I think you will agree that some of those Indians have been rustling cattle. It is necessary for the proper person to procure the evidence at the pueblo, even if that does

A ROUND KIVA

CEREMONIAL DANCERS LEAVING A KIVA

necessitate the searching of suspected houses. You can do this. You are the proper official. I rely upon you to attend to the matter."

"Well, what about this 'taking up of arms,' 'projecting a riot,' and other high crimes and misdemeanors? Will any action be taken against the Domingos, sighting, as it were, from the point of view of such charges?"

"Should those charges be pressed against the Indians, — it is a pity we have not that preposterous search warrant, — then we may proceed to prosecute in the Federal Court of the United States all those who took up arms against the pueblo of Santo Domingo. Remember, 'it is a communal title; not to the Indians of Taos, but *to the pueblo of Taos.*' However that may be, you should present to me all the evidence possible to be obtained concerning those who have butchered Mexican-owned cattle at the pueblo. Good morning!"

And this was exactly in line with our contentions. Stay off the pueblo grants and permit the proper authorities to adjust all complaints against the Pueblo Indians. You cannot accomplish your ends peacefully, to say nothing of accomplishing them legally. We can. It was up to me.

The task was not difficult to one having the confidence of the people. I simply relate what happened to show the position in which an Indian Agent finds himself now and then. I proceeded to the pueblo of Santo Domingo, called on the Governor to assemble his headmen, and placed the matter before them, thus: —

"There are nearly one thousand Indians in this town, and they are all suffering as suspected thieves because of several who have killed cattle belonging to those Mexicans of Pena Blanca. Now you know the guilty persons, or you can find them, and you should prevail on them to come to my office in Albuquerque for a talk. Otherwise, I shall have to search the whole pueblo for evidence, and arrest a number of people, among whom may be innocent persons. If these men have any excuses to offer for their conduct, I shall see that their pleas are placed before the Court. The whole pueblo should not suffer for the misdeeds of a few fellows."

On the day appointed, the Governor of Santo Domingo appeared in my office with six men.

"These are the men who killed the cattle," he said. "They will tell you about it."

"I will take their names," I said, "but I do not want them to tell me about it. They may tell the Court about it."

"But you are our Agent, and we should tell you about it," the several men insisted. They were Indians, and they refused to be silenced when I told them I feared the information would be used to convict them. This made no difference, since they were determined to have the matter settled for the good of the pueblo. So, one after the other, they presented all the details. Among them were the two who had sought to throw the hides into the Rio Grande, and thus brought on the unfortunate hostilities. But it was quite evident to me that three of them, following the impulses of Indians everywhere, had acted as accomplices after the fact. All six were indicted. I still did not relish my position as Indian Agent. So I went to the District Attorney on the day of trial, and told him so.

"But these men have admitted their guilt," he said.

"To me," I said. "I am convinced that three of them are, viewed from the Indian standards, innocent, and should not go to jail; and for that matter, considering all the circumstances, that none of them should be punished."

"Well, what is your position? Do you propose to defend these rapscallions who placed the county in turmoil, when you know they are guilty?"

"No," I replied, "I do not look on them as wholly innocent persons, but I think the circumstances should be considered. They are Indians, and, having confessed to me, will stolidly plead guilty to the charge. I can summon counsel and have them plead 'Not Guilty,' which will mean an expensive trial, and the time of the Court turned from bootleggers."

"I will have no difficulty in proving three of them guilty," he said.

"How will you do it?"

"Your evidence will convict them promptly."

"But suppose I refuse to testify against them?"

"You will be in contempt of Court."

That is a part of the joy of an Indian Agent's existence. One day guide, philosopher, and friend, and the next day stool pigeon. I have sometimes regretted that I neglected to test the matter out. Judge Ben Lindsey was braver in a similar situation. At that time, however, I saw no good cause to be served in going to jail for them.

"What about the three men who are practically innocent of this charge? They were simply on the ground, and an Indian can never resist packing off portions of fresh meat. He does n't believe in wasting it."

"Will the three others plead guilty to the charge?"

"They will if I tell them to; and, for that matter, they are guilty of having killed the cattle, and you can convict them."

"Have the guilty three plead 'Guilty,' and I will quash with respect to the other three."

"Very good!" I said, thankful that I had rescued three

hombres at least. "But see here, I have several reasons why the three guilty men should not receive severe punishment. They are criminals because of circumstances. The guilty party is the United States."

"And you think such a criticism would appeal to the United States Court?"

"It should."

"Then I will request the honorable Court to hear your statement."

The District Attorney then informed the Court that he had decided to dismiss the indictments against three of the Indians charged. The remaining three entered their plea of guilty to the charge. The District Attorney stated that their Agent wished to make a plea for them, being in possession of facts that might be of interest to the Court, and his request was granted. In my judgment there were four excellent reasons why these Indians, who were ignorant of our laws, and who had been plainly offered as a poultice to the injured political feelings of New Mexico, should not be held accountable. Briefly they were as follows: —

1. The exterior boundaries of the pueblo of Santo Domingo were not fenced. The lands were in extent 92,398 acres, and the Indians were too poor to finance a cattleproof fence. The various Indian Agents had petitioned time and again for moneys with which to purchase wire for fencing these grants, the Indians having agreed to furnish all the posts and to do all the manual labor incident to construction. The Indian Bureau had failed to procure such an appropriation from Congress. Therefore, the lands of the Indians were open to all straying cattle and constantly furnished grazing free of charge to outside owners.

2. The principal industry of the Indians was farming. They

were too poor even to fence their little fields against trespassing cattle. The Agency no longer issued wire for labor, as in the past. The Agent was barred by a ruling of the Department from impounding trespassing cattle and holding them for a fine, as on "reservations." We could only drive trespassing stock from the pueblo lands, and, as these owners were on the immediate border, this would have to be done every day.

3. The Indian Bureau allowed but one employee in the nature of a resident sub-Agent at Santo Domingo; and the salary was so small that the position was filled but part-time, and nearly always by a temporary employee drafted from among the very people whose cattle preyed on the Indian lands.

4. The Government would not make available moneys with which the Agent could employ additional line riders from among the Indians themselves.

Therefore, the Santo Domingo pueblo and its people, entitled to the "fostering care," and so forth, of the United States Government, were left unprotected, and denied the right to protect themselves. They could not impound cattle, and the Agent could not impound cattle for them. The same situation applied to every other Indian pueblo in New Mexico. The Indians could not always be restrained from killing trespassing cattle when they saw their crops destroyed and their means of sustenance vanishing. How many white men would stand idle, and watch a vandal destroy the fruits of their labors? And the same ruling that prevented the Agent from impounding stock also prevented him from suing for damage, because it was doubtful if the one Federal statute enacted to protect "savage" Indians, could be invoked to the protection of the so-called "civilized" Pueblo Indians.

The Indians each received a sentence of three months' imprisonment, a very mild one under all the circumstances; and that ended the war at Santo Domingo. But it did not end trespass at Santo Domingo; and Santo Domingo, together with the other pueblos of New Mexico, is still unfenced. Of course, to the casual observer, one familiar with good Mid-West farming lands, it may be argued that semiarid desert lands are not worth fencing. But I beg of you to remember that these Santo Domingo lands support one thousand people and their stock, people who have no other means of subsistence, and who would be public charges without those lands. The "fostering care" of a Supreme Court decision should have something behind it other than printer's ink.

IX

CONQUISTADORS!

The camp and train each eventide heard their *oración*;
When weary captains turned aside, the Cross went on, alone!
A rock their altar by the trail, their trust — a litany,
And simple *Aves* could not fail to touch old Cochiti.
— "The Bells of Cochiti"

It is odd that so many of my own adventures in the desert should cluster about automobiles. It was a misdirected auto that presented me as a crippled wayfarer to the Franciscan padres, and they played the Good Samaritans they are. This was at the St. Michaels Navajo Mission, close to midnight, in that eventful year 1914. Things had happened across the world at Sarajevo, and a monstrous war was emitting its first wails, and I came very close to passing out without knowing whether or not Britain would toss its beaver into the ring. But for a bridge that did not exist, and the earnest effort of a nearsighted Spanish chauffeur to drive across where the bridge once had been, I should not have met that affable gentleman who fought with Alan Seeger in Flanders, and who later wrote "A Soldier of the Legion." Already crippled, I boarded a train at Gallup and found it full of French reservists moving eastward. There was great talk of Alsace and Lorraine.

But I anticipate. That was after I had been succored by the desert Franciscans. Having determined to proceed to Washington, I had hired a car to convey me and my baggage to the railroad, a hundred and five miles distant. It was a Ford in the last stages of decay, but the driver of it, through the liberal use of gasoline, managed to urge it forward at a pace. Darkness had fallen over the lonely desert when we reached the St. Michaels hospice, and we had about twenty-seven miles yet to travel to reach Gallup. On the way we had picked up a tourist, who chatted with me about the country and wondered where they put the cattle at night. The chauffeur and the tourist occupied the front seat, while I was cramped amid baggage in the rear one. At the mission we stopped for water, and I did an un-desert-like thing that probably saved a man's life. Another car came up, also headed for the railroad, and having but one passenger, a woman. The chauffeur of this second car requested me to take the passenger and her additional baggage in my car, and thus save him the night journey to the town. I refused, because we were already crowded, and that necessitated his completing his agreement with her. But for my refusal, we should have had the lonely road to ourselves, and should not have been rescued that night, for my car started out first, the other to follow.

The road from St. Michaels to Gallup crosses many narrow arroyos, and in those days the bridges were of the sort that a depleted county treasury compels. The arroyos are deep cuttings between clay banks that do not erode very much. It is an adobe country, and the mud rolls up like a carpet to enmesh wheels. After a rainy season, cars have to plough laboriously through this mass. It had been raining that week and the road was still soft. My driver forged ahead under considerable power, and to make things interesting for him and his fares the county road men had decided to move one of the bridges to a point elsewhere on the arroyo, leaving only a handful of desert brush in the road as a warning. There was no moon, and with the usual confidence of the Spanish, under full head of gasoline, my Jehu drove merrily down the familiar road, of course expecting a bridge — to be disappointed. The little car bravely dived off the old abutments and crashed on its radiator in the arroyo bottom. It did not turn over, the narrow space between the arroyo banks preventing that. The chauffeur and the tourist went down with it, and were hopelessly mixed with a steering-wheel, windshield glass, pedals, and floor board, while the baggage and I continued on up the road in the general direction of Gallup, New Mexico. Of course friction, acting as a brake, stopped me and the baggage within a hundred yards; regaining consciousness, I found myself completely out of breath, with blood issuing from my mouth and nose, and a distressing absence of feeling in the solar plexus. And to make matters worse, that second car was coming up the same road toward our place of accident, and traveling fast. I feared that its driver would enjoy the same experience, except that he would drive in on top of my companions. That would never do. So, gasping like a porpoise, I struggled to get enough air into my lungs to warn him against this error.

My excitement was wholly unnecessary, for the driver of the second car knew of the detour and, having full sight in his eyes, had taken it. He heard me calling, and approached slowly. Together we scrambled down into the pit and untangled the tourist, who, groaning mournfully, floundered under his own power up the bank. The chauffeur was a different problem. He was not groaning, and after extricating him we had to carry him to the road level, where his limp form stretched out as one uninterested in mundane affairs. We threw water on him and he did not come to. For all traveling purposes, it seemed to me that his ticket had been cancelled. When we were about to fold his hands across his breast, he suddenly opened his eyes and asked what had ambushed him.

The second car promptly returned all the wounded to the St. Michaels Mission. The next nearest point was Fort Defiance where were several government physicians. But for that second car we would have remained in the desert all night, perhaps with an injured woman, since the tourist would not have known his way to either place of rescue, and I was scarcely able to attempt the walk. The good padres put us all to bed, summoned a physician from the Fort, and in the interim furnished various stimulants from their cellar that were gratefully received and promptly disposed of. This is just a suggestion to those who motor through the Southwest. If you must disdain bridges and endeavor to leap arroyos, then arrange your schedule so that its finish will be in the neighborhood of a Franciscan monastery. These good men are prepared for emergencies, and are resourceful, being able to administer excellent first aid, and to sing a requiem later if that should be necessary.

I had met Franciscans before, and had greeted them casually. At the Hopi Indian Agency I had extended to them the same courtesies that other guests received, and one or two of them I had indirectly and unconsciously offended, perhaps; but after that smash-up beyond the Haystacks of New Mexico I felt that Franciscans should receive more of my consideration and respect. Going into the Peublo country, I found them at nearly every pueblo of the Indians, either residing on the ground or frequently visiting from their near-by stations. I rented houses and school buildings from them where the Government possessed none, bought hay and grain from their farms, and on several occasions was delightfully entertained by the good Sisters at Jemez pueblo, where the Indian School is conducted by them and partly financed by government funds allotted to the Pueblo Agency. Thus I have had Franciscans of one Order as my employees. Sister Mary Boyle and Sister Stephania Schramme came to these Indians as teachers in 1906, from their mother house at Lafayette, Indiana, and have continued in the work ever since. And, too, I could always rely on the Franciscan padres to further the work of education, and to coöperate with me in other ways for the benefit of the Pueblo Indians.

It is not possible to give an exact record of the Franciscans who served in this dangerous field between Coronado's time (1540) and the coming of Benavides in 1621. We know that at least six of the friars had been martyred in this period — those three who remained after the departure of Coronado, and the three who were escorted to Tiguex by the soldier, Chamuscado. There may have been others to meet death, for after the martyrdom of Juan de Padilla several Franciscans sought permission to enter the country, and they may have contributed to the red list of honor; but we have no positive record of them. Between Oñate's colonization and the *Memorial* of Benavides, Hodge has traced the records of thirty-five Franciscan friars and four lay brothers who served in these provinces, some of whom established missions, died naturally, and were buried in their churches.

About the year 1617, Zarate-Salmeron appears on the scene, to labor with the Jemez Indians, and at other times with those of Sandia and Acoma, the major part of his ministry being in the San Diego Cañon. He returned to Mexico in 1626, some five years after Fray Alonzo de Benavides came to the Pueblo Indians as *custodio* of the Conversion of San Pablo, and later wrote his *Relaciones*. Thus the Franciscans began to record their work, an activity that is still proceeding among them. The *Relaciones* of Zarate-Salmeron, and the *Memorial* of Benavides form the initial volumes of their New Mexican history. Salmeron claims that he baptized 6566 Indians in the faith, and that more than 34,000 had been baptized when Benavides presented his report to Philip IV. In 1628–1629, even before the departure of Benavides for Spain, came Fray Estevan de Perea, who succeeded to the custodio, and there is record of twenty of the twenty-nine friars who accompanied him. Thus we have knowledge of nearly seventy Franciscans who labored in this pioneer field, a number of whom sacrificed their lives to the work. Perhaps Lummis, in *The Spanish Pioneers* (1893), has presented the most striking picture of those times: —

They had to furnish their own vestments and church furniture, and to pay for their own transportation from Mexico to New Mexico — for very early a "line" of semiannual armed expeditions across the bitter intervening wilderness was arranged. The fare was $266, which made serious havoc with the good man's salary of $150 a year (at which figure the salaries remained up to 1665, when they were raised to $330, payable every three years). . . .

Arriving, after a perilous trip, in perilous New Mexico, the missionary proceeded first to Santa Fe. His superior there soon assigned him to a parish; and turning his back on the one little colony of his countrymen, the friar trudged on foot . . . to his new and unknown post. Sometimes an escort of three or four Spanish soldiers accompanied him; but often he made that toilsome and perilous walk alone. His new parishioners received him sometimes with a storm of arrows, and sometimes in sullen silence. He could not speak to them, nor they to him; and the very first thing he had to do was to learn from such unwilling teachers their strange tongue.... If they decided to kill him, there was no possibility of resistance. If they refused him food, he must starve.

What manner of men were these early Franciscans? Were they adventurers too — religious zealots, seeking only the loot of baptisms and the treasure of long conversion records? Did they go about singing psalms and, like pagan devotees, spending their every hour in the recitation of credos and litanies? We have but two things to guide us in an estimation of their labor and its worth: the sketchy records of several that have been resuscitated from old chronicles, and the remains of that which they produced when they were not singing Masses, preaching, instructing, succoring the sick, and burying the dead. One may discount for the moment their necessary efforts to subsist themselves meanwhile.

Hodge notes briefly the type evidenced by one Martin de Arvide. He was born at Puerto de San Sebastian, Cantabria, Spain, and made his vows in the Convento de San Francisco at Mexico on June 2, 1612. He went to New Mexico and was assigned to the pueblo of Picuris. He must have spent many years in that distant pueblo, which is little known to-day. From Benavides, who arrived in 1621, and Governor Zotylo, Padre Arvide obtained permission to reëstablish the Jemez in their pueblos, when they had deserted their towns and gone roaming in the mountains. He accomplished this, remaining with the Jemez for several years, beginning in 1622. In 1632 he departed for the unknown country of the Zipias, a tribe of Indians then existing somewhere between the Zuñi and the Hopi, very likely those who inhabited the ruins to be found along the Little Colorado River. On the way he visited with Padre Letrado at Zuñi, and then continued his journey westward. Aside from Letrado, his nearest white neighbor would be that Fray Porras, then ministering to the Hopi at Awatobi. Santa Fe would be quite three hundred miles distant from him when he reached his lonely destination. But he never reached the Zipias, for he was slain by Zuñi on the road, and Letrado was murdered by them too, five days later. He had given twenty years of labor, and finally his life, to these Pueblo people.

With Fray Estevan de Perea came a priest known as Roque de Figueredo. His superior wrote of him that he

pleaded exceedingly to remain there (at Zuñi) to convert these gentiles. He is well known in this kingdom for his great prudence, virtue and letters; endowed with so many graces and the principal and most necessary ones to minister and teach these Indians in the divine worship which they now are; for he is eminent in the ecclesiastical chant, counterpoint and plain; dexterous with the instruments of the chorus, organ, bassoon and cornet; practiced in preaching many years in the Mexican tongue (*i.e.* Nahuatl, Astec) and in Matlalzinga; of clear understanding and quick to learn whatsoever difficult tongue.

Hodge comments, "It seems a pity that a man of such versatility should have wasted any part of his life in an endeavor to convert a people who are almost as far from Christianity to-day as in his own time." It would appear that this friar remained in New Mexico as late as 1632, for he wrote an account of the murder of Letrado and Arvide which occurred in that year; and he was stationed probably at Hawaikuh, the first of the Zuñi pueblos to be reached by Coronado.

The testimony of the works of these men is to be found in the Acoma church and convento, and the ruins of the Jemez Abbey in San Diego Cañon. When the visitor remarks the astonishing proportions of these monuments, the thought at once occurs to him that the Indians were enslaved and held by force to such extraordinary tasks. And in a certain sense they were. There was the shadow of a military force in the background, and there was the memory of those terrible defeats the Spanish soldiery had inflicted on Zuñi, Acoma, and the Tiguex pueblos. These facts were as spectres to a people having little of pronounced decision to-day. But Indians seldom do anything of themselves; that is, without patient organization, liberal exhortation, and exemplary practice. The leader must work too. A colorless personality never succeeds in persuading them to accomplish anything. So the padres must have been wonderful organizers and most stimulating leaders. And it is rather hard to believe that whole communities, who had to subsist themselves by toiling in the semiarid fields, went to work raising the missions unless attracted by some appealing vision. The meagreness of the Spanish Military Department argues against slavery in our accepted meaning of the term. I am rather drawn to Bandelier's theory that, once the padres were firmly established, or seemingly so, the Indians became interested in their new form of ritualistic magic — simply the substitution of one mythology for another, a gentle, virtuous one for a vicious, demonic one; and I add to it that Spanish methods in constructing these huge shrines to the new God and His satellites invited their admiration and enthusiasm. The application of the lever, the mystery of a windlass and of a block and fall, the shaping of stone and the carving of wood with new, and to them wondrously efficient, tools attracted their childish interest. Their vanity could be enlisted too. The Navajo and the Plains tribes had no such powerful God, and no such places for His worship.

Nor was the Indian so wrapped up in his old gods that he failed to recognize the advantages that accrued during these early years of the padres. The Pueblo Indians had gained allies against savage maurauding enemies. The Spanish, largely through the missionaries, introduced the horse and other beasts of burden, thus lightening the toil of the native. They brought in domesticated sheep and goats, thus producing raw materials for fabrics and a food supply. They advanced the primitive knowledge of weaving, very likely improved the cultivation of grains, and presented the Indians with fruits and the grape. From flints and stone axes they led the workers to tools of metal. The friars undoubtedly possessed whatever knowledge of medicine the Spanish had, another tremendous hold on a people who had depended largely on chants and exorcisms. And they were advocates in defense of the natives whenever Spanish civil or military power became oppressive.

Finally, the religion the padres offered, however harsh it may have proved to the obdurate cacique and sorcerer, presented mercy and gentleness and justice to the heretofore helpless and unchampioned individual, simply by his superficially observing forms and ceremonies not singularly different from his old ones. The difference was of such color and drama as would naturally entice him. And such qualities, particularly justice, were practically unknown among these tribes. As to the forms, consider the Lenten fasts and the penances. Did not the old pagan religion prescribe much fasting and include much penance? When witnessing Indian ceremonies in the Southwest, it is not difficult for one versed in Catholic ritual to find the graft of it on native rites, even in those zones from which the influence of the padre long since disappeared. Such things do not prevail unless more or less welcome; and to-day, in the Pueblo country, they go to form the *Pueblo-Catholic compromise.*

The Pueblo Indians, however, were not without their Dissenters, to whom this Spanish intrusion, its civilization and religion, made no appeal. As the great chain of missions expanded, colonization increased, the Military Department seemed unnecessary and was permitted to become weak, and forty-odd years caused the memory of Spanish vengeance to become vague and legendary. It is probable that the legend would not have been revived but for the explosion of August 10, 1680, when the curtain arose on a tragedy staged by a group of these Dissenters — Popé, Catiti, Jaca, Tupatú, and Francisco — when twenty-one of the Franciscans sealed their life's work with their blood.

Popé was a native of San Juan "of the Gentlemen," but he established his revolutionary headquarters at the pueblo of Taos. He was ably assisted in his ferocious agitation by Tupatú of Picuris, Jaca of the Taos pueblo, Francisco of San Ildefonso, and a charming fellow known as Catiti, from Santo Domingo. Uprisings had threatened the Spanish before, but had been abortive because allies sought among the Apaches, the Zuñi, or the Hopi, at different times, had not appeared; others had been betrayed in the planning, and severely suppressed and punished. In 1643–1646, Governor Arguello became aware of a conspiracy of the Jemez, and he caused twenty-nine of the Indians to be hanged for the murder of a Spaniard. In 1650, Governor Concha discovered that the pueblos of Jemez and Cochiti, with Apache allies, planned to rise during Holy Week devotions and massacre the Spanish in the churches. Nine of those accused as ringleaders were hanged, and others sent into slavery for ten years. The Piros killed five Spaniards in the Magdalena Mountains, and at first the Apaches were blamed for the incident. Then the Indian Governor of the Salineros towns and several of his compadres were hanged in retaliation. Not all of the frontier troubles originated among the Pueblo people, however. About 1672, the Apaches increased their assaults on pueblos, destroying one at Zuñi, while the towns of the Piros and Tompiros were decimated and several friars killed. The result was that some mission points were abandoned.

Popé first appears as one of those involved in threatening Governor Trevino, in 1675, when it is related that natives were hanged, others whipped, and others enslaved for having killed Spaniards.

Popé prepared a rope of palmilla fibres with knots to represent the number of days that should elapse before the uprising of his followers. This rope was carried from pueblo to pueblo by runners. He himself traveled about to stir up rebellion against the Spanish, and his four lieutenants were likewise employed. The matter of the rope and knots has been confused through different descriptions. Some have written that when a pueblo signified its willingness to join the conspiracy one of the knots would be untied, as one might sign a written document. As I have regulated a great deal of Indian business by the counting of days to elapse, to me their

A JEMEZ DOORWAY

SIA MISSION

Sia was the seat of a mission as early as 1635

method was simple. When a date for the uprising had been agreed on among the leaders, a rope was prepared with a knot for each of the days to elapse. During the journey of the runners, as each day passed a knot would be untied in the rope carried, so that each pueblo in turn was correctly informed as to the number of days yet to elapse before the day of the uprising. Undoubtedly the pueblos then prepared their own rope calendar, the number of knots agreeing with the rope carried by the messengers when they appeared. Their own rope they unknotted daily for themselves. Thus all the pueblos, from Pecos on the eastern frontier to Oraibi the farthest west, proceeded to their business as native patriots — or murderers, as you will — on the appointed day.

Or they should have; but despite Popé's secrecy (no woman had been admitted to the confidence of the leaders, and Popé killed his own son-in-law whose loyalty was doubted), the plot was betrayed. The plan was revealed to Fray Juan Bernal, custodio at Galisteo, who refused to leave his post; and another friar, Velasco of Pecos, had word of it in the confessional from a converted Indian. Velasco was killed on his way to the Galisteo convento; apparently he had intended to consult his superior about this rumored danger. And, too, the Spanish alcalde at Taos sent Governor Otermin a warning, which was confirmed when two envoys of the conspiring Indians were arrested at Tesuque, on their way to the Tanos and Queres of the south. Governor Otermin sent messengers to warn the Spanish at the distant posts, advising those of the south and west to rendezvous at Isleta, and those of the north to retire on Santa Fe. Realizing that their plot was suspected, the Tihuas of Taos and Picuris, and all the

Tewas of the north, at once attacked the northern settlements. This was on the tenth of August, 1680, the feast of San Lorenzo. In this fashion, Picuris honored its patron, as did the Tesuque pueblo; murdering the Franciscans, Rendon and Pio, to accept the dispensation of Popé and Tupatú three days before the fatal date appointed by the rope calendar.[1]

South of San Felipe pueblo many of the Spanish and friars managed to reach Isleta; but of the outlying missions in the north, east, and west, only the padre at Cochiti and perhaps one at Zuñi escaped this massacre.

On the fourteenth of August, Governor Otermin was advised by his scouts that the Indians were advancing on Santa Fe. There was a parley in the fields near the chapel of San Miguel. The rebels claimed that they had killed God and the Virgin Mary, and that the Spaniards must leave the country or suffer extermination. Otermin engaged them in battle, but after a day's fight, large reënforcements coming to the Indians, he retired into Santa Fe and prepared for a siege. For five days the Spanish held off the army of Indians, which was reënforced constantly, principally by the Tanos and Queres from the districts of Galisteo, Santo Domingo, Cochiti, and San Felipe. By this time the Indians had cut off the water supply. The church and convento had been burned. Otermin and his refugees were confined to the barricaded plaza and its remaining buildings. There was no hope of rescue; starvation and thirst faced them; the horses were already dying; so Governor Otermin determined

---

[1] A tragic anniversary of this revolt was celebrated 157 years later, when Taos Indians, assisted by numerous Pueblo allies, joined Mexican insurgents against the rule of the Mexican Governor Perez, whose forces were defeated. Perez was beheaded, his officials tortured and killed, and Santa Fe captured. On August 10, 1837, these rebels set up a Taos Indian, one José Gonzales, as Governor of New Mexico. Early in 1838 the rebels were defeated, and Gonzales shot without trial.

to cut his way out. On the twenty-first of August, the Spaniards issued from the capital. There were about one thousand in all — soldiers, men, women, and children, including three friars of the eleven who survived the uprising. Five of Otermin's captains had been killed in the fighting about Santa Fe.

The Indians held the foothills and made no attempt to attack the column. It is likely that the desperate resistance they had encountered caused them to ponder on the price extermination would have cost. Otermin marched by way of Santo Domingo, where the bodies of three friars and five Spanish soldiers were found; thence to San Felipe, and through Sandia pueblo to Isleta. He arrived at Isleta on the twenty-seventh of August; quite seven days had been consumed in moving his column of fugitives this distance of about seventy-eight miles. No doubt there were anxious camps and some little rear-guard fighting. At Isleta he found that the other Spanish refugees had moved on farther south. By the end of September they were all encamped below Las Cruces, where they spent the winter enduring great privations. Report of the disaster was sent to the City of Mexico, petitioning for relief and reënforcements, which the Viceroy promptly set about furnishing; but these supplies and additional troops were not received by Otermin until early in 1681.

Apparently the Indians did not seek to harry the column as it went south from Isleta, contenting themselves with returning to the captured city of Santa Fe to celebrate this great victory. They destroyed the records of the capital, wrecked the churches, and held high carnival in the vestments of the priests. Popé set himself up as a barbaric emperor.

Then the old silence settled over the desert and the hills and along the Rio Grande, inviting a return of the twilight gods; a silence broken only by the dull booming of drums, songs of savage exultation and mockery, as Popé and Catiti held their satanic feasts and pledged each other and their cause in the sacred chalices.

There would be no to-morrow . . . the Spaniard had disappeared over the horizon. His civilization had been snuffed out as had that of Pompeii, and his religion, with its impotent Deity, buried deep in the ashes of a pagan volcano. The Cross was succeeded by the kachina emblem, the friar by the cacique, the colonist by the native whom he had dispossessed. The Province of Nuevo Mexico, its garrisons and temples, had been obliterated, and in its stead the many divisions of the Indians separated to their pueblos and kivas, split into their undecisive factions, and restored promptly all the fetishes and cruelties of the old barbarism. They found, or at least many of the helpless did, that Popé would graft all of Spanish severity on an unrestrained heathen growth that it might serve his personal ends; that instead of an inflexible master they had accepted a variable despot, who, aided by the fanatical caciques, would revive every injustice and machination of the savage. Perhaps the triumphant caciques wondered if the mailclad Spaniard would ever come again, and no doubt many a tortured unfortunate longed to see the gleam of Spanish steel in the sunlight along the drowsy Rio Grande.

The concerted uprising of the Pueblo Indians against the Spanish has been ascribed by different writers to a variety of sources; and it is possible that each of these alleged causes may have contributed something to the

Photo. by H. F. Robinson

THE BELLS OF COCHITI

general effect. One could say that it was an unsuspecting minority, lulled into security by eighty years of unchallenged rule, suddenly smothered by a wakened and savage majority; and one could add that it was inevitable — that this noble captain, that simple friar, this humble soldier, that struggling colonist, was no more to blame individually than the dawn or the sunshine. The Spanish spearhead was too far from base, and had prepared no secure line of communication with the actual Spanish frontier. From a strategic point of view, their method of colonization in this instance had been a folly. Only the friars may be excused from this criticism, because such was their means of combating a gentile enemy — lone forays into his provinces, desperate chances, forlorn hopes. As for the charge of ruthless military despotism, one reads that in 1617, when the friars had built eleven churches, there were but forty-eight soldiers in the province; and in 1676, when pueblos and churches had been destroyed by the Apaches, and many converted Indians and Spanish killed, the different stations on the frontier had but five soldiers each, and these poorly armed and mounted.

Pretty generally, beginning with Bancroft, the modern commentators have selected the religious, and the hatred of them by the idolatrous natives, as the main cause for the insurrection. In my opinion, the Franciscan chroniclers themselves are largely to blame for this impression. Their writers, and there were few others, invariably stressed that this whole campaign was against the demons and the Devil, his works and pomps. It was dangerous and difficult enough, because of heathenism, but their reports made it even more so, and attracted to themselves the principal criticism of the historian. As sectarians, they seemed to be blind to the fact that oppressive secular rule, military errors, and scarcely to be avoided economic influences, may have helped to ignite and fan the flame of savage rage. As an instance, in commenting on the delays suffered by Oñate in 1596-1598, when his expedition was handicapped by political cabals and private jealousies, Zarate-Salmeron charged His Satanic Majesty with having engineered the whole thing in order to handicap and delay the friars in their work of converting Indians and saving souls. For fifteen years after the return of the Spaniards, testimony of natives was taken to ascertain what had produced this rebellion, and Bancroft says that the evidence given "shows a general agreement . . . whether from secular or ecclesiastical sources . . . everyone attributed the revolt to demoniac influences brought to bear upon a superstitious and idolatrous people."

Again Bancroft says: —

The friars had worked zealously to stamp out every vestige of the native rites; and the authorities had enforced the strictest compliance with Christian regulations, not hesitating to punish the slightest neglect, unbelief, relapse into paganism, so-called witchcraft, or chafing under missionary rule, with flogging, imprisonment, slavery, or even death. During the past thirty years large numbers of natives had been hanged for alleged sorcery, or communion with the Devil, though generally accused also of projected rebellion or plotting with the Apaches. The influence of the native old men, or priests — sorcerers, the Spaniards called them — was still potent; the very superiority of the pueblo organization gave the patriotic conspirators an advantage.

He says that, because of the penalties inflicted, the natives were given to practising the rites of their aboriginal religion in secret, as they do to my personal knowledge to-day when no one is permitted to inflict penalties on them because of this habit; and I too have given some little testimony as to the ferocity of the modern savage when the mood seizes him, a condition to which the friars have contributed nothing. I have seen it at Santo Domingo and San Felipe, and unpleasant evidences of it at the pleasant little pueblos of Cochiti and Santa Ana. And I believe that, when it comes to religious persecution for the sake of an idea, the Pueblo cacique can maintain a position to equal any Dominican that ever existed. The friars had the most to show for the eighty years of labor among these people; they were in the limelight; they were the shining targets.

I will now suggest a reason for the rebellion as powerful and as potent among Indians or any other race as that of religious differences. Here was an effort at civilization that, despite the remonstrances of distant Spanish statesmen, who intended that its several departments should be kept separate, became in the wilderness hopelessly intermixed — military control, colonization, exploration, religious fervor, taxation, trade, even, each and all heavily dependent on the closest relationship between the two dominant governing bodies. It was not until 1608, after Oñate's resignation had been tendered, and the close of his contract was in sight, that the Crown assumed the support of the garrison and the friars. It has been shown with what little efficiency the Military Department was upheld. Thus the military, such as it was, and the colonists, neither class as disciplined or as frugal as the friars, were thrown on their own resources to maintain themselves. Peralta, who succeeded Oñate as Governor, was furnished twelve soldiers who were to receive $450 a year as pay; and Benavides speaks of the taxes levied for the support of the Villa of Santa Fe, and its presidio, "where reside the Governors and the Spaniards, who must number as many as two hundred and fifty" — this in 1621–1630. Oñate had with him but eight friars, and these were feebly augmented through the years; but Oñate entered New Mexico with an army of 400 soldiers, 130 of whom brought their families, and other colonists arrived later; so that, at the time of the revolt, the Spaniards numbered nearly 2400.

I have considered those capable of bearing arms as "soldiers," of which class there were 228; of friars there were 32; leaving more than 2000 persons to be classed as officials and colonists. These people were not settled under the walls of missions. There was a terrible slaughter of colonists along the Rio Grande, in the vicinity of San Felipe, where the Mexican hamlet of Algodones now stands, and where the land susceptible of irrigation is still valuable. One hundred padres could not have stirred up so much daily misery as these 2000 unwelcome guests of the Indians. To-day, were the Santa Fe Railway to cease running its huge freights, New Mexico would begin to starve in a very short time. The comparison is not odious.

The padre may have been hated by the cacique and his disciples, but the padres were not so intensely hated by the mass of the natives as we have been led to believe. Witness those who were warned of prior uprisings, and even helped to escape the great one. It was the "colonist" who put fear into the heart of the Pueblo Indian, and who had generated a hatred from the days of Oñate, for the colonist had to subsist himself from the soil — failing this, he had to be sustained by the tribes. First he was allotted the choice tillable lands, and of course as much water as he thought he required, thus dispossessing the Indian. In this land of harsh conditions and uncertain seasons, even among the Indians existence was a struggle. Now it is not likely that these colonists made a much better showing than some Indian Service farmers sent out to teach the Hopi how to grow corn. In a strange country, facing the bitter problems of new soils, harsh climate, short growing seasons, themselves ignorant of the tricks of irrigation, it is not likely that the colonists raised bumper crops. And when their crops failed, or were immature, the Indian suffered extraordinary levies on his, which had been raised laboriously, in many instances on second-grade land. It is true that the Pueblo Indians killed twenty-one missionaries in the 1680 revolt, but at the same time they slaughtered nearly four hundred colonists, men, women, and children, who were in possession of their choice lands, no doubt unpaying guests. .

Land and water! The precious elements of existence in a semiarid country. Men will fight for land when no other cause appeals to them. If the demons must be included, then it should be remembered that the pagan gods the Pueblo Indians placated were all connected with fruition, the lifeblood of the tribe, extending surely to the levee, the ditch, the field, and what could be charmed out of it.

And it was land and water, still being filched from them by Spanish influences in a patch-quilt Spanish atmosphere, that brought the Pueblo Indians before the Sixty-Seventh Congress of the United States in February 1923. These bones of contention had been chewed and fought over for three hundred and twenty-five years, and matters had quite nearly approached bloodshed again in 1922.

It seems to me that the best evidence of Franciscan virility, faithfulness, and sincerity is to be found in the bare and unadorned fact that they were in New Mexico in 1540, and are to be found there to-day. The several breaks in their ministry, and the loss of time and the chaos that resulted, may not be charged to them, since, as soon as permitted, they returned.

For themselves they ask nothing, and it is plain from their progress that they have received much. They no longer go about barefoot, *solo con su breviario y una cruz*, being now accustomed to the use of the train and automobile; but they do without comforts, eat plain food, and wear coarse clothing; and the black is often covered with the desert dust.

Indeed, I have heard it remarked that some of them have a careless or unkempt appearance, depending on how few necessities they have restricted themselves to. Bare, quite cheerless quarters mark their stations in the desert. But at no place in the Enchanted Empire of the Pueblo and Navajo Indians have all the other creeds combined produced a showing that is comparable to theirs. The boasts of Benavides have been sustained.

Whereas these friars once preached to the entire Indian field, in our day they have not resumed the work of missionaries at all the pueblos of New Mexico. The Jemez mission has that pueblo and Sia and Santa Ana as visitas; the mission at Pena Blanca has the pueblos of Cochiti, Santo Domingo, and San Felipe as visitas; a resident Franciscan ministers to the towns of the Lagunas with Acoma as a visita. The little pueblo of Tesuque is a visita of Santa Fe, the Cathedral parish. Zuñi has a resident Franciscan. Nine other stations serve the Mexican communities. These missions require thirty-five priests and nine lay brothers.

The headquarters of their mission to the Navajo is at St. Michaels, almost on the boundary line between Arizona and New Mexico, north of Gallup. Its visitas are Fort Defiance, Tohatchi, Wide Ruins, Ganado, Chrystal, Fort Wingate, and Keams Cañon. A second Navajo mission has been established at Chin Lee, close to the Cañon de Chelly. It has three visitas — Naazlini, Red Rock, and Lukachukai. These twelve points are all Navajo Indian locations on the original great Navajo Reservation, except that Keams Cañon, where is the Hopi-Navajo Agency, does not offer a fertile field, owing to the old Hopi animosity to the friars and their faith. Indeed, the Fathers make little effort to cultivate this obdurate soil, and if they reach the Navajo of the district, it is from the Chin Lee Mission, distant about sixty miles from the First Mesa settlements of the Hopi. This Navajo work employs eight priests and two lay brothers.

The importance and success of this Navajo mission effort reflects the life work of the late Father Anselm Weber, who died in 1921, after having labored among the Navajo Indians twenty-two years. The St. Michaels Mission was founded in October 1898, Father Weber being assistant to its first director. In 1900, Father Weber was made superior of the mission. No other missionary in the Southwest in our day has exercised an equal influence over the Indians and knowledge of their affairs. Whether or not the Navajo have absorbed and profited by his spiritual counsels, they have enjoyed many temporal advantages because of his championship of their causes; and his influence was felt in the Pueblo provinces too.

The scientific world is indebted to him and his assistants, since at this mission important ethnological contributions have been assembled and published. The Arizona Fathers have issued *An Ethnologic Dictionary of the Navajo Language* (1910); *A Vocabulary of the Navajo Language* (1912), and *A Manual of Navajo Grammar* (1926). From 1913 to 1922 they issued an annual illustrated magazine, *The Franciscan Missions of the Southwest*. Their *Dictionary* is, considering the peculiarities and scope of the Navajo language, an extraordinary production. But two hundred copies of it were printed, and, like the *Memorial* of Benavides, it is well-nigh priceless.

> What though the Indian heart conceals its pagan mystery?
> Each Desert dawn on high reveals the Cross at Cochiti!
> At evening, when the sun's last red halos each purple hill,
> Across the Rio Grande's bed the Bells are ringing still!

There may be those to despise and ridicule the thing I have termed a "compromise" between Franciscan dogma and pagan forms. Many phases of this apparent compromise I do not like, but I am unable to suggest an effective cure that would not be worse than the disease. Practically all primitive peoples have employed the dance to depict their emotions and sensations, or to commemorate events. Christ Himself preferred to teach in parables. Perhaps the present Fathers, aware of the fact that the pagan dance form, like so many other things inherited from the dark, reappeared in the early Church notwithstanding the early Fathers, have thought best to tolerate it among the heathen of the New World rather than abruptly to sever communication with them, as many other equally sincere missionaries have done. And it has lived too as a remnant of old Spanish influence, for we find that even after the middle of the eighteenth century there were traces of religious dancing in the cathedrals of Spain and Portugal. There is that Dance of the Blessed Sacrament, performed by ten little boys, still to be seen in the Cathedral of Seville, at Benediction, on the Feast of Corpus Christi.

I have wondered why this compromise should not have been carried even further. If an Indian refuses to be baptized with water, why not humor him and baptize him with corn meal? It seems to me that several of the faiths, as well as the earnest padres, have overlooked this means of attacking native reticence. At the more primitive pueblos, one finds a bowl suspended at the door, or in a niche of the plastered wall, and in it corn meal. The orthodox scatter a pinch of it on leaving the house. This may be pure Indian ceremony, and then it may be the last trace of some imaginative padre who sought to connect the sacred meal with the *asperges*. Certainly some of them would appear to have thought that, if the Indian did not comprehend all of Catholic mystery, — neither did Sir Thomas More, — they would get him into the sanctuary with as much as he knew, for, like the man in jail, he could not be in a safer place. One should not deny to the early Franciscans the saving gifts of fancy and humor. Occasionally comes a critic who is fearful that these padres were ill-equipped for the pioneer mission work. Their present champion and venerable historian, Father Engelhardt of California, pauses in his splendid account of the period to observe: —

> This particular Bible pedlar is very much concerned to know whether the first Franciscans in the State had any Bibles. . . . Why should they? They had equipped themselves by studying the Bible for many years, and especially by practicing its commands.

He might have pointed out that the Luther schism occurred in 1520, and that Luther's translation of the Bible was completed in 1534. In those days, expresses of new publications to the New World were not speedy; there was no Book-of-the-Month Club; and, while the first Franciscans in New Mexico probably had word of the event, no missionaries were sent to them. By 1618, Zarate-Salmeron, at Jemez, was preparing a *doctrina* in the Jemez language, using the feeble materials at his disposal. Now should these Franciscans have imported and distributed Luther's Bible, after teaching the Pueblo Indians to read in the German language? The religious works arranged and printed in Spanish at the monasteries of Mexico were equally useless among an unlettered people; and that tremendous influence, the American Bible Society, would not be founded until 1816.

That was in the past, a time of little education; but if you feel that the Indians should pack a Bible, which many of them to-day cannot read, then stress government education through your Congressman, who may be studiously curtailing the Indian appropriations. I failed to build four day schools among the Peublo Indians because of Congressmen. And you will find the Franciscan as eager for schools as anyone else. At St. Michaels there is a boarding school for 275 Navajo, and in 1922 428 Pueblo Indian children were in Catholic mission schools at Bernalillo and Santa Fe.

Inasmuch as the Pueblo Indians have been decided wards of this government, their education should be thoroughly supplied by it, which implies, coincidently, sanitation and medication.

You cannot endow an Indian with intelligence by pre-

MISSION OF SAN ESTEVAN AT ACOMA
Probably dating from after the Pueblo Revolt of 1680

ST. MICHAEL'S CHURCH AND MONASTERY
The Franciscan Mission to the Navajo, founded 1898

senting him a neatly indexed Bible, nor can you salve syphilis with *McGuffey's First Reader*.

Tuberculosis does not yield to arithmetic, and grammar has never been known to have the slightest effect on cancer. Reflect, though, that when the local government physician was helpless, when the Agent was handcuffed, when Washington was indifferent to either of them, the syphilitic of San Felipe still had Father Jerome Hesse.

Should we expect of the friar that he will assume somehow the duties of government? On occasion, when impatient ones have done this, they have been branded as meddlers or propagandists. Should we expect that the friar continue miracles, like Porras at Awatobi, and by simply saying "Epheta" make our burdens the less? The days of miracles are over, and to the everlasting credit of the Franciscans in the desert, even in the early days, they claimed and credited few miracles.

Yes, the friar has a Bible, originally prepared by Saint Jerome in the fourth century, commonly known as the Vulgate. The official English translation is the "Douai Version" of 1609. Considered simply as a Bible, it seems to stand the wear and tear of time; and in it one finds this significant passage, reported from a most high Source: —

Show me the coin of the tribute. And they offered him a penny. And Jesus saith to them: Whose image and inscription is this? And they say to him: Cæsar's. Then he saith to them: Render therefore to Cæsar the things that are Cæsar's; and to God, the things that are God's.

Franciscan Martyrs in New Mexico

Year	Station or Pueblo	Indian Nation	Name
1542	Tiguex	Tihuas	Juan de la Cruz
1542?	Pecos	Pecos	Luis Descalona (lay brother)
1544?	Quivira	Vaqueros	Juan de Padilla
1581	Tiguex	Tihuas	Juan de Santa Maria
			Francisco Lopez
			Agustin Rodriguez
1631	Taos	Tihuas	Pedro de Miranda
1632	Zipias	Zipias	Martin de Arvide (killed by Zuñi)
1632	Hawaikuh	Zuñi	Francisco de Letrado
1633	Awatobi	Hopi	Francisco de Porras
1670	Hawaikuh	Zuñi	Pedro de Avila y Ayala (killed by Navajo)
1675	Senecu	Piros	Alonzo Gil de Avila (killed by Apache)
1680	Taos	Tihuas	Antonio de Mora
			Juan de la Pedrosa (lay brother)
	Picuris	Tihuas	Matías Rendon
	Tesuque	Tewas	Juan Bautista Pio
	Nambe	Tewas	Tomas de Torres
	San Ildefonso	Tewas	Luis de Morales
			Antonio Sanchez de Pro (lay brother)
	Pecos	Pecos	Fernando de Velasco
	Galisteo	Tanos	Juan Bernal (custodio)
			Domingo de Vera
	San Marcos	Tanos	Manuel Tinoco
	Santo Domingo	Queres	Juan de Talaban
			Francisco Antonio Lorenzana
			José de Montesdoca
	Jemez	Jemez	Juan de Jesus
	Acoma	Queres	Lucas Maldonado
	Zuñi	Zuñi	Juan de Val
	Awatobi	Hopi	José de Figueroa
	Chimopovi	Hopi	José de Truxillo
	Oraibi	Hopi	José de Espeleta
			Agustin de Santa Maria
1696	Taos	Tihuas	Antonio Carboneli (killed at San Cristobal)
	San Ildefonso	Tewas	Francisco Corbera
	Nambe	Tewas	Antonio Morena

FRANCISCAN MARTYRS IN NEW MEXICO (*Continued*)

YEAR	STATION OR PUEBLO	INDIAN NATION	NAME
1696	San Cristobal	Tanos	José de Arbizu
	Jemez	Jemez	Francisco de Jesus Maria Casanes

The visitor to the Pueblo provinces may be curious to know of those early missionaries who served at the missions, and who sleep in the ruins of churches they constructed. There is record of the following: —

Juan de Escalona, comisario 1599–1605, buried on June 22, 1607, in the church built by him at Santo Domingo.

Cristóbal de Quiñones, established church, hospital, and monastery at San Felipe; died there April 27, 1609.

Gerónimo de Pedraza, died at San Felipe, May 5, 1664.

Alonzo Peinado, converted the pueblo of Chilili, and died there after 1617.

Asencio de Zárate, died at Picuris in 1632; his remains removed to the Santa Fe parish church (now incorporated in the Cathedral) 1759.

Benardo de Marta, died at Sia, September 18, 1635.

Francisco de Acevedo, built the churches at Abo, Tenabo, and Tabrira, and was buried at Abo, August 1, 1644.

García de San Francisco y Zúñiga, founded the mission of Socorro; introduced the first grapes in New Mexico; buried in the pueblo of Senecu, January 22, 1673.

Estevan de Perea, who succeeded Benavides as custodio of missions in 1629, and who may have served in New Mexico earlier than Benavides; founded the church and monastery at Sandia, and was buried there.

X

THE CRUSADER

> Sometimes the winter stars reveal
> A symbol that Old Spain concerns;
> A martial figure clad in steel —
> His vigil keeps, and then returns
>   To where, beneath cathedral lamps,
>   Eternally De Vargas camps.
>   — "El Palacio"

Thirteen years were to pass with the City of the Holy Faith in the hands of the Tanos Indians who had occupied it on Otermin's retreat to the southern borders. With the possible exception of its buildings of adobe, everything that the Spaniards had accumulated was ruined, if not destroyed, we may be sure. Whatever had been constructed in Santa Fe, raising it above the level of a squalid frontier settlement, had centred about the plaza. There is no reason to believe that Santa Fe, from Peralta's to Otermin's administration, a period of seventy years, had grown into an inspiring capital; but there is no doubt that Spanish civic pride, and the labors of the padres, had made of it a pleasing oasis that the wondrous beauty of the Sangre de Cristos enhanced. There were trees to break the desert glare, and gardens, and orchards. One may be certain that the ornamental gardens soon disappeared, and that the trees were speedily turned into firewood.

Into the plaza every feature of an Indian pueblo was

promptly introduced, beginning naturally with a kiva or *estufa*. The Palace of the Governors became very like a caravanserai of the Old East, with dogs and fowls and burros lending it both aroma and primitive attractiveness, and the church a stock pen. Transfer the plaza of Santo Domingo to the plaza of Santa Fe to-day, and the visitor will have a picture of what the town was in the years 1681 to 1693, when it sank to the level of a Galisteo pueblo.

But, even in the Indian mind, Santa Fe had become a Mecca, the centre of their independence, the symbol of their victory over the oppressive white. As for the Spanish, the lure of fabulous cities in New Mexico and northern treasure mines no longer drew their imagination — only Santa Fe, the despoiled capital of a King's province, the place of a shameful defeat, the shrine of a hideous massacre, must be recovered. There had been Seville and Granada in the Old World; the New would furnish a similar tradition.

But Spain and the King were far away. As for the Viceroy, the Spanish frontier in New Spain had suddenly shrunk to El Paso del Norte, a lonely presidio, and its officials were busy holding it against other tribes of Indians. Ambitious captains and impatient friars, who visioned the triumph of redeeming Santa Fe from the heathen, found it difficult to invite interest, because interest of an active sort meant the assembling and financing of forces.

It was not until December 29, 1693, that Spaniards again held the plaza and the Palace in Santa Fe. Don Diego de Vargas, the last of the Conquistadors, on that day recaptured the ancient Villa, bearing his standard of the Virgin. It is said that he raised the very banner that Juan de Oñate had borne through New Mexico in 1598.

For eleven succeeding years this soldier of Spain was to influence New Mexico and the affairs of the Pueblo Indians, and then be taken ill in the Sandia Mountains, as he pursued Apaches, to die at Bernalillo in April 1704. He was to spend those eventful eleven years touching "both extremes of fortune," being first the all-powerful conqueror and Governor, then in disgrace and chains in the Santa Fe prison, charged with peculation and extortion, at the very time the King of Spain was awarding him the public thanks and a title in recognition of his conquest; then again Governor of New Mexico and Marques de la Nava de Brazinas until his death. His body was carried to Santa Fe and interred under the altar in the *parroquia*, where he had, some years before, reverently deposited the bones of the Jemez martyr, Fray Juan de Jesus. This was the original parish church of the town, now incorporated in the Cathedral. Each year a religious procession carries his statue of the Virgin from the Cathedral to the Rosario Chapel at the town's edge, in fulfillment of a vow he made should he be victorious in the conquest. His name will ever be linked with the colorful history of the ancient Villa Real de Santa Fe de San Francisco.

Four governors prior to De Vargas had their opportunity to achieve this immortality. Otermin, who had suffered the siege and evacuated the capital, naturally wished to recover his kingdom. In the latter part of 1681 he managed to collect 146 soldiers and 112 Indian allies for a campaign. Marching north, he found the pueblos of the Piros deserted. Isleta was the first inhabited town he came to, and, after meeting with a feeble resistance, he captured it. A scouting party learned that Cochiti, San Felipe, and Santo Domingo had been abandoned by their inhabitants, and the leader of this party parleyed with these Indians in the hills. Otermin considered his force too weak for conquest, and returned to El Paso. Nothing is of record concerning the official acts of Governor Ramirez, appointed to succeed him. In August 1683 began the administration of Don Petroz de Crusate, and for about three years Don Petroz had a stormy political time of it, to say nothing of his campaigns against the Jumanos and Apaches. Apparently the Franciscans, busy with new missions in the vicinity of El Paso, did not like him, and assisted in his removal from office. Don Pedro Reneros de Posada succeeded him. Hodge records that in 1687 Posada stormed the pueblo of Santa Ana and burned it. At that time Santa Ana was situated about midway between the present pueblo of that name, and San Felipe, on the "great black mesa of San Felipe." Posada ruled until 1689, when he was accused of inefficiency, and again Crusate entered upon the office. Evidently Crusate thought that some determined demonstration should be made against those triumphant Pueblo Indians, for he assembled a force and marched to Sia. In a battle at this pueblo six hundred of the Indians were either slain or burned to death; seventy were captured, and some of the old men were shot in the plaza. While various dates are given for this fight, it appears to have occurred in August of 1689. In the following year Crusate made plans for another vigorous campaign, but his time and energies were sapped by a revolt of the Sumas Indians. He was thus delayed, and before the accounts of his valor at Sia and elsewhere could reach Spain, De Vargas had been appointed to the governorship of a province that he must conquer before ruling.

Both Otermin and Crusate had occupied themselves while in the north with the recording of voluminous testimony respecting the causes of the insurrection of 1680 — Otermin doubtless to justify his own course at Santa Fe, and Crusate with the idea of doing something as a long-distance bureaucrat. After the battle of Sia, one of his prisoners, Bartolomé de Ojeda, a native of that pueblo, suffered cross-examination as to the temperamental conditions among the distant apostate Indians, and procured for certain of them allotments of land — perhaps the original Spanish grants. The United States Land Office Reports for 1856 contain reprints of a series of documents found in the Santa Fe archives. They refer to the pueblos of Picuris, San Juan, Pecos, Jemez, Cochiti, San Felipe, and Santo Domingo, being summaries of the testimony of this prisoner given before His Excellency, Don Petroz de Crusate, upon which it would appear these grants were made, "by proxy" as it were, the Indians concerned being far away in the, as yet, unconquered north, busy with their harvest ceremonies, if not watching the trails for the next invasion. Along with these documents is one referring to Acoma and Laguna, containing language that causes one to doubt the whole series, since Bartolomé is quoted as giving "the Cubero mountain" as an Acoma boundary, as one of the landmarks fixed by Popé, the rebel leader, when he assigned territory to the various groups after the rebellion. We know positively that the place was not given that name until Cubero made his march to the pueblos of the west, ten years later — after the first administration of De Vargas, when he first visited the newly founded pueblo of San Jose de la Laguna. How could Bartolomé have known of such a name? In his testimony before the Congressional committees of 1923,

Twitchell declared that certain of these documents had been discovered "as spurious," but he was not asked and did not explain whether any of them had been accepted as genuine.

If they are genuine, then His Excellency Don Petroz de Crusate is to be credited with having recorded to certain of the pueblos their grants of four square leagues, and greater or less areas to others. Santo Domingo had a very large and irregular tract assigned to it (92,398 acres), whereas San Felipe and Cochiti were restricted in area, the latter with the explanatory statement: "This they owe for being rebels." Crusate was but human, and the inhabitants of old Cochiti had made themselves a trifle more than unpleasant to persons of Spanish descent. They were to bother De Vargas considerably, even down to the second revolt of 1696, when they sincerely did their best to murder their missionary, Fray Alonzo Ximenes de Cisneros, and would have added him to the list of martyrs but for protection he received at San Felipe.

Don Diego de Vargas Zapata Lujan Ponce de Leon was more energetic. He did not waste time taking the testimony of prisoners or in describing grants of land for rebels who were uncomfortably loose in the field. In 1692 he made a swift preliminary reconnaissance through the Pueblo provinces, with but two hundred men in his command. Twenty-three days after leaving El Paso he reached Santa Fe, and, having surrounded the town and cut off the water supply, persuaded the Indians to yield. Perhaps this early success in diplomacy, rather than by force of arms, accounted for the leniency of Don Diego on later occasions, and in the end caused even more bloodshed. Having visited all the pueblos, even the Hopi of the west, De Vargas returned to El Paso to collect such a number of people as would justify an attempt to recolonize New Mexico. In October 1693, he began his second entrada with about one hundred soldiers, seventeen friars, and seven hundred colonists. This time he was not able to advance so rapidly, the colonists and baggage retarding his marches. The food supplies became exhausted, and persons perished from hunger and exposure. With the military, De Vargas pressed on ahead of his suffering column. At Isleta he learned that the Indians holding Santa Fe were preparing to resist, and that this feeling of war was spreading to other pueblos, notably Sia and Cochiti.

The Spanish arrived in Santa Fe on the sixteenth of December, having left Santo Domingo two days before in a heavy snowstorm. The Indian occupants were called on for supplies of corn, and furnished one hundred sacks, but they did not welcome a second demand for food. While there had been evidences of contrition, the Tanos did not vacate the plaza. De Vargas informed them that they must return to their former Galisteo homes, whereupon the Tanos closed the entrance to the plaza and prepared to defend it.

On December 29, 1693, De Vargas assaulted these defenses, and after a spirited battle carried the plaza. The Governor of the Indians, seeing the fight going against his people, hanged himself from the rafters of the Palace, and seventy of his followers were executed. Four hundred women and children were held by the Spanish as captives.

The year 1694 opened with the majority of the pueblos in active revolt. The Tewa Indians, having arrived too late to reënforce the Tanos at Santa Fe, fortified the Black Mesa, a rugged dome rising from the plain beyond the pueblo of San Ildefonso. This meant a hostile force within striking distance of Santa Fe, occupying a natural fortress nearly as strong as Old Acoma. They began to raid the Spanish live stock, to attack any small parties that left the capital, and they also turned their attention to the punishing of those pueblo communities that had not again raised the battle standard. Santa Ana, Sia, Pecos, and San Felipe, who had kept the faith made with De Vargas, were soon forced to defend themselves. The Apaches too became active in the field. Then the Cochitis rebelled and fled to their mountain fastness, the Potrero Viejo.

De Vargas besieged the Black Mesa for fifteen days in March, but failed to take it. He then moved against Cochiti, assaulted the Potrero, killed twenty-one Indians, and captured more than three hundred of their women and children. Fearing that the garrison of Santa Fe would be surprised and perhaps overwhelmed by the Tewas in his absence, he hurriedly returned some of his men from the Cochiti field, remaining with but thirty-six to collect supplies of grain. The Cochitis promptly surprised him and recovered many of the captives. De Vargas fired the pueblo and retreated; and the Potrero was never thereafter occupied.

In May he again appeared before the Black Mesa, and again failed to accomplish the reduction of the place. Going north, he found Picuris and Taos deserted, and was attacked by the Utes, losing eight men. He did not return to Santa Fe until July. The Black Mesa was still like a hornet's nest on his flank; but he found it necessary to proceed against Jemez, where the heights of San Diego Cañon had been fortified. With a force of one hundred and twenty men he attacked the Jemez, killing eighty-four of them, many of whom threw themselves from the cliffs.

He then burned their habitations, after removing large stores of corn, and returned to Santa Fe with more than three hundred prisoners. A little after this the Jemez sought pardon, throwing the blame on a principal chief, who was sent to slavery in the mines.

In September, aided by both Queres and Jemez allies, De Vargas again assaulted the Black Mesa, and failed to storm it. He lost eleven men of the Spanish and some of the allies; so he settled down to besiege the place. After their supplies were cut off, the defenders became discouraged and treated for peace. With the understanding that they would return to their homes and abandon war, pardon was granted them. As a reward for their assistance, De Vargas returned the Jemez women and children to their people. It would appear that it was his policy to hold such prisoners as hostages only, and that the term "sold into slavery" often meant less than it literally describes. Slavery among the Spanish meant labor at the presidio or among the colonists, a system of peonage. No doubt hundreds of the prisoners had been employed in cleaning up the wreckage of old Santa Fe.

By the end of the year 1694, the Pueblo Indians had all submitted to De Vargas, and he made a tour of inspection. Seemingly there were no more rebels, and he began establishing the friars in their several missions. He also returned all the women and children he held as hostages, thinking this good policy, but it was a policy his colonists resented.

Now again the colonists, and their need for lands which could be cultivated, were to foment trouble. Santa Cruz de la Canada was resettled, thus depriving Indians of tillable land. The friars protested this action. And the lands of certain pueblos, practically depopulated by the wars, were granted as rewards to successful captains.

THE BLACK MESA OF SAN ILDEFONSO

THE PLAZA IN THE OLD PUEBLO OF SIA
Tradition has it that on the two rocks De Vargas and his lieutenant sat when receiving the submission of the pueblo

Rumors of trouble were received. It did not develop at once, although the Indians of San Cristobal and San Lazaro departed for the mountains; but the other pueblos were not ready to lend active assistance. Then came the famine of 1696, when the colonists were reduced to starvation. The Viceroy forwarded cattle, arms, and ammunition, but admonished them to rely on themselves rather than upon the general government. While it had been forbidden, the settlers began selling arms to the natives, and an unfortunate incident occurred at Pecos, where one of the friars accidentally shot an Indian. Perhaps these things aided and ripened the second revolt and massacre.

On June 4, 1696, the old rebels of Taos and Picuris, the Tewas, the Jemez, and the Queres of Cochiti and Santo Domingo, rose against their conquerors. They promptly killed five of the friars, and twenty-one others, and fled to their mountain retreats. Again De Vargas took the field, to engage in fights with the Jemez, and at Acoma, and at Taos and other pueblos of the north. He reported later to the Viceroy that once again the Pueblo Indians had submitted to his authority, although he doubted the loyalty of certain divisions. In the midst of this uncertainty and anxiety, politics intervened, as it often does. De Vargas's term of office expired, and in July 1697 Don Pedro Rodriguez Cubero succeeded him. Cubero began to make war on the reputation of De Vargas, rather than applying himself vigorously to ruling the natives. It was not until November 1703 that De Vargas again entered Santa Fe as its Governor, to remain until his death. Indeed, he is there now, in the crypt of the parroquia, within the walls of the Cathedral, peacefully camping in the city he restored to his King.

XI

THE PUEBLO INDIANS OF NEW MEXICO

> To-day — the sheep stray from the fold upon those quiet hills;
> The search for amethyst and gold no mercenary thrills;
> The sand that drifted o'er their graves each summer's corn now yields;
> The Captains and their Spanish braves are dust with Spanish shields.
>
> — "The Bells of Cochiti"

By admirable researches into their dialects and modes, the Pueblo Indians have been traced to four philological divisions of natives in the Southwest: these four being the Shoshonean, the Zuñian, the Keresan, and the Tanoan. Their present neighbors and former bitter enemies, the Apache and the Navajo tribes, are of the Athapascan stock. We have therefore a sharp division between the two groups that have enlisted and compelled the attention of the whites since 1540. Unfortunately, neither of the groups has been able to preserve its ancient history in a form intelligible to the modern peoples, or, if interested at all in the matter, each group has been content to rely on oral tradition.

The deserts and cañons of the Southwest have produced so far but one record of early times that may be deciphered with accuracy; and that is El Morro, or Inscription Rock, situated between Acoma and Zuñi, the bulletin board of the Conquistadors. These great captains were not unaccompanied by men of letters and intelligence who were moved with curiosity to learn of the antecedents of their interesting captives. It would be especially foolish to assume that the early friars made no effort to unravel this riddle. They, or at least many of them, were men of erudition and scholarship. They had before them more of cabalistic decoration to decipher than we are likely to have inherited; and yet, all we have to guide us are the folk tales of the people, varied, involved in symbolism, and withal childishly similar.

Naturally, the first question that arises in connection with this culture is — whence did the Pueblo Indians come? Bancroft scouts the Aztec theory, believing their Montezuma legends offshoots of Spanish times. Dr. Edgar L. Hewett has sought to separate and to classify skeletal remains to justify the possibility of different sources within their New Mexican period. And John Gunn, unhampered by traditions, traces them definitely to the ancient Cushites and the dawn before Babylon.

The commonest answer is that they are descendants of the cliff dwellers. If so, and it seems that they inhabited at times the cliff-dwelling region, using the honeycombed cliffs too, then who were the cliff dwellers? To be perfectly plain about it, we do not know, and are not likely ever to know. I have no material facts with which to increase the store of ethnological research, and few fanciful ideas. The potsherds and corn refuse of the Rio Grande ruins, and the mute sandstone foundations of Hopi pueblos, were long since thoroughly sifted and catalogued by far more capable hands. Indeed, it is my view that analysis of Indian culture must ever be superficial, and that one strays far into imaginative fields when he essays it with the serious intention of proving anything. In so far as this book may represent a contribution, it seeks to present a clarification of ten thousand elusive footnotes.

My purpose has been to present a picture evolved from an Indian Agent's contact with the Pueblo Indians, and to deal with living men and their problems. This has necessitated a glance at the old properties of their stage, and shadowy — almost mythical — dramatis personæ, the heroes of a long-lost empire. Should I seem to eulogize the Spaniard and to idealize the Franciscan, surely they invite it as the great figures of a not inglorious era.

The first were vigorous and dramatically colorful, the second zealous and heroically faithful, — adventurers and fanatics, if you will, — but the two groups together possessed these four engaging qualities that our modern government, however it may have demonstrated them in other scenes, has lacked in its dealings with the Pueblo Indians.

Having met and opposed, by one feeble means or another, four divisions of stronger mankind, without suffering extinction, these Pueblo people present to us a unique chapter in our Indian annals. Their story is not ended, and there is too little of permanent record concerning their more recent adventures with our type of civilization.

Apparently they were never very numerous. Let us compare the earliest record of seeming worth with the latest of scientific investigation. The exaggerations of Fray Alonzo de Benavides, the first custodio of missions, in his *Memorial* to the King, 1630, may not have been intentional, and they are milder than earlier estimates.

It is the most difficult thing to approximate accurately the numbers of native peoples when having no machinery for the compiling of a census. I can personally testify to the terrors of census-making, and I believe that I evolved, finally, a clerical method for procuring most accurate censuses; but then I had at the Agency many times the help available to Benavides. Bandelier says that the *Memorial* was "a campaign document," citing many gross inaccuracies, particularly that concerning the penol of Acoma, the rock top being about seventy acres in extent and entirely too small to sustain 2000 people conveniently. The *Relaciones* of Fray Zarate-Salmeron states that there had been 34,650 baptisms prior to 1626, "as I have counted on the baptismal records." This is very easily explained by one who has struggled with Indian censuses, and in accounting for the identity of unlettered Indians in other ways. Fray Salmeron undoubtedly saw the records, and I do not mean to insinuate that they had been indifferently kept. In 1919, the government census for the Isleta pueblo held between 1100 and 1200 names; and, after a complete revision of it, following very careful methods, the list totaled 988 living persons, a reduction of about twenty per cent. Simply, dead ones had not been removed, although births had constantly been added; and the one Indian had been counted several times under different names. I have not the slightest doubt but that the one Indian was exposed to baptism many different times, because Indians like ceremonies, and many of them sought to please the earnest padres, and so, whenever self-interest, ingratiation, a rush of religion, or desire for display swept them, they would offer themselves.

Benavides's figures, when charted to enable quick comparison, are very interesting:—

DESERT DRUMS

The Historic Pueblos, Now Extinct

Nation	Pueblos	Conventos	Churches	Souls
Tompiro	14 to 15	6	6	10,000
Piro	14	3	3	6,000
Tano	5	1	5	4,000
Pecos	1	1	1	2,000
	34	11	15	22,000

The Present Living Pueblos

Nation	Pueblos	Conventos	Churches	Souls
Jemez	2	1	1	3,000
Tihua	15 to 16	2	2	7,000
Picuris	1	1	1	2,000
Tewa	8	3	8	6,000
Taos	1	1	1	2,500
Queres	7	3	7	4,000
Acoma	1	1	1	2,000
	35	12	21	26,500

He listed the Zuñi and the Hopi as each having from eleven to twelve towns, and a total population of 20,000. These two tribes and the extinct pueblos give a total of 42,000, and his grand total, 68,500. Of the nations known to us as "the Pueblo Indians of New Mexico," Benavides estimated that the population was, therefore, 26,500, and this should be compared with the census figures of two other periods. (See table on page 225.)

Therefore, in my judgment, 26,500 in 1630, fifty years before the Pueblo Revolt, with no battle casualties and many pueblos not named still in existence, was no whopping guess, despite Bandelier's campaign suggestion. We must ever keep in mind that Bandelier, like any other savant immersed in sepulchral statistics, never had anything to do with the management of living Indians, and while recognizing with all due reverence his preëminence in the scientific field, I would not have given two hoots for his services when arranging for, constructing, equip-

THE PUEBLO INDIANS OF NEW MEXICO 225

COMPARATIVE CENSUSES

1630 BENAVIDES		1805 SPANISH GOVERNOR ALENCASTER			1922 UNITED STATES PUEBLO CENSUS		
Jemez	3000	Jemez	264		Jemez	561	
		Pecos	104	368	Pecos (extinct)		
Tihua	11,500	Taos	508		Taos	580	
		Picuris	250		Picuris	114	
		Sandia	314		Sandia	92	
		Isleta	419	1491	Isleta	988	1774
Tewa	6000	Nambe	143		Nambe	116	
		Tesuque	131		Tesuque	107	
		San Juan	194		San Juan	422	
		San Ildefonso	175		San Ildefonso	91	
		Santa Clara	186		Santa Clara	336	
		Pojoaque	100	929	Pojoaque (extinct)		1072
Queres	6000	Sia	254		Sia	146	
		Cochiti	656		Cochiti	251	
		Santo Domingo	333		Santo Domingo	959	
		San Felipe	289		San Felipe	515	
		Santa Ana	450		Santa Ana	219	
		Laguna	940		Laguna	1808	
		Acoma	731	3653	Acoma	900	4798
	26,500			6441			8205

ping, and later filling a Pueblo schoolhouse. At the time for toothbrush drill after enrollment, he would have been found very likely over against the Manzano Mountains, with a Spanish manuscript in one hand and a fragment of skull in the other, endeavoring to place the ancient site of Encaguiagualcaca. Probably he would not have returned to the station for lunch, and as for a monthly report showing average attendance! As a commentator on Pueblo culture, all my imagination fails to encompass the vision he would have had of me.

DESERT DRUMS

But I am sure the figures of Fray Benavides and modern statistics have never before been presented in this fashion. Indeed, there may have been something like accuracy in his estimates concerning the early Zuñi and the Hopi, since we have to-day: —

```
Zuñi . . . . . . . . . . . . . . . 1833
Hopi (Tusayan pueblos, and including Tewa
    among the Hopi) . . . . . . . . . 2483
Hopi at Moencopi . . . . . . . . .  369
                                   ─────
                                   4685
The Pueblo Indians of New Mexico: —
Under Northern Agency . . . . . . . 3344
Under Southern Agency . . . . . . . 5690   9034 [1]
                                          ──────
                                          13,719
```

Thus we have between thirteen and fourteen thousand pueblo-type Indians, and the Reverend Father Custodian, three hundred years ago, totaled them at approximately 68,500, of which 22,000 (the extinct pueblos) have disappeared from the scene and record within historic times.

Nearly everyone quotes Mindeleff's *Aboriginal Remains* as the modern answer, and I have no recourse: —

A band of five hundred village-building Indians might leave the ruins of fifty villages in the course of a single century. It is very doubtful whether the total number of Pueblo Indians ever exceeded 30,000.

When Coronado was still at Hawaikuh, only shortly after he had discovered and reduced Cibola (Zuñi), we find a delegation from Cicuye, or far-off Pecos, waiting on him.

---

[1] Figures taken from the 1927 Annual Report of the Secretary of the Interior. I do not vouch for their accuracy, it appearing that too many Pueblo Indians proper have been born since 1922, when 8205 was their census total.

Examination of the various accounts of the early explorers would seem to indicate either that the Pueblo Indians were a very curious people, or that they sought to entice suspicious strangers farther and farther on with accounts of more wondrous places, either to rid themselves of a temporary menace by the easy expedient of unloading them on neighbors, or to gain time in their rear for organization against them. Organization among the slow-thinking pueblo-type peoples was always complicated and doubtful of success. It required more than eighty years of hatred of oppression to culminate in the revolt of 1680, and the last thirty years of this time were spent in active preparation (1650–1680). This proves one thing definitely, that these Indians had very little national feeling.

Their factional differences and jealousies brought about the divisions that we find to-day. One should note the losses and accretions of living pueblos. The Hopi have split and split when not menaced, the last time as late as 1906. But for the modern grants fixing the Pueblo Indians proper to one abode, and the pressure of civilization around them, they would migrate to-day, to the Hopi possibly, or to the cliff dwellings along the northern borders of Arizona, as fancy seized them. The urge on individuals is common. Only yesterday Lagunas have removed to Isleta, and vice versa; Isletas have taken up their abode at Sandia; Acomas have penetrated Santa Ana; and a few of the northern Pueblo people may be found among the southern ones. Stray Hopi have lived for years at Santo Domingo, nearly four hundred miles from the First Mesa, and members of the Pueblo tribes have intermarried with the Hopi. The last concerted move was that of the San Juan Tewa to the Hopi provinces in 1700. It was during and following the revolt when occurred the admixture of the Pueblo stocks.

Bandelier says in his *Final Report:* —

With the exception of Acoma, there is not a single pueblo standing where it was at the time of Coronado, or even sixty years later, when Juan de Oñate accomplished the peaceful reduction of the New Mexican village Indians. The great insurrection of 1680 wrought an important change in the numbers and distribution of Indian villages.

Lummis is convinced, however, that the pueblo of Isleta should be added to Acoma as occupying its original site since the early Spanish times.

I have never been so fortunate as to see a map of New Mexico giving in one sheet the locations of all the ancient pueblos, so as to fix them approximately in relation to the modern ones and the younger towns of the white men. The scale of it would be too large for the pages of a book. And perhaps the savants who have this information have hesitated to graph their beliefs and theories. When one wades through Bancroft's catalogue of the early pueblos, he becomes conscious of a dull mental depression. I have tried to digest the potpourri with an auto horn tooting in the next compound, three parrots across the street mocking the universe, and a musical genius in the next apartment arranging "My Wild Irish Rose" on the piano with one finger. Bancroft may have used a bombproof during the course of his investigations, but he laments the bales of trash he had to sift through to write his work. Or perhaps he did suffer these disturbances, relatively, since his list of old pueblos is about as comprehensible as the usual government Indian census. We wade through Emexes, Emeges, Ameies, Amejes, Emmes, Emes, Hemes,

Jemes, to reach the present Jemez. We have our choice of Tiquex, Tihuex, Tigueq, Tiguex, and, thank God! Hodge has pronounced it for us as "Tee-wesh." We may select from Cicuique, Cicuye, Cicuic, Acuique, Ciciuio, Ticuique, Tienique, and we get, finally, Pecos. We have Tucuyan, Tuzan, Tusan, Tucano, and Tusayan; and we ought not to complain when reading of the Mohoce, or Mohace, or Mohoqui, later Hopitu, to gather in the Americanese Moki and Moqui (both wrong) to gain the Hopi Indians.

Even F. W. Hodge, a scholar one would expect to revere each tiny tendril of ancient lore, complains somewhat bitterly of this nomenclature, quoting Oñate's two lists of the Jemez towns, cataloguing nine supposed pueblos of this thickly populated region and nominating them in two distinct fashions, so that we have eighteen to guess at. He points out that Bandelier, "of exceptional astuteness in the identification of such names, numerates them as seventeen distinct villages." The experience has very nearly won me over to simplified spelling.

There is a certain feeling of triumph in following through Braba, Urabá, Yuraba, Valladolid, and Tayberon to reach the present art centre of Taos. But greater satisfaction is to be found in speculating on the "lost tribes" of the Pueblo Indians, those four factions or nations now completely extinct, the Pecos reaching their end in 1916. About twenty-two miles south of Santa Fe one reaches the locality of the Galisteo pueblos of the Tanos. Galisteo was the seat of the mission of Santa Cruz as early as 1617. In 1680 its population was 800. It was the residence of the Father Custodian of Missions, who, with several other priests, was killed in the revolt. In 1706 its name was changed to Nuestra Senora de los Remedios, known also as Santa Maria. In 1712 its population was 110. By 1749 its numbers had increased to 350, but owing to decimations of smallpox and Comanche depredations, Galisteo lost its pueblo importance, many of its people going to Pecos and others to the Queres. Soon thereafter we find it a visita of Pecos, and by 1782 there were but 52 inhabitants. In 1793 the pueblo was abandoned, the last remnant removing to Santo Domingo. Bandelier gives it as his opinion that all the villages of the Galisteo region were of the Tanos, and Lummis comments that, if this be true, the five pueblos of this tribe alluded to by Benavides were possibly Galisteo, San Marcos, San Lazaro, San Cristobal, and Cienega. All have disappeared. Floods of the Rio Galisteo destroyed one or more of these once important towns. A relatively short distance from their sites the Galisteo, much of the time a wide sandy wash, enters the Rio Grande at the present pueblo grant of Santo Domingo.

There were also the groups of the Piros, and those of the Tompiros or Salinas. The first of these occupied numerous pueblos along the Rio Grande south of the present Isleta and extending to San Marcial, one of them being named Sevilleta by the Spanish, who, at the end of a trying march, saw in its setting something pleasantly reminiscent of the ancient city in Spain. This town was the place of a church and monastery dedicated to San Luis Obispo; but in 1680 it contained only three families. Apache raids had caused abandonment of some of the Piro settlements, and when the Spanish retreated from Santa Fe they were joined by numbers of the Piros (who had taken no part in the revolt), who went south with them to be settled in what is now Texas and Chihuahua. Hodge says that a remnant still survives there, although their language is practically extinct; and that some of the Piros were absorbed by the Tihuas. Thus we should find traces of them at Isleta.

The Tompiros inhabited the saline slopes to the eastward of the Piros, where we find the ruined missions of Abo, Tabira, and Tenabo. In 1629 the Franciscans had extended their work to these people, and to their neighbors, a seminomadic tribe called the Jumanos, of Caddoan stock. The ruins of Tabira are known as Gran Quivira, causing some to confuse this locality with that mythical Quivira that Coronado sought. The Tompiros were wiped out by Apache raids before 1680, even before their massive missions were completed, and the friars sought other fields.

And we should not forget that vanished section of the Tihuas, of the pueblos of Chilili, Quarai, Tajique, and others in the vicinity of the Salinas, situated to the north of the Tompiro division, and called by Hodge "the pueblos of the Manzanos." He says that Isleta received important accessions of population from these pueblos, which were abandoned between 1669 and 1674 because of Apache depredations, so that, according to Vetancurt, in 1680 Isleta had a population of two thousand.

A great deal has been written about the splendid organization of the Pueblo people. Even Bancroft accepted this vision of a Pueblo republic, and one receives the impression that there was something noble and inspiring about it. This was simply the result of Spanish effort to concentrate them for military and mission control, to make some identified group of headmen in each community responsible to their masters, who were in a feeble minority. This too helped to reduce the number of Pueblo communities, but we may assume from the number of visitas found to be necessary by the friars that the concentration was not complete. In my opinion, judging from what I have seen of them and their organization, it was, prior to Spanish times, simply that described by H. G. Wells as the Old Man form of government — his dominant Old Man being represented among them by the all-powerful cacique or Dalai Lhama. The cacique, being protected and revered and pampered, managed to live to a great age, and long exercised his cruel sway.

The present native form of government, with its gobernadors and their fiscals, was a construction begun no doubt with the best intent. A fantastic evolution of it was suggested to the Indian Bureau in 1912 by one Barbara Freire-Marreco, who came to New Mexico and Arizona with the endorsement of former Commissioner Valentine. It is a pity that this skillful designer could not have remained on the ground with authority to put her scheme into practice — necessarily becoming responsible for it; and I should like to have seen her living under its restrictions, as a citizen of a pueblo. It promised Utopia, if the Pueblo Indians would suddenly expand into Utopians. But it is only fair to state, however, that Barbara Freire-Marreco put her finger precisely and prominently upon the one necessary ingredient that the Indian Bureau always shied away from — that of just and arbitrary control, to be exercised by the native governors, to be sure, but *with Government recognition and support*. She simply overestimated the *average of intelligence* to be found in the pueblos.

It is not likely that the Spanish military authorities were hesitant in giving a native governor full sway in punitive measures. They could scarcely do otherwise.

THE PUEBLO INDIANS OF NEW MEXICO

Benavides has mentioned the size of the Santa Fe garrison in 1630, and by 1676, when Apache and Navajo warfare threatened to extinguish the pueblo civilization, the Spanish had but five fighting men at each frontier station. When Otermin retreated from Santa Fe before the victorious rebels, his column, receiving accessions en route, numbered 1950 persons, including eleven friars, and but 155 men capable of bearing arms. As seventy-three of his soldiers had been killed, Otermin's entire military force, prior to the revolt, could not have exceeded 228 men.

The result of giving arbitrary power into the hands of a native governor, flanked and advised and dominated by a cacique, may be illustrated by some of the ancient customs, showing the severity with which their young men were trained to endure hardships. They were given only dry food to eat over periods and nothing to drink, to inure them against thirst. Until comparatively recent times they must go to the river each morning, winter included, — and the winters along the upper Rio Grande are severe enough, — make an offering to the water gods, and take a plunge. On returning home they were not allowed to approach the fire, but had to remain in a far corner of the room to thaw out gradually. Benavides relates how captains were selected, the candidate being tied to a pillar and flogged with "cruel thistles" (cacti); and Hodge caps this by describing the initiation of one to membership in a Zuñi lodge — the test of endurance being to sit all day naked in the broiling sun on an ant hill. I have described the variations of several charming punishments inflicted on those who offended the pueblo elders at Santo Domingo and elsewhere — skinning alive, hanging until almost dead, and other methods of enforcing obedience; and I do not go along with the suggestion of entrusting an entire community to those who turn most easily and naturally toward a cacique for guidance.

And we have the testimony of Twitchell, given in January 1923, before the Senate Committee on Public Lands, to this effect: —

A good many years ago I happened to be district attorney for the Territory of New Mexico. . . . I was waited upon by an Indian of the [San Juan] pueblo who wanted to go before the grand jury and have the Governor of the pueblo indicted for assault and battery. . . . I inquired into the details, and the facts were that the Governor had notified him that the piece of land he had been cultivating for a long period of years, but which in more recent years he had not cultivated to the satisfaction of the Cacique or the Principales or the Governor, he must turn over to another Indian. This he declined to do . . . and he was tried before the pueblo authorities, and he was strung up by the thumbs, and in a way tortured. . . .

For the actual foundation of this despotism, we must consider the religion of the cacique; and Bandelier has this to say about it: —

There is no greater slave than the Indian. Every motion of his is guided by superstition, every action of his neighbor suspiciously scrutinized. We wonder at many strange actions of the Indian, at what seems to us lack of consistency, of truthfulness, an absence of moral consciousness. We punish him for crimes which he commits without any regret. . . . In this we fail to understand the motives of the Indian. He is not his own master. Nature, deified by him to the extent of innumerable personalities and principles, exacts from him the conduct which we blame. His religion, notwithstanding the promise of coarse felicity beyond the grave, reduces him to utter helplessness so long as he has not crossed the threshold of death, makes him a timid fettered being, anxiously listening

Photo. by H. F. Robinson

THE EAGLE DANCE AT SAN ILDEFONSO
The man facing the camera is beating a *tombe*

to the voice of Nature for advice. These voices stifle the silent throbs of conscience; they are no guide to the heart, no support for the mind.

To-day these sedentary aborigines of New Mexico ... believe in the possibility, not only of apparitions, but also of the transformation, through witchcraft, of men and women into animals of some kind. . . . For the Indian there is nothing more dreadful than sorcery. He believes in it, lives partly through it, and punishes it in secret as severely as possible. . . . Any disaster of magnitude, like drought, epidemic diseases, or flood, is quickly attributed by the Pueblos to witchcraft. In consequence of this, suspicion sets in, and many crimes are committed which are kept secret, but contribute slowly and surely to depopulate the village. Certain pueblos, like Nambe, Santa Clara, and Sia, owe their decline to the constant inter-killing going on for supposed evil practices of witchcraft.

He rejects the idea that these Indians conceived of a merciful Great Spirit. I have no positive means of confuting him in this respect, their own folklore bringing so much proof to his support in the matter of demons and the lesser materialistic gods. I personally believe that all the Indian tribes have dimly felt a Great Spirit, something vaguely superior to their kachina mythology, whether they petitioned it or not, but that they have been without ability to express their Indian idea of it. Now that we have educated some Indians to our conception of monotheism, they accept this picture as a sufficient definition of their once inarticulate theory.

To support his charges of sorcery, Bandelier offers in evidence the decline of certain pueblos in population. In another book I have shown the reason for the decline of Hopi populations, and I know that this applies as well to the pueblos of Sia and Sandia. In addition to the evil of sorcery, which I have no doubt still permeates the elders, there were other evils sufficient to cause decline in population — their self-imposed isolation (retirement even from their common kindred) and the resultant inbreeding of small groups, as at Sia to-day; their restless migrations when they knew little restriction; hostile neighbors, as shown by the fate of the Piros and Tompiros; and epidemics that ravaged them, especially because of their housing and modes of life. And while hostile neighbors and migrations are things of the past, the other two evils are still potent. What chance have Sandia and San Ildefonso for extended life, considering their 92 and 91 inhabitants, respectively? We have record of very terrible smallpox decimations, and it would seem now that the pueblo-type peoples have become practically immune to this disease; but the Spanish influenza of 1918 decimated them all, and it is quite probable that tuberculosis and syphilitic sequelæ are constantly weakening the resistance of a very large proportion of these people.

I am fully aware that the ideas presented in this chapter are fragmentary, culled principally from other men, and present them simply as primary views of the Pueblo culture. It would be a triumph to offer something definite and precise to the student; but I fear that is impossible in the wake of Bandelier, Hodge, and others who have tilled this field. Few people will accept the estimates of the Conquistadors, or of earnest Father Benavides, as to Pueblo populations; fewer still will travel with the interesting Mr. Gunn to the borders of ancient Ethiopia in an effort to trace their antecedents; but most of us will agree that Bandelier's views and Mindeleff's suggestions are within reasonable bounds. Therefore, of the 30,000 pueblo-type natives who once roamed these mysterious

SAN ILDEFONSO DANCERS

THE PUEBLO INDIANS OF NEW MEXICO

deserts, we have present-day knowledge of and communication with nearly 13,000, of which a trifle more than 8000 form "the Pueblo Indians of New Mexico." And for the purposes of a new book, it seems to me that the most important question respecting this remainder is to be found in that query of the fiscal's guard, standing at the mission portal: —

"Heizonarshro?"   (Whither?)

XII

"INFERNAL AFFAIRS"

> José Jesus Juan Ortiz —
> That's his name in Spanish lingo —
> Cleaned the ditch for fiscal fees,
> And polished beads at Sant' Domingo;
>   When he sought a change of work he
>   Peddled pots in Albuquerque.
>   — "The Politician"

SANTO DOMINGO, at first sight, seems a sleepy place. It is a broad pueblo of many streets, and courts, and plazas. In the winter it has a gray, cheerless, even dreary appearance; but through summer and harvest it mellows and yellows in the New Mexican sunshine, with drying corn everywhere and rustling husks blowing around and through the many corrals and dooryards. Smoke wreathes up from pottery chimneys; there is the strange odor of smouldering cottonwood; and burros and half-naked children wallow in the dust. There are several impressive kivas, the largest one finds among the Pueblo Indians, like huge cheeses with long poles protruding from the parapets of their flat roofs. Its mission stands apart from the pueblo proper, hedged by an adobe wall, and wearing an appearance of great age. The phallic horses decorate its balcony. But this church is not very old. Lummis states that this building dates from the last devastating flood of the Rio Grande, in 1886, and that several earlier churches have been destroyed by floods. The pueblo itself has been moved a number of times.

Santo Domingo exhibits many inconsistencies. Notwithstanding its apparent sleepiness, the people may buzz out like hornets should a tourist appear with a camera; and for that matter the bunch buzzed out once at me, their appointed Agent, and for a moment or two it looked as if one very fine picture-making machine would crown the consecrated head of the worthy sacristan. I am not able to report that those lay members of the pueblos who have attained semi-Orders in the Church are always of the deepest humility. Sacristans have had, more than once, serious altercations with their anointed Fathers and spiritual guides — when they proposed to officiate and solemnize marriages, for instance. But much of this attitude, as with most of the people of the pueblos, consists in bluff toward officials and mentors, and is quickly quelled if treated with no showing of weakness.

On the other hand, I have known Santo Domingo to welcome and entertain those who came only to fleece them. True, the Indians bought no gold bricks, and fake turquoise was not offered; but on occasion they came to me with petitions that former guests be traced to unknown lairs. One had arrived and ingratiated himself; had collected a considerable amount of turquoise ornaments and robes and other curios, and then had told the owners to be patient until his return, it being his announced plan to sell these articles at a price and to invest the money for them in cattle. They permitted him to depart with the loot, and, strangely, he disappeared. After waiting several months for the cattle, they sought the Agency, for they feared that something had befallen him. They gave me a list of cities in which this man claimed residence, but the chiefs of police of those places failed utterly to find him. He has not as yet been discovered;

but it may be that some day in the future he will reappear at Santo Domingo, driving ahead of him those cattle, well fattened; and then again it may not. Unless he has the cattle, though, I should advise him to remain away from Santo Domingo, because they are a people given to misunderstandings and abrupt action.

The fiesta at Santo Domingo is a very colorful event. It attracts a large number of their Mexican-type neighbors, and the hatchet is buried courteously for the period of this feast. Saint Dominic rules in the plaza, in a booth decorated by Indian tapestries, and lighted by candles, its floor strewn with meal and loaves of bread. The Governor sells concessions for lunch stands, and confection stalls, and lotteries. There is that old friend, the merry-go-round, with its battered grotesque wooden horses, its asthmatic organ, and piercing whistle. But the feature of such a time is the dance floor. During the day the Indians have held gorgeous tribal dances in the plaza, the actors numbered by hundreds, and marshaled by relays. The Mexicans do the dancing by night. And they dance all night. These Mexicans have a method all their own, and from a financial standpoint it is admirable. At dusk the orchestra of mandolins and guitars parades through the streets, and immediately thereafter dancing begins in one or more of the long, narrow Indian houses that have been rented and in which rough board floors have been laid temporarily. It costs each cavalier ten cents for not more than one round of the building, dancing with his inamorata as well as he may within the crowd of watchers, four or five deep against the walls. As the crowd increases, the dancing space is reduced, naturally, for the adobe walls will not expand and the pressure must be extended inward. Gayly the orchestra emits about four bars of fandango music, and quits. The dance stops. The master of the ceremonies then hurries through the crowd and diligently collects another ten cents per head of the cavaliers; whereupon the orchestra is revived instantly on signal, plays another four bars, and quits again. This keeps up until daylight heralds a new day on the irrigation ditches. The atmosphere is one of rice powder and very cheap cologne.

The Honorable Justice for the United States District Court for New Mexico, in a momentous decision that wonderfully strengthened the power of the appointed Indian Agent, uttered a few significant words concerning the "ancient laws, customs, and usages" of the Pueblo people, which constitute their "internal affairs." Such customs were not to be disturbed so long as they did not appear to be in conflict with law. Now this decree seemed very simple, until its implications were carefully examined; and then appeared the catch.

What were the "laws, customs, and usages" of the Pueblo people, of Santo Domingo, let us say for example? A casual glance at this decision seemed to justify the impression that the Honorable Justice knew; but when one began to discover that each pueblo had differing customs, such as they were — customs that no other pueblo was bound to respect; that there were seventeen living pueblos; and that their varying customs were not of record, but were embalmed only in the skulls of seventeen or more different caciques, who, like the Deity, would n't tell — what chance had an Indian Agent to reflect light on the problem? The Honorable Justice had retired to his chambers, and one could not hammer on the door and request specific information.

One could, however, sit back and await what might

occur; and if what occurred in the pueblos was on the bias with the law, then it need not be respected as belonging to the "ancient laws, customs, and usages" of the people. But the Indians, and especially the Indians of Santo Domingo, thought differently; and they had been allowed to indulge themselves in such thoughts for a good many years. They deferred to the cacique, come what may, and the unfortunate Gobernador and his assistants bore the brunt of any unpleasantness arising with Federal officials. Pretty generally, though, the news of whatever they secretly plotted and carried through within the pueblo did not leak out. When they stoned a physician, the medical officer discreetly made tracks, concluding that he was neither a policeman nor a Franciscan martyr. When they ordered a well-digger to cease work and leave the pueblo, he packed up his tools and departed obediently, the result being that Santo Domingo had few wells. When they told their resident farmer to stay at home on a certain day, he found something to occupy him in the environs of Pena Blanca, and forebore to disturb them. When they placed an obstruction on the Santa Fe main line, with gentle intent of wrecking "the Limited," the guilty person or persons could not be discovered, for the pueblo of Santo Domingo never yielded information.

Somehow or other, these things did not appeal to me. If there was someone ill at the pueblo, I wanted the doctor to investigate; when the schools opened in September of each year, I desired that the pupils arrive unescorted by the police; and when business called me to Santo Domingo I firmly intended going into the town, and I expected the resident farmer to exercise the same freedom of movement. It was rather a bitter struggle at first, and unpleasant things were said on both sides; and then I was assisted in the matter of control through the immolation of a woman from a distant pueblo. After that, Santo Domingo became quite mild, even obedient, and, after a fashion, would come up and eat out of the hand.

This Santa Clara woman married a Santo Domingo man. They were both young, and probably they were married after Mass on the morning of the fiesta, with the padre's stole placed around their necks as a symbol, all after the custom of Santo Domingo. This young woman had been to school and had learned something of the ways of the white man. She dutifully took up her residence in Santo Domingo, her aged mother accompanying her; and this was an unusual thing, for the bridegroom should go to the home of his bride. Perhaps the mother-in-law made some of the trouble, for Indians suffer in this respect far more than white men. Anyway, after some years of wedded life, the husband began to absent himself from home evenings. The wife became suspicious of him; and she refused to sit by the hearth in tears. She was determined. She picked up his trail one evening and traced him to the house of a colorful Santo Domingo woman, who possessed one husband, but whose reputation, even at Santo Domingo, was not above village comment. The lawful wife from Santa Clara emitted a "holler" about these meetings. She disapproved of them, and in the pueblo-woman fashion, a mode not altogether unknown to the white race, she put on a show for the benefit of the neighbors.

Returning home later, she was rather ashamed of herself, and perhaps she received some good maternal advice; for early the next morning she busied herself harnessing the household team to the community wagon, loaded her mother into it with the children, and together, like Ruth and Naomi, they departed, vigorously shaking the dust of Santo Domingo from their feet. They would return to Santa Clara, where the people possessed some knowledge of humanity, made decent pottery, and were Christians.

The team was not of the best, being the usual lanky, ill-fed pueblo span of ponies, and it took a long time to reach the foot of the rugged trail up La Bajada; but up the trail they toiled slowly, and at the very top of it they encountered a peacemaker, an old Indian, kindly disposed, one of the very witnesses to the wedding. He was naturally curious as to their mission, as Indians always are, and they related all that had happened. He thereupon volunteered some very poor advice. He remonstrated with the injured wife, counseled her to return to her husband's roof, and promised to use his influence in procuring an amicable adjustment of things. No doubt he was an excellent old man, and I have known of many fierce differences smoothed away by these elders. So, not without some misgivings, the wife turned the team about, and slowly they returned to Santo Domingo.

Several mornings after this the telephone in my office tinkled persistently, and a clerk said: —

"Domingo calling."

The physician at that station had called from the trader's store, and his message was not reassuring.

"We have one of those malicious torture cases up here," he said. "The victim is a woman, and she's in bad shape — fit subject for a hospital. Think you would do well to come here and see her for yourself."

"What has happened to her?" I asked him.

"Pretty nearly everything. I think they must have hanged her, after making a very good effort at skinning her alive."

"Will she accept your treatment?"

"Oh, yes. She happens to be an educated girl; a Santa Clara woman. But I cannot hope for good results in that dirty pueblo house. She is infected already, and she should be removed from the pueblo at once."

"Will she tell who illtreated her, do you think?"

"Being a Santa Clara, I think she will. I have told her that I meant to send for you, and she has n't raised any objections."

Now here was a chance to learn something of "laws, customs, and usages"; and, moreover, the Grand Jury was in session, and the Federal Court sitting just around the corner. I departed promptly for Santo Domingo.

With the physician I went to the house of Monica Silva. The old mother puttered about doing what she could for the patient, and two little children played and wailed at intervals. I had thought it possible that the doctor might have been unduly excited, inasmuch as he had had several unpleasant experiences in the pueblo; but I found that he had rather understated the conditions. Monica Silva was a sight. She looked like one who has fallen foul of a threshing machine. She spoke excellent English, and seemed very glad that someone in authority had arrived. Had she been a Santo Domingo woman, I should have been received with sullenness and few words, and then silence. But Monica was ready to display her wounds, and to tell how she came by them.

About her neck, from ear to ear, the flesh was raw in a strip an inch wide. It was the sort of wound that would result from the twisting of a rough sisal rope about one's throat and then sawing it to and fro. The skin was entirely gone from the undersides of her arms and legs, her chest was covered with bruises and lacerations, and a number of these places showed the dull gray of infection. Her face had not been injured, and with some effort she could walk.

"Now I want to know two things," I said, scarcely expecting that she would consent to either. "Are you ready to go to a hospital? Your mother and the children may go along. And then, will you tell me who did these things to you, and later tell them at the Court?"

"Yes, I will tell you all about it, and I will go to the hospital."

So the next train took our little party into Albuquerque, and at the hospital she unfolded this story:—

She and her mother had arrived at the pueblo house about dark. They had something to eat and then waited for the husband to come home. He did not arrive, so they went to bed. In the night there was a knock at the door, and Monica admitted a number of the pueblo officials. Their manner was very stern, and, after reprimanding her for leaving her husband's house, they served notice that she should appear next morning before a council of the elders, when the Governor would consider her case.

At first she told them that she had done nothing justifying a pueblo trial, and that she would not come; but they became angry, and she was advised by her mother to agree. She said her mother would come as a witness to the fact that she was the injured party. The men said her husband would be there. She inquired if that woman would be there, also, and was told that she would.

Next morning she and her mother went to the council place, and found the Governor and his officials sitting. Her husband, and the scarlet woman, and other witnesses appeared. The door was closed. Monica was then called to account for deserting her pueblo home. From

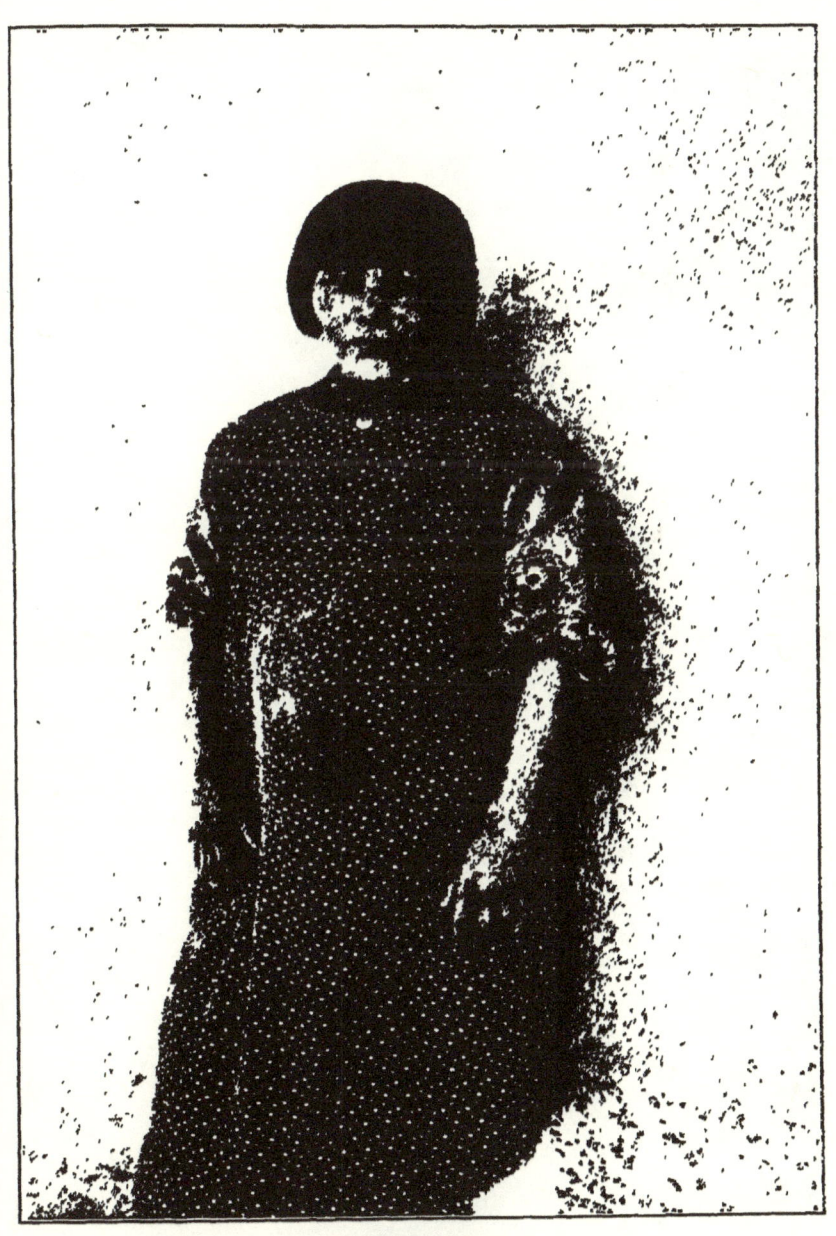

MONICA SILVA

the very beginning it was apparent that nothing was likely to happen to her husband for his misbehavior, or to the other party involved. The husband was a much injured individual. She had decamped with his chattels, and left his home in solitude. As a matter of fact, Monica, by working at the school, had contributed more than he had to the purchase of the wagon and harness, and, according to pueblo common law everywhere, the children were her property. She outlined these things to the pueblo fathers, but without convincing them that she had any grounds for displeasure. Becoming aware that they did not mean to give her a fair deal, she arose and told them this was no trial, and that she was going home. Her mother arose too, and they departed. That is to say, they passed through the doorway, her mother leading, and had gained about five yards from the house when the sheriffs ran out and seized Monica. They made some effort to catch the mother, but the old woman managed to escape. Monica struggled and fought, but was dragged back into the house. She caught at the rough sides of the adobe doorway, bracing herself with arms and legs, which accounted for the skinning of those members. The clothing was fairly torn from her body. She continued to struggle after being dragged inside, and declared that twice she reached the door, to repeat the operation of skinning herself. Finally she was thrown to the ground and remembered that someone, or several, had kicked and walked on her; then she became unconscious. She could not explain the decoration around her throat, but I could surmise the method of this. A rope was twisted about her neck, and she was either dragged around the floor or else hanged and dropped, and hanged and dropped, just enough to instill discipline and not quite enough to choke her. Later, she came to herself outside the house, and crawled home.

And would Monica give the names of all those present? She would and did — the names of Eliseo Calabassas, the Governor; Francisco Cate, the Lieutenant Governor; San Juan Tenorio, Venturo Coriz, Antonio Garcia, and Nicolás, Ignacio, Santiago, and Cruz, of the Lobato family, who were officials of the different grades. Monica did more than that. She managed to struggle around to the Grand Jury rooms, where the District Attorney exhibited her wounds to those gentlemen, and promptly, with some evidences of delight, had the whole bunch indicted.

And now, the pot having been prepared and the fire burning brightly, with the chef and his assistants standing by, forks and spoons in hand, it was only necessary that some skillful individual go forth and fetch in the rabbits. I consulted the District Attorney about this, as I had other district attorneys concerning other native delinquents. In this instance I found a gentleman with some appreciation of conditions, although he approached the matter along old lines.

". . . Er . . . that is to say, Mr. Burkhart, these indictments, calling for one Eliseo Calabassas, the Governor of Santo Domingo, to wit, and numerous of his official cohort — how about it?"

"Why," he observed, looking up from a law book and reaching for his box of Turkish cigarettes, "those men should be apprehended, and brought before the Court now sitting in this city."

"But whose job is it?"

"You are the Indian Agent."

"That is what I thought. But, have you ever been to Santo Domingo? I mean, have you ever gone there and endeavored to snake a Governor and his entire native staff from their official kivas? The population is 959 persons, according to our ineffective count. We may have missed a few. I have a police force consisting of half a dozen nicely dressed messengers, and two men who may be depended on to arrest an equal number of these accused Indians."

"You have Louis Abeita."

"I had included him as one of the two; and I have myself, and I can summon half a dozen rangemen who will serve as deputies if properly commissioned. I should like the moral help of a few United States deputy marshals, for I cannot expect that three men, however determined and duly commissioned, are likely to intimidate nine or more who may object to being removed from their native village. It has been known to occur. In fact, I have witnessed such objections accompanied by violence. No one was killed, but it was a messy affair. So I will summon my white men, if you can have them commissioned."

"You know very well that cannot be done. We have the United States Marshal for New Mexico at hand, but even he cannot summon a posse of more than three special deputies without incurring such expense as might be frowned on by Washington. But I will see the Marshal, and have him serve those warrants."

A little later I was told to be in readiness for the journey to Santo Domingo, together with such Indian police as necessary for the identification of the accused. When my car drew up before the Federal Building early one morning, there were numerous other cars being loaded with men. I noticed that these men were in uniform. It looked very much as if a section of Pershing's army had reported for duty. The United States Marshal was a wise official who knew something of Indians. Perhaps he had read of Perez's episode in the Domingo region, a scene rivaling the French Revolution. At any rate, he had collected a squad of ex-Service men, requesting that they appear in their old regimentals; and they did; and we went to Santo Domingo and procured Eliseo and his satraps without the slightest fuss. Moreover, we procured them without calling a council of the ancients, without wasting two days in instructing the Governor that the Sandoval Decision of 1913 and the Neblett Decision of 1919 meant that the "laws, customs, and usages" of the pueblo of Santo Domingo had been found on a slant with the law.

And now came other conferences.

"These men will immediately offer bail," I said, "so please arrange to make it high enough to inconvenience sympathizers."

"But they cannot give bail," said someone else, meaning that the Santo Domingos had nothing to offer as security for their kind.

"There will be plenty of bail forthcoming, speedily and promptly, if the amounts are nominal, such as one hundred dollars per man. You'll see."

And see they did. Nine hundred and fifty-nine Indians, living in a community, require a great many more things than dried corn and river water. They purchase, when in funds, such materials as flour, sugar, coffee, canned goods, clothing, tools, rope, ammunition. The trade of such a community is considerable — therefore traders — therefore bondsmen.

My telephone rang, and a familiar voice was heard:—

"Those Santo Domingos have been seeking bail, and I

have been approached in the matter. Now, if it will help you —"

"Help me nothing! I have just had that crew arrested, and its bail, I hope, will be fixed in strong figures. You're not helping me by tendering bond. You're fighting me."

"Why, I remembered the last case —"

"Sure! And I thank you again. Then the state of New Mexico was endeavoring to railroad five ignorant Indians for having killed their own deer on their own lands. And you acted nobly. But in this case the United States wishes to have nine savages punished for having tortured a woman."

"Excuse me! I hereby retire from the bonding business."

But there were other traders. They came forward, and then they went home again. The amount of bond fixed was too tall a hurdle. At this point readers may become confused. They will think it strange that an "Indian trader," under bond of $10,000 to the United States, guaranteeing his good behavior and honest methods and the minding of his own business in "the Indian country," would scarcely dare inject himself into an Indian case, whatever his sympathies. But you must remember that the Pueblo Indian country was not "reservation" in the sense that the Zuñi, Hopi, Navajo, Apache, Mohave, and other Indian homelands are "reservations." For many years it was doubted that the Pueblo grant-lands could be "Indian country." The title never was in the United States. And its traders are not licensed and bonded and regulated as are the merchants conducting businesses on reservations. And they do not reside and transact their affairs on Federal or Indian grant-lands. They have very skillfully installed themselves *adjacent thereto* — on state lands, or railroad rights of way over which the United States has lost control. What did a trader care about the proper regulation of a pueblo so long as his trade was not affected? There was but one exception to this attitude — the gentleman who had first offered to furnish bail; and he had called the Indian Agent to be sure that his believed help would not prove embarrassing.

So the Governor of Santo Domingo, and all his Cabinet, remained comfortably in jail.

But other things happened. Monica Silva recovered sufficiently from her wounds to receive visitors, and sympathetic pueblo neighbors arrived who could not be denied admission to the patient; and they conversed in their native tongue; and Monica began to petition the Agent to be allowed to return home. It was explained that this might not be for her eventual good, since the men were in jail, and their pueblo friends might feel aggrieved if they received punishment at the hands of the Court; but Monica could not well be held against her will, and she had recovered from her original fright, and, what is more to the point, someone had talked to her. I posted about to my legal mentor, the District Attorney, and admitted my fears.

"You are afraid that she will not stand by her story?"

"Exactly so. When an Indian complainant receives visitors from the home town, and the elders are involved, there is likely to be a change in tactics, often startling, occurring on the witness stand, and Indian testimony is a strange and fearful thing at best. Should that gang be acquitted, the result will be worse than having taken no action on her complaint."

"Quite true. Suppose you agree to waive prosecution,

A KIVA OF THE SQUARE TYPE.

providing that I arrange, if possible, to scare the daylights out of them."

"I shall be entirely satisfied with having the daylights scared out of them. The effect of discipline is all that I am interested in."

And so, somehow, a little scene was staged that accomplished more in its direct effect upon obstinate Indians than all the other Federal Court proceedings I have observed. The Honorable Justice gave instructions that on a certain day the Indian offenders should be presented in Court. Word of this brought in a group of their compadres from the pueblo, who were not involved, but who were interested. The accused were seated in a long row inside the Court railing. There they sat for some time, observing the trial of another case. They appeared a trifle apprehensive. Then they were lined up before the Judge's desk, at one end of which the Spanish interpreter took his station.

"Where is the Agent for these Indians?" the Judge asked.

I arose from among the spectators.

"Come up here!" ordered the Judge, and I stood at the opposite end of his desk.

Then he delivered a speech to the Indians concerning their recent actions. Such things were not in conformity with white man's law, no matter what the ancient traditions of their "infernal" pueblo institutions. He was very brief and very stern about it. Moreover, in size, demeanor, and vocal intonation he embodied the traditional idea of a judge. The Indians received the impression that they were before a judge who could, and might, send them somewhere far from the pleasant and familiar scenes of the pueblo of Santo Domingo. He closed with an effect that I had not expected.

"Here is your Agent. He has been appointed to that post by Washington. He is expected to manage all things for your pueblo without interfering with your native ceremonies. If he is not able, then Washington will procure another man who is. From this time forth you will transact all business through him, and do nothing of any consequence without first having consulted him. He has brought you here charged with most serious offenses. I should send you to jail, but I am going to put you on probation this time. But if he ever presents you to this Court again you will receive long terms in the penitentiary."

If the Honorable Justice did not use these exact words, that was the brief effect of his oration. Please observe — it had nothing in it of legal verbiage. Even a Santo Domingo Indian could understand it, and did.

After that, I had some small troubles with ignorant outsiders who wished to control the destinies of Santo Domingo; and the Santo Domingos had one big trouble with the posse who paid them a Christmas visit; but as between ourselves, the Santo Domingos and the Agent, all was serene. They did exactly as I counseled them, with no more than trifling dispute over the cigarettes at informal councils; and when anything worried them they came to the Agency for advice, where they were cheerfully received and speedily heard *by the Agent*.

It has occurred to some of the historians to suggest that *autos-de-fe* were celebrated in the Pueblo country by the early Spanish, and probably at Santo Domingo, where in 1663 the Custodio of Missions was also the Commissary for the Inquisition, and had his residence in the neighborhood at Galisteo. Bandelier, Twitchell, and Father Engelhardt arise to defend the Franciscans from this accusation; but it seems to me that the charge of an Inquisition at Santo Domingo would have some foundation in fact, provided that we accuse the natives and absolve the Franciscans. Affairs of this kind cause one to suspect the real reasons for secrecy in connection with the native religion. Archbishop Salpointe, in his book, *Soldiers of the Cross*, does not credit the charge of gross immoralities and indecencies gracing these "secret dances"; but the files of the Pueblo Indian Agency hold the affidavits of those who witnessed some very foul things at certain of the backward pueblos of New Mexico; and in 1916, Inspector Henry S. Traylor made an investigation and incorporated his findings in a scathing report filed with the Department. Traylor's report should have alarmed a mummy; but perhaps it would hardly disturb a political mummy. And the affidavits collected by Agent Lonergan to illustrate an atmosphere affecting the innocent, and especially children, were embalmed as a pornographic record and interred in the mausoleum of dead things. It is sufficient to say that they were approached only by the statements of Captain John G. Bourke, who, during his army experiences, observed some distressing sights among the decadent Zuñi Indians.

These things appear to be confined to the communities that reject progress, some of which have declined almost out of existence, such as Sandia and Sia. One is justified especially in suspecting both San Felipe and Santo Domingo of these practices. And certainly it is most probable that those who contrived to put the fear of the cacique into Monica Silva would not hesitate in stamping out any growing preference for education and the white man's standard of morals; for behind the subtle construction of the pueblo native government, protected by the immunity of "Internal Affairs," the cacique and his cohort are free to go as far as they like, until caught — and it is very difficult for any Agent unaided by timid natives to catch them. There is no doubt that in the majority of the pueblos this high priest of paganism continues to influence the life of the community profoundly, and that he often thoroughly controls the native Governor and his principales. Beneath the interesting paint and feathers of the Pueblo dance, behind the gourd rattle and the tombe, there is still a great deal of barbarism. The fact that Santa Fe trains pass within sight of the plazas, and that airplanes often cast their shadows on pueblo roofs, affect these things not at all. New Mexico has to-day a dozen areas where, though the day proclaims the twentieth century, the events of the night are still those of the sixteenth.

XIII

FRIENDS AT COURT

> MAKE no treaty with the Padrone! Trust no man who
>   calls him friend.
> He is just another Judas, and should meet a Judas end.
> He will walk the streets with Arnold, who had quite a
>   cheaper fame —
> And while you may live on corn husks, he will eat the bread
>   of shame.
> — "Lincoln's Counsel"

AN effort, however honest and sincere, to deduce facts from folklore usually meets with failure. It is a deluding method. According to it, investigators of the year 5000 may prove that the early inhabitants of the upper Hudson region were Japanese, since the story of Rip Van Winkle may be duplicated among the legends of the Aino.

Following this method, Mr. Gunn, in his book, *Schat Chen*, ingeniously compares words of the Queres language, and their pronunciations and meanings, with the geography of the archaic Mediterranean of ancient history, trying to identify ancient philology with that of the Queres legends. I have been entertained by his exposition, and while I do not follow him blindly into the dusk of Phœnicia, still there may be something in his theory, for we are told that history is given to repeating itself. I may sustain him in a measure by a modern chapter, drawn from the time when the Pueblo Indians of New Mexico paid tribute to a Dynasty.

One day I met a traveling official, and he said: —

"Have you heard of the great labors in Washington recently? The Bureau summoned its minions and worked all day of a Sunday."

This was extraordinary news to one who had worked in the Bureau.

"In Heaven's name, why?"

"To find vacant positions," he explained.

This was the year 1921, only shortly after March 4. I pondered these words en route to the Agency. "To find vacant positions." And I rejoiced that my pay roll was comfortably filled with regulars; but there was one vacancy in the position of resident farmer at a certain pueblo. Few cared for the place, as the quarters were even worse than poor and the pay did not resemble great riches. I was not to be left in peace, however. That position was vacant. I could not deny it. So when I received a call from the recently appointed Chief Inspector for the Interior Department, I felt that the plot was thickening. He did not have far to come, for naturally, a fat post like the Chief Inspectorship had been promptly filled by a "native citizen" of New Mexico. This particular citizen had distinguished himself in the past by killing a number of men — or at least he so testified on one occasion under cross-examination in the Federal Court. He appeared to be worried about vacant positions. He had a son. Now it seemed to me that, should I graciously immure this son in the depths of the undesirable pueblo, I should be relieved of pressure and unwelcome visitors; and I could report to my superiors in Washington, who at least had killed no men, that all positions were filled, clinching the matter by noting in the report that the scion of the Chief Inspector for the Interior Department had been just favored with a job. It would be a so-called "temporary" appointment, always subject to disturbance when the Bureau selected *an eligible* from the Civil Service lists; but considering what had been done at times, and considering the Chief Inspector for the Interior Department, I felt somehow that an eligible of sufficient eligibility would never be discovered.

It is immaterial, but I should state that the son proved to be a good average employee, as such things go in New Mexico, and that he accomplished the routine work at the pueblo as well as those who had preceded him.

Now there was an excellent Agency employee, who had labored nine years at a miserable wage, and who had sought this position and had been denied. Actually, he had once been fired by telegraph, the Agent not being consulted as to his worth, virtue, experience, or condition of health, so that it required about one year's time and part of a trip to Washington to accomplish his reinstatement in the old and meagre place. Along with his reinstatement, which sheer justice demanded, the Bureau had issued a proclamation to the Agent that under no circumstances would this employee ever be considered for promotion in rank or salary.

But the man was cunningly advised by somebody; and notwithstanding his lack of an English academic education, he drew on his knowledge of excellent Spanish, plus a shrewd mentality, and passed a Civil Service examination, by which he automatically gained a Civil Service rating. Thus, in a wholly Machiavellian fashion, he became *an eligible!* It was an awful situation. An eligible had been discovered, not in farthest Maine or distant Oregon, but right at the New Mexican home corral.

I reported these things, as was my duty, and suggested

that inasmuch as the son of the newly appointed Chief Inspector for the Interior Department (who was without a Civil Service rating) might be needlessly worried by the spectre of this eligible dogging his heels, the eligible should be promoted through an increase of wages to a similar position in rank, and thus silenced. Lo! it was promptly done. Thus justice in a triumphant democracy.

Then I met another official at the club, and he seemed torn between a feeling of amusement and one of anguish. He confided in me thus: —

"I am to have an additional clerk in my office."

"You had a nerve," I said, "to request additional help when the country is struggling beyond normalcy."

"I did n't request it, and it is not help. It is a gift. I have been instructed to prepare a home for a protégé of the Secretary's, all swept and garnished, something suitable to her station in life."

When a man finds himself in a position of this kind, the rest of us should sympathize with him, and I did.

"Come out and see the place I have arranged," he invited.

I went and surveyed a very comfortable abode, much better than many of our "old faithfuls" were enjoying.

"Do you think she will be satisfied?" he asked, anxiously.

"She should be, but you won't be," I told him.

I do not know how much of government funds, appropriated for the education of Indian children, this official expended; but I can say without fear of successful contradiction that the protégé was *not* satisfied. And for many reasons. The designated place of her labors was situated beyond the city limits, remote from the festivities of society, and gave the impression that those employed there would, let us say, be placed in the menial position of having to work. It was inconvenient, requiring an expenditure of foot power to connect with the nearest tram car, unless one should maintain an automobile or have the courage to commandeer that of the superintendent. But the protégé took the oath of office, to connect with the pay roll, and departed. She did not reappear.

The Pueblo Indian Agency, an entirely different place, and with an entirely different director, stood not far from the centre of the city, had a street-car line at its door, could produce several autos, and was not remote from theatres, women's clubs, and other diversions, if one cared for that kind of life. My pay roll was filled, but that was a trifling thing to overcome. My chief clerk was very ill, and had requested furlough. There was another clerk skilled in the handling of governmental accounts, and there was a "financial clerk." In order to assist the faithful chief clerk (an Indian, whose days in the land were few), his wife had been assigned to my office force as a "financial clerk." This is an old graft of the Indian Bureau. Once upon a time, when Indian Agents were paid very little, and when they complained of their salaries, a "financial clerk" would be granted. It was a position without Civil Service status, created especially for the relief of underpaid Indian Agents, who could then nominate their wives, sons, daughters, or daughters-in-law, if they were fortunate enough to possess them, to this sinecure. Sometimes the "financial clerk" worked, but more often made only a pretense of working. While the graft had been frowned upon, it could be revived; and it was revived for the benefit of my chief clerk, a faithful fellow, who would never recover his health.

But when I was questioned from Washington about quarters for *another* "financial clerk," it seemed as though the practice were being carried too far.

On an Indian reservation, the Agent either has quarters for his staff of employees or may construct them; but in a city office, removed from the "Indian country," he must rent or lease such domiciles. I reported that no quarters were available, and could not be unless leased; and that if leased such quarters would require furnishings, as my commissary did not contain the supplies; and that my allotment of funds would not cover such expenditures, if authorized, to say nothing of an additional salary. Came the answer, promptly, "How much will you require for leasing of quarters, furnishings, and salary of twelve hundred?"

Right there I made a hideous mistake, for the mails had brought in one of those blue-tinted appointment sheets showing that the very person who had been dissatisfied with the rural location was to be assigned to my staff, in a newly created position termed "financial clerk," at twelve hundred dollars per annum, plus the Congressional bonus, and all perquisites. I should have wired in answer, "Six thousand dollars will cover all needs." For you may be able to perceive that six thousand dollars, less the salary of twelve hundred (the Congressional bonus came from different funds) would have left $4800 annually for house rent, furniture, miscellaneous fittings, service of water, light, fuel, and telephone. It would have covered ice, even; and perhaps a man servant.

Did not the Secretary of the Interior desire to provide for this clerk, and were not Congressional appropriations for the benefit of the Pueblo Indians of New Mexico available to cover the bills? Do not ask stupid questions.

This was the Harding Administration, not the Coolidge. There was a little green house on K Street; there were master minds; there were little black bags, and packages of Liberty Bonds that went hither and thither and yon, only to turn up eventually in New Mexico. Six thousand dollars! A mere "opener" on a pair of Jacks and one Queen.

But I am penurious. I thought that three thousand dollars should be sufficient. I might have known that nothing would satisfy the Dynasts — nothing save debacle, a thing that a lean and hungry-looking editor, then penciling copy around the corner at the Albuquerque *Morning Journal*, would finally accomplish.

When I met Albert Bacon Fall, there were no public dinners awaiting him in Albuquerque, for none had been arranged. He came simply to see for himself how comfortably off his protégé, my "financial clerk," had been made with Indian appropriations.

Albert Bacon Fall, being Secretary of the Interior, was the Great White Father of the aborigines of New Mexico. He had always been interested in the natives of his state. The Indians did not vote, but their neighbors did; and it was but natural that an ambitious man, with his eye on the political horizon, should wish whoever voted to vote for him. As early as 1917 he had devoted valuable time in the United States Senate to the unhappy conditions existing among the Pueblo Indians of New Mexico. The *Congressional Record* of that year reports him as saying:—

He [the Indian Agent] has gone to one of the Pueblos and there selected a favorite of his own as Judge, overturning all the traditions and customs of the Indians, interfering unwarrantedly with them, and he takes from one pueblo 250 miles away an Indian to try him before this Pueblo Indian Judge.

Each of these pueblos or settlements of Indians is as separate and distinct from the others as is one State of this Union separate from the others as a State. The Commissioner of Indian Affairs here in your city of Washington did not know that the Pueblo Indians of New Mexico did not speak the same language. He did not know that there were nine different languages spoken, and that the Pueblos could not understand one another. . . .

When I myself asked the Commissioner of Indian Affairs in Washington if he did not understand that this Indian brought from 250 miles away could not understand the language of the Indian before whom he was tried, he did not know; he thought all the Pueblos spoke the one language.

The Commissioner referred to was Cato Sells, and when Sells thought all the Pueblo Indians spoke the one language he was perfectly and correctly informed. They all speak Spanish, many of them approaching, in their diction, the Castilian — a much better variety of that tongue than the sort one picks up in Tularosa bars.

The Commissioner had appointed a Judge of the Indian Court, a common custom among the tribes and clearly provided for by Act of Congress, to preside over those petty Indian cases that, if presented to the Federal Court, would have turned it into a police court. And the native court, conducted or supervised by the Indian Agent, also safeguarded the petty delinquents from the tyranny of State Courts.

No one of the Pueblo Indians then or now could be removed from his home and presented before an Indian magistrate two hundred and fifty miles away. The farthest remove possible in the Pueblo jurisdiction (Taos to Acoma) is two hundred and thirty miles, and the judge complained of was located actually at Isleta, his district including only Isleta, Sandia, Santa Ana, and infrequently San Felipe, Santo Domingo, and Cochiti, these last named being the farthest from him, in no case more than sixty miles. There were other native judges for the other districts, or, where they were not, the Indian Agent acted as magistrate. Of the pueblos within the Isleta judge's district, all were Queres save Sandia (and that was Tihua), and the judge was Tihua, who spoke Queres as well as English and Spanish and several additional Indian languages or dialects.

Again, the Pueblo Indians do not speak nine native languages, but four, with slight variations in dialects — Tihua, Queres, Tewa, and the Jemez or Pecos languages.

When Mr. Fall had satisfied himself about the comfort of his protégé, our conversation turned on the New Mexican Indian muddle and the proper methods for controlling the several reactionary pueblos, such as San Felipe and Santo Domingo. The cases of Monica Silva and the incident at Santo Domingo were cited to him. He told me that such control as I had endeavored to preserve, with the assistance of the United States District Attorney and the United States Court, might embarrass his policies, and that he did not wish to be embarrassed by such horseplay. He was of the opinion, however, that the Pueblo land situation, an entirely different but closely related matter, demanded prompt clarification if the Indians and their squatting neighbors were ever to enjoy peace; and said that he had arranged for the assembling of wisdom on these questions with a view to ending the dissension that had troubled New Mexico for seventy-five years.

It should not be difficult for the layman to understand that control of Indians had nothing to do with the validity of land titles; although even the Indian Bureau, during various waves of political expediency, of which this last was the most threatening, had never been quite able to separate land tenures from the duties of constables. When New York takes drastic steps to protect its citizens from the danger of gun men, the municipal officials do not begin by conferring on the moot question whether Peter Minuit paid a sufficient and equitable price in 1626 for the Island of Manhattan. And complete control of the Pueblo Indians by the Indian Agent stopped further encroachment on their lands.

Now Franklin K. Lane and John Barton Payne, perhaps inferior Secretaries, had upheld the Agents for the Pueblo Indians; and Cato Sells, although ignorant of Pueblo linguistics, had maintained during 1919–1921, to my personal knowledge, a most consistent policy with respect to these matters. It is possible that I am not a good judge of men, and view these retired superiors through glasses befogged with partisanship and an underdone culture not gained in New Mexico. Fall, however, who is still before the public, would not lend his support, and said so. He would, when he had filled all the vacant positions with nonentities and created a few wholly unnecessary posts for persons of his choosing — all at the public expense — end this riddle of title, imposition, and contention. He would do it, as developed shortly thereafter, through the Bursum Bill.

Just what animated Holm O. Bursum, former superintendent of the state penitentiary at Santa Fe, to lend his support to this plot will probably never be known. He had a great opportunity to ingratiate himself with both Indians and honest citizens who had ignorantly purchased of them, and might have maintained himself in the United States Senate for many years because of this act alone.

One should not, however, expect the impossible; and it is difficult in New Mexico for a political stream to rise above its source. He finally cast in his lot with his former political enemies, perhaps in accordance with the old doctrine of Sir Henry Morgan, who said to timid and murmuring souls among his crew: "If our number is small, our hearts are great, and the fewer persons we are, the more union and better shares we shall have in the spoils."

To add a touch of dignity to the array that finally assembled, the Secretary had Ralph Emerson Twitchell, of Santa Fe, an authority on Pueblo history, appointed a Special Assistant to the Attorney-General for the United States. This was easier than at first blush it seems. It was arranged, no doubt, in the little green house on K Street, prior to the demise of one Jess Smith. Jess himself may have been of the company. For Harry Daugherty, you may remember, a figure from Washington Court House, Ohio, was the Attorney-General for the United States; and these gentlemen seldom denied each other anything.

And other appointments were made; for instance, that of the "South Seas" Attorney. If this expression chances to be vague, permit me to explain. Legal lights with offices in Honolulu and Pago Pago were no doubt canvassed with a view to their accepting this position of Special Counselor to the Pueblo Indians. But it would seem that they declined the honor. Then a young man, filled with admiration for Secretary Fall, accepted the post. He opened no office in Albuquerque or Santa Fe, where the most negligent counsel had made some pretense of maintaining an office in the past; nor did he install himself in an adobe at Picuris or Laguna. He contented himself with remaining largely at home, in a town as difficult of access and as unknown as he was. If the Indians wished to consult him, or if the Agent needed advice in an emergency, they could indite missives to him, or motor to his distant residence, or await the time when he might have shopping to do in Albuquerque. They seldom bothered him. Thus another position was filled *away* from the Pueblo battlefield.

About this time, too, my companion Agent, who acted for the Northern Pueblo Indians above Santa Fe, was transferred suddenly to the arid regions of Nevada, and disappeared from the scene. Unable to read the handwriting on the wall, he had been industrious in endeavoring to press action for his wards, and he had been so unwise as to call the "South Seas" Attorney a Squatters' Attorney paid from an Indian appropriation, claiming that he had advised adverse claimants among the native citizens not to worry about "those suits," since Albert would never forsake them. I do not charge the man with a familiarity of this sort. That was all right for Palm Beach and "Ned" McLean, but I do not believe the attorney had that degree of intimacy. I do think, however, that he was perfectly satisfactory, as Pueblo Indian Counsel, to Messrs. Albert Bacon Fall and Holm O. Bursum.

And so things drifted along in the little town of Albuquerque, with the Chief Inspector for the Interior Department lounging in hotel lobbies, or sunning himself on a corner, thinking of *mañana* when Fall's grand colonization scheme across the border, in the land of the real Mexicans, would unfold into a dream of empire and lift even his lieutenants into prominence.

Returning to the Pueblo Indian Agency, one entered an atmosphere radiated by the Secretary's protégé whenever she condescended to appear for duty. Being a "financial clerk," she asked for the combination of the safe, and wanted to know when she should begin disbursing the public moneys. This was a surprise to me. There was nothing in the safe, other than government numbered forms and a few aged papers evidencing a right of way, or perhaps the yellowed patent that some Pueblo had filed with me for safe-keeping. And while I was steadily, day by day, growing older and more infirm, still my right arm held out sufficiently to sign checks. I explained to her that the Treasurer of the United States was not familiar with her signature, and that it had taken him some time to become familiar with mine; also, that I feared he would demur to a sudden change in methods, and that if he did not, I must, since I was accountable under bond. And I went on acting as Indian Agent, Purchasing Agent, Legal Agent in the absence of the "South Seas" Attorney, Judge of the Indian Court, Judge of the Appellate Court, Chief of the Indian Police, Special Constable — well, in short, as Pooh-Bah for the Pueblo Indians of New Mexico in their daily affairs.

But this atmosphere ceased to be amusing. I had never installed a time clock for the clerks and assistants, and seldom reprimanded them for tardiness. In fact, I seldom had occasion to be so unpleasant. But subordinates do not appreciate favoritism; and when one of their number would arrive at ten in the morning, go at twelve, and reappear, if at all, at two in the afternoon, to depart without a word of comment or adieu at three or four o'clock, a feeling arose that the Indian Agent was somehow losing his grip.

This necessitated the keeping of a time chart — not a bulletin on the open wall, but nevertheless the keeping of it. Commissioner of Indian Affairs Charles H. Burke was asked for a decision as to the working hours for clerks at Indian agencies, a thing that he could not avoid transmitting, and his decision did not check up with the ideas that seemed to be prevalent among employees sponsored by the Secretary. As this fact would have been embarrassing to the Commissioner, nothing was said about it. Outside his door in Washington was a mat with the word "Welcome" neatly stenciled across its face; and it was quite possible that the Secretary himself often used this mat. One should exercise some sort of crude diplomacy.

But I was not without advisers. Albuquerque is a little town, and you may understand what a small town is. Things get around and about, even though there are no party lines connecting the business and professional offices. There was the Big Fellow. He knew everything there was to know concerning politics in New Mexico, and this was clearly one phase of a political condition.

"Crane, you are an idealistic ass!" he declared on one occasion. "You haven't the first faint indications of a politician. Now, this is what you should do: Dispatch a letter to the Bureau recommending that they at once allow this protégé an automobile. Relate, as you can, the indignities suffered by one of her station in walking through the common streets, to and fro, from work, as the case may be. Go to the florist's and arrange that flowers be delivered at her home daily. Have your chief physician certify that one so delicate should be exempt from the regular hours of service, and keep no records as to leaves. Simply keep a record of her address, so that you may accurately forward each month the slip of blue paper calling on the Treasurer of the United States to pay a certain salary.

That is New Mexican politics, and that is what this man Fall has been accustomed to, and what he expects."

"Wouldn't you add that I should lease the Masonic Temple, so that she may have a bridge room and an audience chamber?"

"The Masons may aid you along those lines, although I am not sure. But as in fishing in the Guadalupe, pay out sufficient line. You are not strong enough for this gang. See how they have inconvenienced Carl Magee. It will be your turn next."

It was good political advice, but somehow I am not composed of that sort of New Mexican Americanism. And things drifted along until the time chart showed that all manner of leave had expired. And the other accounts showed:—

To salary, August 1, 1921, to April 30, 1922	$ 984.00
To rent of quarters, August 1, 1921, to June 30, 1922	825.00
To purchases of furniture and fittings for quarters	638.41
To service of gas and electricity	129.97
To water service	41.65
To telephone charges	22.50
	$2641.53

Or, to put the case another way:—

Cost to the United States and the Pueblo Indians	$2641.53
Daily remuneration (actual number of hours on duty, 800, or 100 days)	26.41
Rate per hour for financial services	3.30

When called on the telephone, at government expense, the "financial clerk" was in no mood to discuss business. After all, hours of labor are vulgar topics. She was informed that all manner of leave had been exhausted, and that, following the regulations, an application for "leave without pay" must be sent to Washington for approval, the Agent having no authority to approve leave of this character. She was assured that it would be approved in Washington. But she did not intend to make an application for "leave without pay," and so stated, more or less acridly, adding that the Honorable Secretary would attend to everything, as indeed he was doing. We had reached an impasse. It was quite similar to the old problem of an irresistible force striking an immovable object. For the Disbursing Officer refused to make further payments.

There is always a way out, however, for those who devote themselves to politics and found dynasties. Within ten days the Bureau notified me by telegraph that a six months' furlough had been granted the protégé at her personal request. The telegram was dated April 12, 1922. It was in that very period when the Teapot Dome leases were signed. And on April 18, 1922, I was transferred to take charge of the Crow Creek Indian Agency, at Fort Thompson, South Dakota, quite close to the Indian Commissioner's home, where I should observe all the miseries of the Lower Yanktonai Sioux. When a number of prominent organizations and equally prominent men interested in Indian Affairs sought information as to the reason for this transfer, they were told by the Indian Bureau, and particularly by its Commissioner, that it had occurred for "administrative reasons."

For the benefit of those who may consider this record an *ex parte* statement, it is no more than just to show in the margin the views of other men who are not likely to have had their judgment warped by personal interests. In a speech before the Maryland Federation of Women's

FRIENDS AT COURT 273

Clubs, at Baltimore, on November 1, 1922, Edgar B. Meritt, the Assistant Commissioner of Indian Affairs, said: —

"The two officials most directly charged by law with the administration of Indian Affairs, Honorable Albert Bacon Fall, Secretary of the Interior, and Honorable Charles H. Burke, Commissioner of Indian Affairs, are sincere friends of the Indian; have long lived among them and know their needs; have served many years on the Senate and House Indian committees of Congress, respectively, and can be depended on to guard and promote most faithfully every interest of our Governmental wards."

Charles H. Burke, when before the House Committee on Indian Affairs in 1923, referring to the "propaganda" that had brought the Bursum Bill to unpleasant notoriety, said: —

"If the charges made and circulated are true, namely, that the officials of the Government have countenanced or contemplated any action seeking to deprive the Pueblo Indians of any property which legally or equitably belongs to them — then the present Commissioner of Indian Affairs . . . ought to be removed from his position and in the future denied the right to hold any office of trust. A distinguished resident of New Mexico, who has been honored by an election to the Senate of the United States, should be expelled from that body. Another eminent citizen of New Mexico, for a time a United States judge . . . and three times elected to the United States Senate, and now occupying the high office of Secretary of the Interior, should be impeached."

The Indian Rights Association sent to President-elect Harding in 1921 an open letter protesting against the selection of Albert Bacon Fall as Secretary of the Interior, charging that his record in the United States Senate had been hostile to Indian interests; and this association presented similar protests to Senators Henry Cabot Lodge and George Wharton Pepper with view to procuring their support. Senator Lodge demurred, as follows: —

"In my opinion he is exceptionally fitted to be Secretary of the Interior, as it is now generally understood that he will be appointed to that post. Senator Fall is a thoroughly upright and highminded man, and utterly incapable of using his office for his own financial interest, which I regret to say is implied by some of the expressions of your letter."

And Senator Pepper ventured a prophecy: —

"It is my expectation, however, that Senator Fall will agreeably disappoint you as a Cabinet officer."

Thus a variety of sources, and a conclusive unanimity of viewpoint — that of the solon, the politician, the statesman, the counsellor. And one should hesitate before accusing any one of them of having strabismus. However, it is illusory to estimate a man's whole fame from the chorus of his friends. Time, an excellent evaluator of reputations, will elevate Fall's to that high position in the sun to which it is entitled, an eminence from which not even Charity may drag it down.

XIV

THE RIDDLE, THE BUNK, AND THE BURSUM BILL

Thou shalt not have in thy bag divers weights, a great and a small.
— Deuteronomy XXV. 13

"Heizonarshro . . . ?" If ever again I journey through the Pueblo provinces, and am so accosted by a native, I shall probably reply in the Navajo fashion, pointing with my lips, and saying: "To Albuquerque." Perhaps I may try to twist my larynx, tongue, lips, nose, and glottis over the actual Navajo definition for that pleasant little city, and emit something like "Beeldil Dasenil," which a poet translates as "The Place of the Bells."

But should I understand him as again seeking counsel of me, and meaning to inquire whither he and his people are going, I shall have to plead an abject ignorance, although I could inform him definitely where they were headed once, and who were their guides.

The Treaty of Guadalupe Hidalgo defined the new boundary between two countries that had been bitterly at war. The line ran through a seemingly worthless cacti-studded desert, relieved only by a treacherous watercourse that was sometimes an inconsequential turgid stream and at others a raging terror of devastation, and by gaunt mountains that served no purpose other than to shield the savage. To-day, many Americans are familiar with El Paso, Douglas and Nogales, Calexico and Tia Juana — not because of musty old treaties and purchase agreements, not because of trade and customs, mining or horse racing, but because they mark places on the Mexican border that eventuated, where the Great American Desert and its terrible thirst now ends. But in 1848 the Treaty was of intense importance to Mexicans and Indians who would never know of Volstead or the Eighteenth Amendment, although the majority of them did not realize the change in their status then, and I doubt if many of their descendants are completely aware of it to-day.

Two Articles of this Treaty affected the fortunes of the Pueblo Indians of New Mexico, simply because of their quasi-civilization and sedentary habits, which prevented their being classed as "savages." They were not named specifically, and, by assumption, were considered as of that class possessing Mexican citizenship. According to the Treaty, those Mexicans who preferred to remain in the ceded territories could either retain the title and rights of Mexican citizens or acquire those of citizens of the United States; but they should "be under the obligation to make their election *within one year*" from the date of ratification; and those remaining without having declared their intention would be considered to have elected to become citizens of the United States; and those who did not elect to remain Mexican citizens would be admitted at the proper time (to be judged of by the Congress of the United States) to the enjoyment of all the rights of citizens of the United States according to the principles of the Constitution.

Article XI was devoted to Indians, and provided specifically for the control, by the United States, of "the savage tribes" within its borders.

Therefore the nomadic and warlike tribes, even then unsubdued, such as the Navajo, the various groups of Apaches, the Utes, and so forth, must have been "the savage tribes"; but what were the Pueblo Indians? The Zuñi were then classed with them, and racially and by habit the Hopi were of this division, whatever its political classification; but the Hopi had never possessed a Spanish title or grant, and by their negatively obdurate conduct had classed themselves as "apostate" and hostile Indians; and they were isolated and surrounded by the virile raiding Navajo, with Fort Defiance as yet unbuilt.

If therefore these pueblo-type Indians (if they were Indians) did not remove to Old Mexico along with other loyal Mexican citizens within one year from the ratification of the Treaty (and they did not), they would automatically become citizens of the United States — to be admitted at such time as the Congress considered proper. It was assumed for them by the intelligentsia of New Mexico, and it was not disputed vigorously by the new American officials, nor by Washington, that whatever of citizenship the Pueblo Indians of Spanish-title lands had under the Mexican Government would be sufficient to confirm to them citizenship under our Government. Calhoun, and others following him as Indian Agents, were estopped at once from classing them definitely as "Indians," subject to all the laws enacted for the *control and protection* of Indians, because it was not until the Act of July 27, 1851, that such laws were extended even over the savage tribes of Utah and New Mexico. Then arose the question whether the pueblo-type people were "Indian tribes." It became the riddle of New Mexico, and for many years the legal lights would wax and wane in the gusts of this perplexing question.

The question should have been — what was the status of a Pueblo Indian under Mexico and Spain? Historical research would have clarified the roiled waters, as it eventually did. The facts are that his status under the Spanish kings had been that of tutelage and wardship, and under Mexico his "citizenship" had been restricted and limited. All this was to be discovered by intelligent men years after the riddle had become legend, like the beard of Barbarossa; and, in New Mexico, once legend is fixed in the public mind even the United States Supreme Court will have to strain itself to unseat it.

In the year 1919, it was not generally conceded that the various provisions of the Act of 1834 (extended over the Territory of New Mexico in 1851) could be applied to protect the Pueblo Indians of New Mexico, because such laws were indicative of safeguards to "savage" or "uncivilized" natives of the reservation status. The Decision File at the Pueblo Agency contained a Departmental ruling, signed by a former Assistant Secretary of the Interior, later the senior United States Senator for New Mexico (now deceased), stating concisely why action should not be brought under Section 2117 of the Revised Statutes against those who trespassed with live stock on Pueblo lands.[1]

This Departmental ruling had successfully handcuffed three former Pueblo Indian Agents. It was one thing to round up a peon-type citizen, grazing a wee bunch of ponies or cattle, to bawl him out, and to eject him from the pueblo environs, and decidedly another thing to hunt down a back-county padrone, an influence in a voting

[1] Section 2117: "Every person who drives or otherwise conveys any stock of horses, mules, or cattle, to range and feed on any land belonging to any Indian or Indian tribe, without the consent of such tribe, is liable to a penalty of one dollar for each animal of such stock."

district, with his name on a bronze courthouse marker, to fine him $3000 for trespassing on pueblo lands with 3000 head of sheep stock. Because, in case of dispute, and the chance of the bluff being called, the Indian Agent would either have to wilt, thus losing prestige among the Indians he sought to protect, or seize the live stock for impounding. To hold 3000 head of sheep on the range without losses until a court would condescend to consider the question (perhaps a matter of years) presented too much of risk — to the Agent, who would become personally responsible for the losses, especially as Washington, and its New Mexican Assistant Secretary, had counseled against such action and would certainly permit O'Grady to swim out solo. Hence Agents had not sacrificed themselves, and trespassers of that type openly and insolently continued trespassing.

But, notwithstanding this dictum, and its high source, I felt that something could be done about it. I had the exterior lines of a pueblo ornamented with large posters, and did this without asking the Government Printing Office at Washington to set the type or the Indian Bureau to edit the wording. When these posters were pulled down and otherwise desecrated, I had the native officials put duplicates in their places, and this was kept up quite patiently. Then I had the trespassing gentleman's stock and employees watched by persons of intelligence, acting in groups of three, and always one of the three would be a white man, for I knew how much courts and juries welcome "Indian testimony"; and I had the sites of his camps marked, with the dates of occupancy recorded, and as if to assist me in this matter his employees obligingly left in the said camps certain bills and papers confirming the dates of occupancy; and I regularly and formally and officially warned him that his sheep were feeding and trespassing on Pueblo Indian lands.

Then I drifted around the corner to consult the United States District Attorney for the state of New Mexico. I found Mr. Attorney Burkhart in a mood. It was a brave thing to challenge this legal authority in his den, but I did it. I felt sure that the Statute could be invoked to protect the sedentary and supposedly civilized Pueblo people, and held to cover sheep, as well as horses, mules, and cattle, for sheep *had to be driven and herded*, thus — considering posters and warnings — proving intentional trespass.

Mr. Attorney Burkhart surveyed me without admiration.

"You admit that the Secretary's Office is of opinion that 2117, of the Military Act of '34, is not applicable . . ."

"I will admit further than that," I conceded, "I will admit that the Secretary's Office has successfully, and for years, protected a bunch of precinct politicians."

Again Mr. Attorney Burkhart surveyed me. There is something about him, when he propounds legal doctrine to an ignoramus, that causes his slight frame to expand and assume proportions — even threatening proportions. He represented in New Mexico all there was of determination in the Wilson Administration, and was respected, feared, admired, and hated by different elements of the heterogeneous population. But I knew that he was a Pueblo champion at heart, and that he had been the terror of precinct politicians. Under his hat reposed perhaps the most erudite and complete knowledge of Pueblo Indian law in the United States. Mr. Attorney Burkhart could not only read the law, but somehow he knew what it meant. As opposed to practically all legal New Mexico, he had known from the beginning what the Honorable Mr. Justice Van Devanter had meant in the "Sandoval Decision," and he could extract subtle meanings from the "Joseph Decision" that had entirely escaped others. I knew that, if there was anything of a solution in the thousands of law books that buttressed Mr. Attorney Burkhart on every side, he would find it. I suggested subtly — would he calmly accept that ruling, probably signed without reading, the production of a clerk just two nights ahead of the law school? Mr. Attorney Burkhart selected a fresh Turkish cigarette and conceded in his turn that the Indian Bureau had a lawyer, once; and he promised to look into the matter for me. In no great while he announced that he had traced a decision under the Statute that could be lugged across the sacred boundary line of the sovereign state of New Mexico to support my contention. Lo! the New Mexican trespasser was summoned to Santa Fe, where the Big Judge sat. He had to employ counsel, a simple but expensive thing in those parts; and he employed very able counsel, who at once went to work dissecting the viscera of the "Sandoval Decision." He faced a suit to recover the penalty of one dollar the head on 3000 sheep. There was no comfort to be found in the works of the "Sandoval Decision," and it was deemed finally to be wisdom to tender the Indian Agent a compromise trespass fee, which his counsel advised him to accept.

The Indian Bureau evidenced no surprise in that the ancient scarecrow had been exposed. Its only interest was manifest in ruling that the fine could be expended "for school purposes only." Such money, it was said, should be viewed as a product of Pueblo lands. But we could not sell alfalfa from Pueblo lands; we could not allot Pueblo lands. As Mr. Attorney Burkhart would chant —

"It is a communal title! — NOT to the Pueblo Indians of Taos, BUT to *the Pueblo of Taos!* . . ."

The money was turned over to the Treasurer for the Laguna Indian Pueblo to become a part of the communal funds.

The Treaty of Guadalupe Hidalgo justified the expectation that the Congress of the United States would determine the rights of all those persons who elected to remain within the ceded territories. But the Congress is a great deliberative body, and, so far as the Pueblo Indians of New Mexico were concerned, enjoyed a vacation of seventy-five years. There were three groups of people affected by the laches of Congress: —

1. The government officials, charged apparently with controlling and protecting the Pueblo Indians (if they were Indians), who were isolated on a seething frontier, and were confused, badgered, helpless.

2. The ceded Mexican citizens (the colonists), who were hopelessly intermixed with these Indian people in trade and lands (who would in some localities Mexicanize them completely), and who would be seriously inconvenienced by any clarification tending to preserve thoroughly an Indian status for the Pueblo people.

3. The Pueblo Indians themselves, who were not unconscious of their burdens in the form of colonists and guests, but who had no means of bringing pressure to bear on politicians, especially as they did not seek to exercise the franchise they could have demanded.

Now it is idle for anyone to say that politics did not enter into this question from the very day Calhoun took

A MOUNTAIN HACIENDA OWNED BY A NATIVE CITIZEN

office as the first Indian Agent. His own reports indicate it; but these reports do not reveal specifically the subtle influences of politics among those newly ceded Mexican-type citizens, who would exercise the franchise in their own fashion, and who would not care to have their customs and landholdings disturbed. I am not referring to the debilitated peon type of Mexican who inhabited the ranchitos of the isolated settlements; but one must remember that there was a baronial class, the padrones, and that this class was intelligent, educated, shrewd with a Spanish shrewdness, and often unscrupulous. This was the former ruling class, and, under the leadership of new captains as shrewd and as unscrupulous as their own worst examples, would be the ruling class again. Where this class did not itself hold sections of Pueblo Indian country, it was allied with relatives and factions who did; and those who wish to swim into political power in a ceded empire must give ear to the groundlings who will vote and carry elections.

This was the powerful and original brake on any progress toward the clarification of Pueblo Indian titles to land, and it grew more and more powerful through the years, until it brought forth the Bursum Bill, an effort to legalize the increased holdings of these "colonists," the descendants of those who had invited and received bloodshed and terror in 1680.

Let us consider land conditions among these Mexican-type people in the areas outside the pueblo grants, accepting the statements of their advocate before the Congressional committees of 1923. Mr. A. B. Renehan said: —

We had no recording system in New Mexico until 1856. . . . They had no system of surveys in Spanish times, nor in

Mexican times. For instance: a tract of land is sold to one Juan Tafoya, and the description is "Bounded on the north by the road which comes down from Tesuque, and on the south bounded by the ditch [that is, the ditch that existed in those days], and bounded on the east by the lands of Tomas Martinez, an individual, and bounded on the west by the lands of Jacobo Montoya, another individual." In the lapse of time, since a deed was made in 1727, with such a description as that, how are you going to connect the present-day description of a piece of land with that ancient description; how are you going to make color of title, because there cannot be color of title where there is no instrument upon which it is based or where there is no instrument containing an adequate identifiable description?

Thus Mr. Renehan justified his argument, under the Bursum Bill, for a twofold statute of limitations — one period of years to cover those instances having color of title, and another period of years to cover those instances showing possession of land without color of title, or color of title that could not be established or related to a prior deed.

Mr. Renehan illustrated another phase of the question. A great deal of alleged encroachment centred about the pueblo of Santa Clara, because the town of Española is on the original pueblo grant.

"A grant [Santa Clara] representing probably the greatest amount of adverse holdings, confirmed, patented, and conveyed for 17,368 acres. The Joy Survey of adverse claims shows 4073 acres, or twenty-three per cent. That is Española, the centre of a magnificent orchard community. Those lands were obtained by purchase from the Indians in most instances, and many ancient deeds . . . are between Indians of the Santa Clara pueblo and individual Mexicans — if they can be identified as Mexicans or Spanish-Americans, because the fact that the names of the Indians are Spanish, and the name of the citizen is Spanish, renders it impossible in these recent times to know what was the national identity of an individual who made a deed one hundred fifty to two hundred years ago."

Question: Do you mean that twenty-three per cent of adverse possession is under deed?

"Much of it is; I cannot say all. Most of that land is under deed. But in many of the cases there is no deed, but title was derived by the present owner or his predecessors in interest by the delivery of title-papers, which came down to him from generations before. . . . They may or may not all relate to the same tract of land, because of the peculiarities of description [cites many instances]. . . ."

Question: Would you contend that that kind of conveyance of realty would carry any kind of title?

"Yes, sir, I contend it. I contend it, *not upon the theory of the Anglo-Saxon, but I contend it upon the theory of the Spanish or Mexican*, for we are not dealing with Anglo-Saxon times or with Anglo-Saxon people. We are attempting to turn ourselves to-day to Spanish jurisprudence and the traditions and habits and customs of Spanish people."

Let us consider another view of this beautiful Spanish-American system of landholding. Many of these lands are valuable because of a river frontage, or because of water rights in the main irrigation ditch from the river. Don José de Aguilar owned a tract of land with one hundred yards of frontage on the Rio Grande and running back from the river one half mile. In the natural course of events, Don José died, leaving this land to his four children. Each of the heirs must have a river frontage, although they seldom left the home ranchito. They would divide the house into four parts, and they would divide the land into four strips, each with twenty-five yards of river frontage and each one half mile in depth. In the natural course of human events, the said four children die, each leaving five children. What these twenty new heirs do to the old homestead can be imagined only; but they again divide the land in the same manner, producing twenty ribbons, each five yards wide and one half mile long. In the early days the simplest way to get around this dilemma was for a purchaser to buy out the rights of all the children with a fiesta and a jug of whiskey. That method settled many otherwise confused and probably clouded titles.

And to the Pueblo Indians came the "Joseph Decision" of 1876. The case arose because the Government sought to eject from lands of the Taos pueblo a man who had made settlement thereon and to recover the penalty provided by Section 2118 of the Revised Statutes ($1000) for every person who makes a settlement on any lands belonging, secured, or granted by treaty with the United States to any Indian tribe. The defendant set up in his petition that the lands belonged to the Pueblo tribe of Indians of the pueblo of Taos, secured to them by patent of the United States. A demurrer to this petition was sustained by the Supreme Court of the Territory, and thence was presented on error to the Supreme Court of the United States. The Court said: —

Were the Pueblo Indians, and the lands held by them, on which this settlement was made, within the meaning of the Act of Congress of 1834 and its extension to the Territory of New Mexico by the Act of 1851?

This question resolves itself into two others: —

1. Are the people who constitute the pueblo or village of Taos an Indian tribe within the meaning of the Statute?

2. Do they hold the lands on which the settlement was made by a tenure which brings them within its terms?

The first question was waived by the demurrer itself, because the petition recognized them as "the Pueblo tribe of Indians of the pueblo of Taos." The Court then recited a splendid picture of the Pueblo people, their history and civilization, such as it was; deftly eluded the question of their being citizens of the United States; inferred that while they looked like Indians, and certainly acted like Indians, they actually might not have the authority, even though a government Agent had been appointed for them; and then turned its attention to consecrating and canonizing the title — showing that it was a communal title vesting in the "pueblo of Taos, in the county of Taos; *not* to the Pueblo Indians of Taos, but the pueblo of Taos." This decision furnished to the legal profession for thirty-seven years the motif of a chant, with numerous variations, always sung *a cappella*, to the end that the Pueblos were Indians, that they were not Indians; that they were citizens of the United States, that they were not citizens of the United States; and, to the horror of everyone who had at heart the best interests of the Indians, that, because of this ironclad title conferring a peculiar status, they could alienate land. For, said the Court: —

The Pueblo Indians hold their lands by a right superior to that of the United States. Their title dates back to grants made by the government of Spain before the Mexican revolution — a title which was fully recognized by the Mexican Government and protected by it in the Treaty of Guadalupe Hidalgo, by which this country and the allegiance of its inhabitants were transferred to the United States.

And finally: —

If the defendant is on the lands of the Pueblo, without the consent of the inhabitants, he may be ejected or punished civilly by a suit for trespass, according to the laws regulating such matters in the Territory. If he is there with their consent *or license,* we know of no injury which the United States suffers by his presence, nor any statute which he violates in that regard.

Exactly what mediæval New Mexico wanted — first, to assure itself of what it had garnered already; and, second, to enable it unhindered to acquire more. There were to be thirty-seven years of harvest. Thus the loss of the ancient pueblo of Pecos, and the loss of the lands of Pojoaque, Nambe, Santa Clara, San Juan, Sandia, Cochiti, and Jemez; thus the horde of trespassers, — "colonists," — ever increasing, and joined even by persons once sworn to protect Indians as Indian Agents, but who, having retired from office, became meddlesome critics and landholders on pueblos. All these were to be assured of their holdings finally by the provisions of the proposed Bursum Bill in 1922.

But why, you ask? Had not the Supreme Court of the United States —

Wait a bit. You are not out of the thorns. In 1913 this same Supreme Court of the United States, using a different springboard, successfully cleared another group of obstacles, *and reversed* the decision cited above with respect to the Government's right to complain. In 1913 it did not find that it was "unnecessary to waste words," but proceeded to slather them around gorgeously.

The question through which the "Sandoval Decision" climbed into view was: —

Whether the status of the Pueblo Indians and their lands is such that Congress competently can prohibit the introduction of intoxicating liquor into those lands notwithstanding the admission of New Mexico to statehood.

Volstead had nothing to do with this. The Pueblo Indians were being debauched, physically, mentally, and morally. Many of them had soused away all the integrity and virtue that, in the opinion of courts and sentimentalists, they had once possessed. And earnest individuals commissioned by the Government as prohibition officers, at the head of whom loomed the determined figure of "Pussyfoot" Johnson, found themselves up against the Pueblo legend as constructed and construed by the state of New Mexico. And this too, notwithstanding that in its Enabling Act, thanks principally to the late Senator Albert J. Beveridge and Mr. Ernest Knaebel, then Assistant to the Attorney-General, the state had conceded the authority of Congress in Indian Affairs.

The Sandoval case went to the Supreme Court on appeal from the decision of Judge William H. Pope in the United States District Court; and the preparation of this appeal fell to Mr. Francis C. Wilson, then Special Counsel for the Pueblo Indians, after the United States District Attorney (Stephen B. Davis) decided that he would not appeal the case. Judge Pope had followed the doctrine of the "Joseph Decision." He too had been Counsel for the Pueblo Indians, and possessed an extraordinary knowledge of their history and legal relations. It was believed by nearly everyone that his opinion of the Indian status would be sustained. Even the Department of Justice in Washington was convinced that Judge Pope's decision was correct, and it would have prevailed but for the arguments of Mr. Wilson. A brief was then prepared following his contentions in the lower court. The Solicitor-General argued the case before the Supreme Court, and the result was the "Sandoval Decision," the opinion of the Court being delivered by Mr. Justice Van Devanter.

The Supreme Court proceeded to declare positively that they, the Pueblo Indians of New Mexico, *were Indians* in race, customs, and domestic government; that Federal moneys had been expended to improve their condition in life; that Agents had been appointed for them, and Special Counsel; that Congress had forbidden their taxation by the Territory of New Mexico, and that the grand state arising out of that territorial agglomeration had found it necessary to accept such a provision in its Enabling Act; that under Spain they had been wards, subjected to restraints and official supervision in the alienation of their property, and had been the beneficiaries of law prohibiting the liquor traffic among them; that under Mexico they must have enjoyed a limited and restricted citizenship; and that legislation enacted by the Congress of the United States (for many reasons given) could be made to apply to the Pueblo Indians without encroaching upon the police power of the state, and without disturbing the principle of equality among the states.

Argal, being Indians at last, and subject to this controlling legislation, it was plain that they could not competently alienate land; *and that they never should have been permitted to alienate land.*

But all was not lost save honor. In 1913 New Mexico had above 300,000 people, of whom but 8000 were Pueblo Indians, and the lawyers had to live. So the Indian Agents, in all disputes other than those over land titles, taxation, and liquor prohibition, had to run their legal barrage as before the Sandoval Decision, unless — unless the Indian Bureau bravely determined to apply *all the legislation* that Congress had enacted for the protection of Indians to the protection of the Pueblo Indians. The squawman said this would mean reducing the pure and democratic state of Pueblo civilization that had received him to the level of the monstrous and ignorant Apaches, and ethically it would have; the politician said that it would play hob in his precincts; those who expected to climb into the Senate, as they did, were wary and watchful; and the Indian Agent was handcuffed. The Indian Bureau swung to and fro as these tides ebbed and flowed, most of the time at anchor, sometimes drifting with the New Mexican winds, always close-hauled, but *never* braving a lee shore, and *never* getting into safe harbor.

Nor was this ignorance. Twenty-two years before the Sandoval Decision the Indian Bureau had received glimmerings of the very doctrine contained in it. The Chief Law Clerk of that time, one Kenneth F. Murchison, had embodied this opinion in the Commissioner's Annual Report for 1891, under the caption: "Status of Indians in Mexican Cession." Therefore the Indian Bureau of later years could demonstrate only expensive and uncaring vacillation. At any time in those twenty-two years it should have seen the folly of seeking to rule by inference, and resolutely besieged Congress for an expression of definite policy.

Before the relief obtained through the Sandoval Decision, the Pueblo situation had become so filled with menace that their Special Counsel and Agents advocated another course of remedial procedure. In order to ensure complete administration by the Federal Government over the pueblo grants, and with the compliance of the Indian Bureau, they sought to have each pueblo cede its title to the United States, the Secretary of the Interior to accept the trust. This trust period was to be for a limited term of years, and the power of the Secretary was limited also.

But the Secretary had no authority to accept such a trust unless authorized by Congress. The Indians agreed to and signed the petitions in each pueblo, and twice delegations of them, headed by their Special Counsel, visited Washington to urge this protection. The Indian Bureau had a bill introduced in Congress to give the Secretary of the Interior the necessary authority, but the bill was opposed in committee by New Mexico's representatives, failed to pass, and the project was abandoned.

I have been assured repeatedly by the two Indian Agents and the Special Counsel who advocated this method that the limitations placed on the authorities concerned would have kept the Pueblo Indians from the danger zone of allotment in severalty and all that implies. But I still view the method as one of rough surgery, and believe the ultimate future would have produced a land massacre. In any case, conditions must have been terrible to warrant the proposal to trade an impregnable charter for the benefits of a variable protectorate. As late as 1920, and in the Indian Bureau at Washington, when I sought to show that Pueblo conditions were alarming, this method of defeating hostile measures was revived and recommended. I had not been in South Dakota at that time, and I knew very little about allotment in severalty, patents in fee, land sales, and their sequelæ; but I prophesied then that never again would the Pueblo Indians of New Mexico seek to pledge their titles to any Secretary of the Interior; and I believe that, considering our modern advantages in appraising Secretaries of the Interior, my judgment was not altogether fantastic.

For it is by no means conceded that Congress has any power to set aside, or limit, or dismember a title that it did not create; but which, however, it has confirmed by

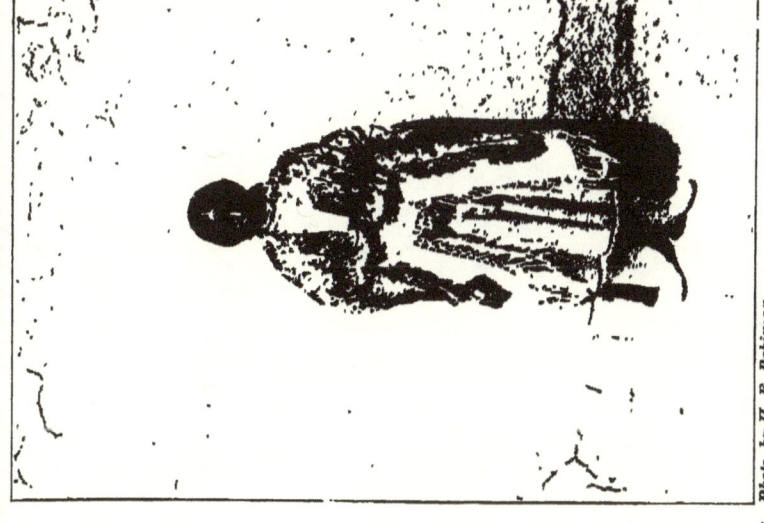

Photo. by H. F. Robinson

SANTA CLARA WOMAN IN FIESTA COSTUME

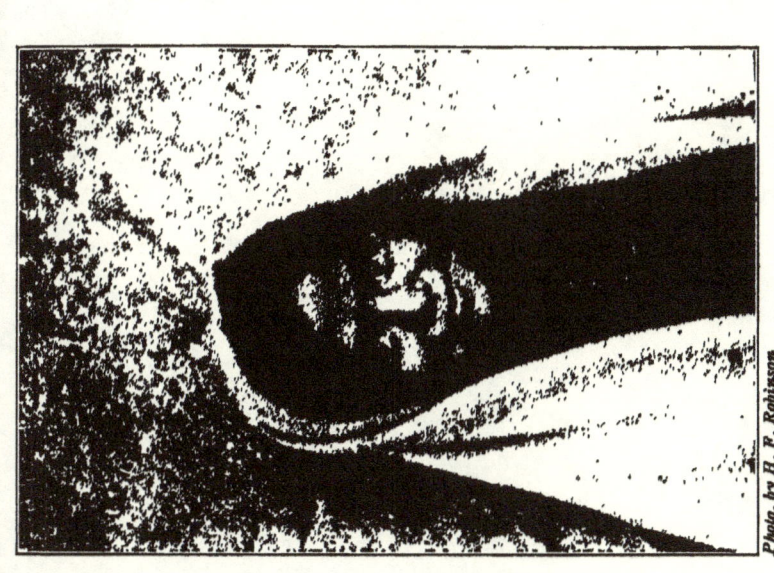

Photo. by H. F. Robinson

"HONEY," A SCHOOLGIRL OF TAOS

had been received from a Mexican President, the patent and the archives of the pueblo. Before the writ was served, the Governor deposited these sacred pieces of furniture with the Indian Agent, who had recognized him as the rightful holder. This Indian Agent, Harold Coggeshall, surrendered them to his successor in office, Philip T. Lonergan, who in turn surrendered them to me. Thus it will be seen that a local row and a legal action which occurred prior to 1912, and which engaged the attention of the Territorial Court, next the State Court, and finally the United States District Court, was settled in 1919. New Mexico having become a state in 1912, the State Court sought to enforce against Lonergan the writ of replevin, and served it on him. Lonergan refused to recognize any jurisdiction of the State Court over him as a Federal official, and was cited for contempt, and for quite some time was "constructively" in jail. Then a writ of habeas corpus was procured from the Federal Court, and the case went to decision there, graduating as stated in 1919, after Lonergan's resignation from office. Naturally, the Federal Court decided that the State Courts had no jurisdiction over questions of internal government of the Pueblo Indians, and the state did not appeal the case.

Next the Agents found that the Pueblo Indians were menaced in their status by various bills proposed to the Congress and designed to confer citizenship on the Indians wherever located, each of which measures would have delivered the Pueblo Indians into the hands of the State Courts. Proceeding under advice of counsel, the agents sought to have enacted a bill specifically outlining the methods of Pueblo control, to clarify by legislation in Congress those matters so indefinitely covered by various Court decisions, and to avoid the necessity of ruling by inference. For a number of years the Counsels had sought to secure Congressional expression of this kind, and had drafted several bills for the purpose. In Washington, I found that the Indian Bureau had accumulated these drafts in a pile that measured at least a foot in thickness; that a guardian had been appointed for them; and that every little while they were taken out, dusted, and looked at. Commissioner Cato Sells was anxious to have the Pueblo situation reduced to some semblance of normality. I carried to him the opinion of Mr. Attorney Summers Burkhart showing how seriously the Carter Citizenship Bill might affect Pueblo status, so seriously in fact as to remove them entirely from Federal protection. The long-neglected drafts designed to establish complete control were revived and boiled into a brief bit of legislation that received the Commissioner's endorsement. It went to the Secretary of the Interior and received his endorsement. Then it traveled hopefully to Capitol Hill. But, along with several thousands of other proposed and doubtless important measures, it fell into a committee wastebasket and expired there; for the Congress was in a hurry to get itself adjourned, and before its next session the whole atmosphere of the Interior Department would change, for better or worse, and the newspaper men of the country would, in no great time, have a lot to write about.

Considering the change of opinion that would so soon thereafter paralyze the remaining solons of the Indian Bureau, it is only fair to record that so long as Cato Sells remained in office, the Indian Bureau supported the Pueblo Indian Agency and defended the Pueblo Indians of New Mexico. Its new attitude may be measured perfectly by a quotation from the Indian Commissioner's Annual Report for 1922: —

Pueblo Indians of New Mexico

In the last annual report it was stated that an attorney had been appointed by the Department of Justice to represent the Attorney-General in matters of litigation, etc., relating to the Pueblo Indians of New Mexico. . . .

The report of the attorney has been received, and after careful consideration thereof it was concluded that additional legislation was needed to work out a fair settlement of matters relating to jurisdiction, land titles, etc., which for many years have been in an unsatisfactory state among those Indians.

Senate Bill No. 3855 was believed to be a practical and fair measure under which to adjust matters, *and has been recommended for enactment.*

Senate Bill No. 3855 *was* practical. It was the Bursum Bill.

Down through all these years of discussion and bitter irritation loomed the necessity for doing something to clear the Pueblo titles. Calhoun had suggested a Commission in 1849. Since Calhoun's time the acridity had increased. The "colonists" possessed the best of the irrigated lands within many pueblos, and, following mestizo methods, were increasing their holdings. It should not be inferred that the Indian Agents did nothing. They sometimes acted vigorously, without waiting for Court decisions; and again they were drawn into unpleasant situations by the unauthorized actions of their zealous subordinates residing on the pueblos, where the atmosphere occasionally became acute and approached actual warfare. But these were isolated flare-ups and could produce no general or beneficial result.

Before the Sandoval Decision it was planned to institute suits to quiet title, one such suit to be filed for each pueblo entity. Before this could be done intelligently, it was necessary to procure definite information of the aggressions, legal or otherwise, which had taken place. About 1912–1913 the "Joy Survey" was authorized by the Department for this purpose. The survey required about two years for its completion, and the plats evidencing its findings were still being received by the Agent in 1919. These plats, following the suggestion of the Pueblo Special Counsel, bore a significant inscription: —

The data shown on this plat are merely a portrayal of conditions existing on the ground at the time of survey in the field, without recognizing, establishing, or admitting any right of occupancy, title, ownership, legal, equitable, or otherwise, in any person or persons whose names may appear hereon, in or to any of the lands covered hereby.

The Joy Survey, therefore, was a governmental instrument to show the locations and the areas of pueblo lands claimed by non-Indians, with view to determining validity of title through subsequent and proper legal action. Each non-Indian claimant was allowed to make his claim, and the tract he sought to hold was surveyed out, regardless of whatever he had in the nature of title, regardless of whatever was claimed by the Indians against him. The survey was simply for the purpose of *graphing* claims against the Indians from the standpoint of the claimant; and this the Indian Bureau knew perfectly, since it had arranged for the making of the Joy Survey, and had paid for it.

A glance at the Bursum Bill (which was believed "a practical and fair measure") is necessary at this point: —

Section 15: That surveys of lands within pueblo grants and reservations held and occupied by persons not Indian, or corporations, as heretofore made under the supervision of the Surveyor-General for New Mexico, and plats and field notes of which have been filed in his office, *shall be accepted as prima-facie evidence of the boundaries of lands herein described.*

This was proposing to legalize by Act of Congress the use of the Joy Survey against the Indians and the Government, conceding its described boundaries as definitive. Taken in connection with other sections of the Bill, this provision would practically have established the survey as mandatory to a decree in favor of the non-Indian. On appeal, the Government would have had the burden of *disproving a survey made by the Government* with an entirely different intent and purpose, and certainly not made as complete evidence of anything. Before a Court, the weight of a government survey as against Indian testimony would ruin the case every time, for much of the Indian testimony would of necessity have to be in the nature of hearsay, "tribal tradition," with regard to alleged titles, some of which had originated seventy-five to one hundred and fifty years prior to the possibility of beginning a case in Court. If there had been no other argument to advance against the Bursum Bill, the proposed use of this survey would have been sufficient to damn it as a slick political production worthy of the atmosphere of New Mexico.

Let us consider a few samples of these non-Indian claims.

The Sandia "Garcia case" will serve to illustrate a mild sort of adverse holding. During the Mexican period of government over this territory, the Sandia Indians had a grievance of some sort, and a kindly disposed gentleman of the neighborhood agreed to carry their complaint to Mexico City with view of securing justice. He was successful as their envoy and advocate, and the Indians were grateful. As a fee they granted him the right of occupancy to a piece of pueblo land close to their town, *a life-interest only.* This man died some years later, leaving a widow, but no children. The Indians then decided that it would be discourteous to evict the widow, and they extended the right of occupancy and life-interest for the period of her lifetime. It was then to end. But it is surprising how many Mexican heirs developed with the demise of the old lady, and the descendants of these inheritors were comfortably ensconced on the Sandia pueblo in the year 1922. Through the years they had made many improvements, and eviction would have meant their losing houses, barns, wells, sheds, fences, and so forth, all of considerable value. Moreover, decision against them (the case had been in the courts for years), and it was not seen how decision could possibly be for them, would have been a tremendous lever of precedent in disposing of other and lesser intruders, trespassers, and "colonists."

And Sandia had other instances. As late as 1917 a non-Indian claimant at that pueblo began extending his fences to include more land. The Indians complained to their Agent (Lonergan), who investigated. The Mexican claimed to hold the land under deed, which he produced, and it purported to date back thirty or forty years; but, peculiarly enough, it was evidenced by the native Governor of Sandia *then in office.* The Agent pointed out this strange discrepancy, cut the fences without going into Court for a ten years' wrangle, and returned to his Agency. But within a short time the fences were restored on the same lines, and again, on being called to book, the Mexican claimed to hold under a deed. He produced the deed, and this time it carried the names of Indian officials who had served *fifty years before.*

Again during the period of Mexican sovereignty, when the Navajo Indians were raiding and plundering and murdering, the Cochiti Indians gave sanctuary to a group of Mexican people of the frontier beyond their pueblo. The Cochiti expected that when the danger had passed these people would return to their former homes. But the guests did not all depart; or, if they did, it was soon discovered by the Indians that the refugees had sold the houses allotted to them to other Mexicans who remained in possession, and documents were produced as deeds. The heirs of these early guests were on the Cochiti pueblo, in substantial houses and holding good lands, in 1922. In fact, the town of Cochiti was about evenly divided, one half being Mexican in its population and the other half Indian.

Such instances will indicate the chicanery that had been practised. But there were four other classes of claims that deserved different consideration in law and equity:—

1. Titles that had originated in the early Spanish times, the persons claiming under them being in quite the same class as the holders of real estate on lower Manhattan Island.

2. Persons who innocently, and many of them upon advice of competent legal counsel, had purchased of the Indians during those thirty-seven years when, under the Supreme Court's decision, the Pueblo Indians had possessed the ability to alienate lands.

3. Combinations of claims, legal and illegal, now represented by a populous town, such as at Taos and Española.

4. Other Spanish or Mexican grants of lands, large in area, which conflicted with and overlapped the Pueblo grants, justifying an investigation to ascertain the earliest title.

These conflicting grants had not been confirmed to the claimants by the Court of Private Land Claims, established by Congress in 1891, which continued its sittings until about 1905, for that Court had no jurisdiction to "interfere with or overthrow any just and unextinguished Indian title to any land or place. . . ."

It was estimated that more than 60,000 acres would be lost by the Indians of eight pueblos (or one seventh of their land area) were these conflicting grants validated — without considering the smaller trespassers or "colonists"; and the Bursum Bill (Section 8) proposed that persons or corporations who had held lands *for more than ten years* prior to June 20, 1910, *with or without color of title*, or who claimed such lands under valid grants from the governments of Spain or Mexico, or under any grant, act of confirmation, or patent of the United States, *would be entitled to a decree in their favor for the whole of such lands claimed* — the Indians to be reimbursed for these losses by equal areas on the public domain adjacent to their pueblo lines, or in cash should such lands not be found available. This carried the matter back to 1900 only, and thus practically all the adverse claimants (as shown by the Government's memoranda survey) would be confirmed in their holdings, and the huge areas under Spanish or Mexican grants (which the Court of Private Land Claims had refused to adjudicate) would be validated against the Indians.

Those who held possession under color of title were to be confirmed in their claims without reimbursement to the Indians, and, in ascertaining and adjudicating the true boundaries of such lands claimed, secondary evidence would be admissible and competent, according to the Bursum Bill.

The public domain adjacent to the pueblos, if any, would scarcely reimburse the cravings of a hungry jack rabbit. Such public-domain lands were not valley lands, and were not susceptible of irrigation; they were semiarid lands offering sparse grazing only in good seasons. For this very reason (the paucity of grazing lands), Executive Order extensions had been made to certain of the pueblos to increase their stock-grazing areas. Even where, by the wildest stretch of an engineer's imagination, sections of adjacent lands could be classed as "susceptible of irrigation," the expenditure involved in conveyance of water would have been so large that the Government could not consider it, and of course the Indians themselves could not finance it. Please keep in mind that the lands under dispute (save the large conflicting grants) were all irrigated, producing lands in the river trough, or lands that could be irrigated once the Rio Grande wastage was conserved. There only could the Indians farm, and they must farm to continue to exist, and they must have an equitable share of the river water.

In this last respect the Bursum Bill sought to throw the adjudication of water rights into the State Courts, thus achieving the effect of preventing the Indians from procuring additional water to their lands whenever additional supplies were reclaimed, developed, and conserved through the drainage of the water-logged Rio Grande Valley and the impounding of water in the upper Rio Grande — projects then in sight and now proceeding to a conclusion. The iniquity consisted in the fact that many of the pueblos had either no water, or an insufficiency of water for their irrigable lands, because available water had been appropriated by the non-Indians to their holdings. The state's statute of limitations (four years) had already run against the Indians, and they would have been barred in the State Courts from recovering waters that had flowed through their ditches for centuries. And their one hope would be demolished — that is, the rule of law that a statute of limitations cannot run against the Government, nor against its dependent wards. Why was not the Federal Court designated as the tribunal for the settlement of water rights? One naturally replies: Would it not be simpler to adjudicate all *conspiracy charges*, for instance, in the courts of the state of the accused?

To illustrate the amounts of aggressions on these valuable irrigable or irrigated lands: At Nambe, where 3000 acres of land were available to cultivation once water was procured, the Indians held 280 acres; at San Juan there were about 4000 acres under ditch, and the Indians held 588 acres of them; at San Ildefonso, out of 1200 acres under ditch, the Indians retained 248 acres; at Santa Clara, of the land under ditch it was estimated that the Indians did not possess more than 15 per cent. One should compare the Indian populations with these figures. San Juan's population in 1922 was 422 people, averaging 1.4 acres each; Nambe's population was 116, averaging 2.4 acres each; San Ildefonso's population was 91, averaging 2.7 acres each. Do not look at the size of the pueblo grant in these cases, for a patent cannot be planted to corn. San Juan had above 17,000 acres as "a pueblo holding" or grant; but its 422 people had but 1.4 acres each of arable land on which to subsist.

The pueblos of Cochiti, Sandia, San Felipe, and Jemez suffered from "colonists" also, but not to the extent shown above. Some of the pueblos were practically free from small holders of lands, notably Isleta, while others were seriously threatened by the validating of the overlapping grants only, notably Laguna. It was the frightful need for land and water at such pueblos as San Juan, Nambe, Tesuque, San Ildefonso, and Santa Clara, where the Indians in poor seasons faced starvation, that brought all the mestizo conditions vividly to public attention — once the public attention had been secured through a "Blue Book."

Immediately on decrees being entered by the Federal Court in these land claims (and in many cases the decrees were mandatory), all the lands confirmed to non-Indians would come within the jurisdiction of the State Courts, thus denying to the Indians the chance for appeal and relitigation in the Federal Court. Twitchell has commented: "The local courts and juries have yet, in my judgment, to show where the Indian has ever received justice." And in this respect reference is invited to the various trials of one Carl Magee, an editor, who interfered with a certain Mr. Fall, and whose editorial freedom annoyed the ruling powers of New Mexico that had controlled the press and the banks, as well as the votes, and meant with the help of Spanish influences and an apathetic minority of Americans to continue such control. Mr. Magee was not an Indian.

And the Bursum Bill proposed calmly and with a certain insolent assurance that those non-Indian claimants who were nothing but squatters, without color of title, and who were in possession, or who might enter into possession by some fortunate hook or crook before the passage of the Bill, *could purchase the lands they could demonstrate as holding*, at a price to be fixed by the Court, it is true, but without the Indians having an option as to sale or no sale.

Finally, Senator Bursum's charter sought to set aside the authority confirmed in the Indian Bureau (authority

Photo. by H. F. Robinson
CHURCH AT SAN BUENAVENTURA AT COCHITI

Photo. by H. F. Robinson
THE NORTH PUEBLO AND BRIDGE AT TAOS

fixed by the decisions of the Supreme Court of the United States) to deal with purely administrative Indian problems, thus throwing all the petty Indian offenses and tribal discontent into the Federal Court. This meant that anything and everything arousing native factional animosity would be expensively litigated, because the Indian is a natural litigant; and this would require the services of lawyers, who would scarcely quiet such turmoils so long as Pueblo fees held out.

Senator Holm O. Bursum became imbued with his mission to clarify the Pueblo land conditions. It was a duty imposed on him through his having been chosen to occupy the Senate seat still warm with the benevolence of Albert Bacon Fall. Senator Bursum prepared several drafts of legislation to accomplish this; but somehow they did not seem to click. Yet it was certain that, given time enough, and a sufficiency of legal help out of Santa Fe, he would evolve an instrument blunt enough for the purpose. Now A. B. Renehan, a learned and astute attorney of Santa Fe, had drawn a bill in 1920, at the solicitation of the Honorable Homer P. Snyder, then Chairman of the House Committee on Indian Affairs, who visited the Pueblo provinces to view conditions, but who was handicapped in this reconnaissance by the fact that mealtime was always bobbing up. Judge Richard H. Hanna represented the Indians then as Special Counsel, and was paid by Congress for his services; but Judge Hanna was not consulted by the Chairman on this occasion. Mr. Renehan had no official status, and later testified before this same Chairman that "he had no fish to fry"; but he had been on fishing expeditions, and had represented one hundred and fifty-five or more defendants in a suit once pending to adjust title to holdings by non-Indians within the Santa Clara and San Ildefonso pueblo grants. And Mr. Renehan had been one of learned counsel in the "Sandoval case," on the losing side.

Then Twitchell was appointed to his position as Special Assistant to the Attorney-General; but his initial report on Pueblo problems, when submitted to the Secretary early in 1922, did not seem to click any more than Bursum's earlier drafts of legislation. By this time the Commissioner of Indian Affairs had in the Pueblo field no official adviser. Those who had learned of Pueblo conditions inside the fold were, unfortunately for Mr. Burke, all outside it. His home, or "Bureau," talent was available, and would strive to please; but as late as 1920 it had expressed itself in another fashion, and a too sudden reversal of form might invite comment. Something of experience from the actual scene of operations was wanted, and so the Commissioner of Indian Affairs sent for Twitchell and Renehan. They should come to Washington for the purpose of going over a bill to be submitted to Secretary Fall for his final approval.

Thus was Senator Bursum's legislative child conceived. It was by Fall, out of partisan New Mexico, assisted by numerous learned but disingenuous midwives. Senator Bursum dutifully carried the bassinet to the Senate and revealed the little stranger. It was labeled "an Administrative measure," and Administrative measures should be like Cæsar's wife; so the unsuspecting Senators told nurse to pass on to the House. But from the corridor a howl of dismay was heard. There sounded sibilant hissing that reflected on the protégé's very legitimacy. As for the terms of endearment used, I can only refer to a brilliant commentary on the times, and ask you to select from those scattered through the pages of *Revelry*.

How did the outcry arise? Were the Pueblo Indians possessed of radio, and did they broadcast these insidious reflections? No! the Pueblo Indians were, as usual, helpless, and just then official-less, since all those who might have raised objections, however forlorn, had been dismissed for political reasons, or, failing that, "transferred for administrative reasons." Nevertheless, a man named Borah heard this clamor, and, notwithstanding that Bursum had assured him of the Bill's purity, demanded that it be recalled for a Wassermann test.

There was a reason; and, like most things that have vitally influenced the Pueblo Indians of New Mexico, the reason emerged from the old Villa Real de Santa Fe de San Francisco. A little association had been formed there, styled the New Mexico Association on Indian Affairs; and its members did not admire the Bursum Bill. Also, in 1921, the General Federation of Women's Clubs, despite the fact that an Indian Bureau representative had touted Mr. Fall to them, had seen fit to form a committee on Indian Welfare, to observe and assist where possible in the improvement of Indian health conditions generally. The chairman of this committee was Mrs. Stella M. Atwood, of Riverside, California, who came to New Mexico early in 1922, and did not find Pueblo conditions, or those things being devised for their correction, pleasing to her state of mind. Mrs. Atwood employed a field representative, Mr. John Collier, who, at the time the Bursum Bill appeared on the horizon, was studying Pueblo problems at Taos. Then the New Mexico association invited legal counsel as to the probable effects of the Bursum Bill; and also invited the coöperation of the Women's Clubs Welfare Committee and its field representative.

Thus it happened that one evening two men sat in a Santa Fe legal kiva to prepare a "Blue Book," a production that became as potent for destruction as was Popé's palmilla fibre rope of knots in the red days of 1680. They labored over this literature from 9 P.M. until two o'clock of the next morning, and that same day it was in the hands of the printer, issued under the auspices of the New Mexico Association on Indian Affairs and the Indian Welfare Committee of the General Federation of Women's Clubs. This "Blue Book" dissected the Bursum Bill with a dispassionate, cold-blooded, legal intensity. There was no sentimentality, picturesque writing, or other blatherskite in the "Blue Book," and no statement of it has been successfully controverted or contradicted. It was the Wassermann test.

The counsel employed was Mr. Francis C. Wilson, of Santa Fe, who had been legal advisor to the Pueblo Indians (1909–1914); who had prepared the winning essay in that Sandoval affair; who had inspired the Joy Survey; and who possessed the confidence of the Pueblo Indians, and the confidence of their Agents, and who has it to-day; but who, one must admit, was most cordially hated by the Indian Bureau that had recommended Mr. Fall. He proved the most vital force in accomplishing all that it was possible to achieve in the way of purified legislation to succeed the Bursum Bill, since, when that unfortunate measure was returned from the House, it was promptly stretched on the rack and mangled beyond recognition.

These sentimental "propagandists," including Mr. Wilson, received a heckling in Washington, because it appeared that there must be something unsavory in any effort on the part of a citizen to flag and fix the attention of Congress. However, Mr. Wilson summed up their intentions in this manner:—

I believe it can be safely stated that, from Calhoun's time down to the present day, every agent, every man connected with the Pueblo Indian situation as an official of the Indian Bureau *in the field*, has recommended some method of arriving at an adjustment of their troubles and a solution of their problems. . . .

What we have said with reference to the present situation can be equally well said of every Commissioner and every official of the Indian Bureau *in Washington* who has had anything to do with it for the past seventy-five years. . . .

We come then directly to the meat of the situation: *that is, the failure of the Indian Bureau for seventy-five years* to take cognizance of reports like Calhoun's which have been before it, and to try in some intelligent manner to solve this situation.

The City of the Holy Faith was well represented at the hearings of the two Congressional committees.[1] Here were Twitchell and Renehan from Santa Fe, earnest advocates, deftly using the same historical materials; and here too was Wilson, also of Santa Fe, an equally earnest advocate, not so well versed in history and picturesque effects, but bitterly informed as to the legal poison of the Bursum Bill.

---

[1] As the result of these hearings, comprising 500,000 words of testimony and argument, an equitable piece of legislation was procured and enacted into law. It provided for the formation of the Pueblo Lands Board, now engaged in doing that which Calhoun proposed in his report dated November 20, 1849. This Pueblo Lands Bill was approved June 7, 1924.

From Secretary Work's annual report for 1927: "The work of the Pueblo Lands Board . . . was continued during the year. Hearings were held for the Pueblo of Sandia and preliminary work done in the cases of Isleta and San Felipe pueblos. To the present time, reports of findings have been made by the board in the cases of the Tesuque, Jemez, Nambe, Taos, Sia, and Santa Ana pueblos. . . . The board has now passed on 1152 adverse claims. Suits have been instituted in the Federal Court in New Mexico to quiet title in the Indians to the pueblos of Taos and Nambe."

The ensemble at the curtain included many eminent figures, who enacted their rôles in the traditional manner. We see the Defender of Congress, who had many times deprived the Pueblo Indians of benefits by talking down appropriations, and who once at Santa Ana, in 1920, had refused to meet with the natives of that pueblo, and their Jemez and Sia guests, who had ridden thirty miles to greet him. We see the Bureau's apologist with his India-rubber schedules of gratuities, stretching over all "Indian country" from Moencopi, Arizona, to the watering troughs of Tres Ritos, New Mexico; and we see another eloquent Burke, but in a different rôle from the part that Edmund played in the trial of Warren Hastings.

Last, — but who could do justice to the monumental figure of the cast? — the man who denounced propaganda and invidious publicity, yet who, ever restrained and temperate himself, was forced by the exigencies of the plot to invoke the shadow of that sinister thing — *conspiracy!* With the well-selected files of the Indian Bureau furnished him, he sought to show that the advocate, Francis C. Wilson, should have been prosecuted for engaging in an alleged conspiracy to defraud the Pojoaque pueblo of lands in 1914, a matter that had been presented to the Department of Justice long before Harry Daugherty became Attorney-General for the United States. I know this is a trifle confusing. Please do not misunderstand me. This was not Francis C. Wilson indicting Albert Bacon Fall for having hatched a conspiracy against the United States; this was Albert Bacon Fall alleging conspiracy on the part of Francis C. Wilson.

It was bad dramatic form, for the climax produced an anticlimax, a thing that all seasoned playwrights struggle to avoid. The limelight turned on a former Cabinet official — one James Rudolph Garfield, of Roosevelt's Cabinet, not Harding's. The Honorable Mr. Garfield was able to recall the Pojoaque case and its charges, and extended himself to produce from governmental files *all the details* of this case. And the Honorable Mr. Garfield was moved to assert: —

The whole record discloses an instance of the bitterness and personal animosities that arise when unwarranted charges are brought against faithful public officials. Unfortunately, such incidents have too often occurred in Indian matters.

It is clear that the charges made against Mr. Wilson *are without basis in fact or law*, and that a grave injustice has been done to him and the organizations he represents by the statement of Secretary Fall.

When this charge was made, Mr. Wilson sought to question his accuser.

"Mr. Chairman! Am I to submit to cross-examination from this man?" cried Fall, his white hair growing whiter at the thought of it. The Chairman said it was unnecessary; and indeed it was, for that cross-examination on the faithfulness of public officials would come later.

Then Fall concluded: —

"We decline to sit down at the council table with those who think we are unworthy of trust!"

Blessed are the pure in heart. . .

XV

THE PEOPLE OF THE LITTLE ISLAND

The pigeons coo and preen upon the tower,
The bees drone in the heat, a parrot calls;
And many a cactus, shrub, and desert flower
Grows in the compound of the mission walls.
A golden pheasant struts, a well-wheel hums,
A magpie chatters, shrills its bitter spite,
As from the cloister now the padre comes
To walk within his garden of delight.
Beyond — the drowsy pueblo suns and dreams,
The Rio murmurs, and a passing train
Shrieks out its warning — then the quiet seems
To charm Isleta once again to Spain.
Who knows? . . . Some ghostly midnight yet may bring
De Vargas back in armor, challenging!
— "Isleta" (1919)

Isleta — meaning an "islet" or little island; a pueblo situated on the west bank of the Rio Grande, thirteen miles south of Albuquerque; a station of the same name on the Santa Fe Railway; population (1922), 988 Tihua (Pueblo) Indians.

Before the Rio Grande changed its course many years ago, the village occupied an island formed by the river and an arroyo; to-day, the great Rio drifts somnolently or boils savagely at their very dooryards. Lummis claims that Isleta is one of two pueblos remaining on the very sites occupied when Coronado made his entrada in 1540,

THE PEOPLE OF THE LITTLE ISLAND

Acoma being the other; but Bandelier does not agree in this opinion as far as it concerns Isleta. The Isletas are styled by their one-time raiding foes, the Navajo, as "Nah-toh-ho," enemies at the water.

This pueblo always appealed to me rather more than others. Some may explain this by saying that Isleta is only thirteen miles from the Albuquerque Agency, and I could get there and back the quicker; but Sandia, the very opposite from Isleta in every respect except that they too are Tihua, is only thirteen miles north of Albuquerque, and I seldom went there at all.

Perhaps Isleta appealed to me because of the writings of Lummis; perhaps it was because I was always so courteously received by the members of the intelligent Indian Council, and the Governor, when he happened to be of the progressive party of the pueblo; perhaps it was because of the venerable padre, who would meet me in his mission garden and call me "his son," before leading to a restful room at the end of the long, cool cloister, where were deep armchairs and a box of genuine "Owl" cigars. Yet I rather think it was because the Isletas preserved more of their Indian appearance, in costume and mannerisms, than even the backward Pueblo Indians, many of whom were content with cast-off clothing except on feast days.

The people of Isleta may have an infusion of the Spanish blood, — that of the early Spanish, — although they reject the suggestion and call themselves pure Indians. Their family records are very complete, and do not lend much support to the theory. Charles H. Burke once made a feeble effort to explain Pablo Abeita's shrewdness thus; and indeed, when before the Senate Committee in 1923, and when questioned by Senator

Bursum himself, who sought to demonstrate that the Indians were to blame for everything, Abeita said: "My grandfather used to tell me that his grandfather was half Spanish."

Well, if so, and considering the history of the early Spanish in the New World, this is nothing to be ashamed of. One will find at all the pueblos Spanish names. There are Aguilars, and Herreras, and Jirons, and Olguins, and Archuletas in profusion. Bancroft tells us that all these names came into New Mexico with the first settlers, the Spanish who formed Oñate's expedition in 1598. And just as surely we find the names of Randolph, and Jefferson, and Washington, and Lee,. identifying negroes in Virginia. What does it prove? In the case of the Pueblo Indians our limited intelligence should recognize first that the Indians were promptly baptized and named in Spanish, partly to incorporate them as closely as possible with the Saints, and partly for quick identification in a familiar tongue. Indian Bureau officials have followed this method in modern times, both on reserves and at schools. I recall one day-school principal who kept a Litany of the Saints for this purpose, and certainly he had no other use for it. My own method was to perpetuate the poetic names of the Old Testament. Those who thought differently had often been before me, so one of my tribes was loaded with great modern patronymics — Walter Scott, Charles Dickens, Abraham Lincoln, Edwin Booth; and, should this writing interest a certain contemporary author descended from a stage family, Izola Forrester. For that matter, there is a Hopi Indian named "Leo Crane," a label that I trust will never be a disadvantage to him.

In brief, the Isletas proudly insist that they are of the

THE PUEBLO OF ISLETA

pure Indian blood, and they deplore any slip of their sons in marrying with aliens of whatever nationality or complexion.

The reactionary element at the pueblo is in the majority; but there is a Bull Moose faction, led by such men as Pablo Abeita, and including J. Felipe Abeita, many times Governor of the pueblo; Frank Lucero, for years the pueblo Treasurer; Bautista Zuñi, José Felipe Abeita, Remijio Lucero, Juan Trinidad Abeita, José Jojola, Pascual Abeita, Andres Jojola, Juan Antonio Montoya, Romaldo Abeita, and others. The Old Native Party, however, is not without its naturally shrewd men and a few well-educated ones who have retarded the more rapid progress of the community. Most of the reactionaries are simply interested in old tribal ways and ceremonies, and allow themselves to be used by cunning "walking delegates" who would like a slice of the fees through election, or rather "selection by the cacique," to public office. Alas! the Isletas are still partially under the domination of a cacique, and their regal to-morrow will never dawn for them until this worn-out symbol of a pagan past is discarded.

The strife between these two factions always culminated in the Court of Indian Offenses, having jurisdiction of all Indian misdemeanors. As that court among the Pueblos has been abolished, insofar as the native judges are concerned, where the battle wages now I do not know. Perhaps the pot simply stews and stews. It was unfortunate that the pueblo possessed no equally well-educated and disinterested patriot to accept the position of Indian Judge; but the fact is that, as all were interested, and few well educated, Señor Pablo Abeita just happened to be the man best equipped for the job, a post he held from

1913 to 1923.[1] This placed a leader of the progressive minority in a governmental place of power and influence, and laid him open to the charge of advancing his party and personal interests through governmental measures. For that matter, it was unfortunate for the British Crown that the American colonists had no servile and uninterested man to lead the Continental forces, being forced to employ one Colonel Washington, a steadfast and perhaps bitter partisan who greatly inconvenienced the faithful military men of the opposing armies. As for Abeita, he wears his hair long and affects the splendor of the blanket, together with the lacelike Isleta shirt with its red wristbands and red-piped collar; but he is not a "blanket Indian," and explains this dress to friends by saying that he can drop the blanket quicker than he could an overcoat should a bear get after him. He is not without a certain trenchant wit.

---

[1] Tihua Indian of the Isleta pueblo, New Mexico. Born February 10, 1871; son of José P. Abeita and Marcelina Lucero; married María Dolores Abeita (second cousin), February 9, 1889; five sons — John, Joseph, Remijio, Ambrosio, Andrew. Educated in the Jesuit School of Old Albuquerque; finished his schooling at St. Michaels College, Santa Fe; in all, ten years. Speaks English, Spanish, Isleta-Tihua, Taos-Tihua, Laguna (Queres), Jemez (Pecos), and Zuñi languages, with some knowledge of Hopi and Navajo. Worked as typesetter on Albuquerque *Morning Democrat*, now the *Journal*, and later as commercial clerk three years; then resident farmer for the Indian Service. In 1905 made the first complete census of the Isleta, Sandia, Santa Ana, and San Felipe pueblos. Conducted store at Isleta since 1907, his people having been in the trading business for many years. Has held most offices of the Isleta native government. Member of the Principales since 1889. Chosen president of the first Business Council at Isleta when it was organized in 1912. Judge of the Indian Court, 1913–1923. Has made many trips to Washington on behalf of his people, and assisted in having restored to them large areas of land. Has met every President since Cleveland with the exception of President Coolidge. One son, Remijio, enlisted in the army during the World War.

The Abeita family claims that the grandfather of Pablo — Ambrosio Abeita — advanced to government or military officials some fifty thousand dollars in the early sixties to pay Federal troops when New Mexico was invaded by the Confederates. Money was raised locally by Colonel Canby. Perhaps this advance was in the nature of subsistence and forage. It has been said that Ambrosio Abeita was reimbursed during the administration of President Garfield, but Ambrosio died in 1879. When at Washington in 1863 Ambrosio was presented a fine field glass by President Lincoln, the instrument now in the possession of Pablo Abeita.

PABLO ABEITA
A progressive leader of Isleta

THE PEOPLE OF THE LITTLE ISLAND

In his speech before the Congressional Committee there was more of it than we find in the language of others. Indeed, Mr. Renehan and Abeita divided the honors in this respect. Referring to the discovery of this continent by the dominant white, Abeita said: —

Columbus goes back to Europe and claims and proclaims that he had found a New World. What right did Columbus have to make such a claim, or what proofs had he that it was a New World he had found? This world was not lost, and may have been and may be as old, if not older, than the one Columbus came from. . . .

Imagine what Europe would have said if some Indian sailed eastward in search of the rising sun, and had come into the Port of Palos, to claim and proclaim that he had found a New World. . . .

The white people may say that he did not take all of this country by force, but in some cases had bought it of the Indian. We will not deny that, but look at the bargains they used to get, and remember that Manhattan Island was sold about three hundred eight years ago for $24 worth of glass beads. . . . Had it been the other way, and some foolish Irishman had sold the British Isles for $24 worth of tobacco, would that have been a good bargain?

Our principal needs to-day are that you eject all non-Indian trespassers off our lands. Instead of reimbursing the Indian for what land the non-Indian holds, why not reimburse the non-Indian trespasser and make him get off? He knows that he is holding the land illegally, only he knows that he won't vote for you if you don't kick us into submission!

He had six other sane and sensible suggestions, but this was his first shaft into the target. It was like throwing the harpoon with an unerring accuracy, and then twisting it around until it revolved freely.

Despite his shrewd understanding and native wit, however, Abeita was at a distinct disadvantage in a colloquy with Senator Bursum. Abeita had not sharp sarcastic replies at his command when questioned concerning the past "fostering care" of the United States Government. An Indian seldom has, for the bulk appropriations and their distribution from a large original sum into various puny streams, over huge states and many tribes, are not known to him. The Indian Bureau, whenever called on to make a showing, lists the expenditures for all the Indians of New Mexico, and some of Arizona, to prove that the Pueblo Indians have not been neglected.

As a matter of fact, the Isletas had received free education for their children, which included some clothing at the local day school, and clothing and subsistence at the boarding schools; free medical attention and medicines; and the financing of some stock-watering wells. There was an expensive steel bridge across the Rio Grande at their pueblo, true; but it was as much a benefit to the state of New Mexico as to the pueblo. And they had their proportionate share in the Pueblo Special Counsel, the Indian Agent, and employee services, such as they were. But in the back of Abeita's mind lived a panorama of many years of official neglect. He was trying to picture the hopelessness of the law between 1848 and 1913, really until 1923, as it had been interpreted for the benefit of a venal and voting constituency; the lassitude of time-serving officials; the inertia of courts; the complacency of the Indian Bureau. Above all, he was thinking of the utter indifference of Congress to this situation, an indifference which was not new or startling, but which was becoming a terrible menace to *his people*, not only to the 988 Isletas, but in grievous measure to the Pueblo Indians as a whole people. Small credit to a United States Senator to argue down a man he should have represented, and whom he had tried to sell out; to put him in the wrong as a neglectful, stupid, vacillating native chargeable with much of the dereliction. But it is ever the manner of wardens.

The Honorable Charles Carter, who once proposed a "Citizenship bill" which would have seriously affected Pueblo interests, thought that the gift of the franchise would go a long way to cure these things. Would it? Let us consider the political conditions in the County of Bernalillo, where the Isleta pueblo may be found on the maps. Bernalillo County embraces both the Sandia and Isleta Indian pueblos, their combined populations in 1922 being 1080 persons. There were 377 male adults, and it is not likely that Indian women would vote. The polling list of voters in this county (1916–1918) showed:—

Americans	2714
Spanish Americans	2480
	5194

Therefore the Indian vote, which would have been for years a confused and ignorant vote, if polled in its entirety, was less than seven per cent; and a very large percentage of Bernalillo County could be depended on to vote exactly as the padrone said.

The governor and his fiscals on an important pueblo of many acres, such as Isleta, are officials who can advance the financial interests of outsiders, through leases, concessions, and the like, unless the Indian Agent thoroughly controls affairs. Before the "Sandoval Decision" of the Supreme Court this was very hard for the Agent to accomplish — in fact, quite impossible. Isleta fees and revenue were dissipated for years. Therefore the Isleta Council was established in 1912, a movement largely of progressive pueblo conception, and supported by Agents of sense, to the end that the business of the community received publicity. This deprived the native governor of his graft, were he that sort of governor; and, the governor being helpless to control the "Congress," many of those hanging hungrily over the pueblo lines were debarred from their believed just prerogatives. It may be interesting to the reader to examine the last financial statement I rendered to the Governor and the Isleta Council, as of May 6, 1922:—

Liberty Bonds of $500 each, one drawing interest at 4 per cent, the other at 4½ per cent		$ 1,000.00
Certificate of Deposit No. 21393, dated May 6, 1922, interest at 4 per cent, on State National Bank of Albuquerque		21,000.00
Treasurer's checking account, same bank		188.03
Bills receivable		
Payment for posts	$150.00	
Fiesta fees	268.25	418.25
Total pueblo funds		$22,606.28

Statement from the Agent's annual report for the period ending June 30, 1922: "September 1, 1919, the Isleta pueblo funds totaled $7106.88; therefore, in less than three years, the account has tripled."

It should not be inferred that all the pueblos of New Mexico were so solvent. Of the others, only Laguna and Cochiti, at this time, had moneys in any appreciable amount, and the funds of Cochiti were in process of collection. Isleta was the only pueblo having a large surplus grazing area to lease, netting them $4500 annually.

Before 1919, the Isletas, expecting the development of great riches, entered into a lease, in utter defiance of their Agent and the Department, for the development of oil from their grant lands. The validity of this lease was promptly challenged, a compromise refused, and suit entered to have the lease canceled. The lessee, however, proceeded to the pueblo lands and began drilling operations. The question of his right, if any, languished in the United States Court. The Isletas, or many of them, were not able to understand why their action was displeasing to the Department, when for years other pueblos had entered into leases and contracts with little or no Agency supervision — for grazing areas and logging sites, for the mining of gypsum, for railroad rights of way, watering stations, track extensions, and other projects, all of which had occurred before the Supreme Court had defined their status of wardship. And, like Isletas, they had proceeded into this oil project on a grand scale, having executed a lease covering 110,000 acres of their territory. The immense area involved was one of the chief reasons for refusing to approve their action, for, if you will permit me, the Departmental officials who challenged its legality and wisdom were those serving under the Wilson Administration. The lands of the Isletas, where tested by this quasi lessee, produced no amount of oil sufficient to justify the sums stockholders paid for the holes, and after a while even suckers become chary of those who prospect for oil and develop a lawsuit only.

The matter was of interest to me in one slight particular. After 1921, I was waited on by a delegation of legal gentlemen, who announced themselves as representing the lessee's interests. They sought, apparently, information as to the progress of the case, and were hopeful that the

Department would change its attitude toward one who so earnestly wished to benefit an Indian tribe through developing its mineral and stock-selling resources. I explained that the Indian Agent could have no influence with the Court; and I knew, although I made no mention of it, that efforts to sell additional stock in the Middle West were meeting with small success, even suspicion; and that rumors of a big strike of oil on the pueblo, a gossip that was being permitted to leak out convincingly through certain Indians, had no basis of fact. But the gentlemen were insistent, and assured me that the recommendation of the Indian Agent would have great weight, especially were he to advise the withdrawal of the suit and the approval of the original lease by the Department. I had never before felt myself so important.

"With whom would my recommendation have weight?" I mildly inquired.

"With the new Secretary," I was informed.

"Would it?" I asked.

But at this late date, I am inclined to believe that my recommendation to cry quits and validate the lease might have been effective; for you see it *was* an oil lease, covering 110,000 acres; and we all know now that oil development in all its phases was a hobby to which the new Secretary devoted himself unsparingly.

Before the formation of the Isleta Council the pueblo had no financial showing. When a governor relinquished office at the year's end, he left an empty treasury as a testimonial to his fiscal acumen. And ninety per cent of the dissention which I experienced from 1919 to 1922 arose through reactionary governors, who sought to repossess themselves of pueblo funds, as they did not succeed in doing, even though one delegation in war paint traveled all the way to Washington and wound up in the council chamber of Secretary Fall. When I departed from Albuquerque the moneys were at the disposition of the Pueblo Council, upon proper vote and showings, thus removing Isleta from the sad situation of many other pueblos, where, without a cent in their treasuries, they at times faced famine and invoked the offerings of sentimentalists.

These moneys were not subject to the rules and regulations affecting Public Moneys of the United States, and were not carried as "Indian Moneys"; and thus the Bureau could not step in, now and then, as was the custom, to use such moneys — or so much thereof as may be necessary — for the building of a school house when a Congressional appropriation was not available. On the other hand, if the Pueblo Council received a petition stating that certain families of the community were in need of food for the winter, owing to sickness, failure of crop, or other causes, it could promptly vote assistance and relief, and its treasurer would sign a check, which, on being countersigned by the Indian Agent, provided immediate succor — without justification to every clerk between Albuquerque and the office of the United States Comptroller General, and approval nine weeks after the beneficiaries had died.

Now the Bureau had never approved of the Council, had never authorized the Agent to recognize or commission or support its membership, had never commended its success, and did not have the courage to order its abandonment. Therefore, when a government auditor found a draft for $2250 in my Agency safe awaiting the arrival of the Isleta treasurer to bank it, he insisted on my taking this sum into the public accounts, thus getting it into the cyclone cellar of the United States Treasury. I refused to do so, and appealed the matter. The money had been received by me as "a pueblo revenue." It belonged "not to the Indians of Isleta, *but* to the pueblo of Isleta." The auditor knew less of this than he did of Navajo grammar, and the Bureau allowed the point to remain like Mahomet's coffin, suspended in mid air, the hope being that time, delay, and indifference would settle it without the precedent of a decision, just as such subtle influences had finished many another important Pueblo question. The payment had been made to "Leo Crane, Agent for the Pueblo of Isleta." So I had it changed to a direct payment to the "Treasurer for the pueblo of Isleta," as were all subsequent payments, and thus virtue was not only guaranteed, but even restored to a pristine glory.

Prior to 1921, the Indian Agents were annoyed by local attorneys seeking to defend Indians before the Court of Indian Offenses. I do not mean the leading legal lights of Albuquerque and Santa Fe, but those who were looking for something to do in their spare time. One such case was given a test at Isleta by my predecessor, during that time when the "Neblett Decision" had not sustained the Agent's authority, and before Secretary Payne's ruling that the Indian Court of the pueblos should be conducted as a military court-martial, the defendant having the right of appeal to the Indian Agent, and again of appeal to the Indian Commissioner. It happened when the Isletas were still brewing their wines, and the Liquor Service officers had not succeeded in discouraging the circulation of such beverages. One night, when many of the reactionary Indians were engaged in a dance and the flowing bowl at the same time, Agent Lonergan sought to disperse them. He went so far as to seize the communal or ceremonial drum, and in the ensuing debate his life was threatened by Indians in the mood to stage another revolt. Promptly Agent Lonergan arrested and charged their leader with inciting a riot. The Indian demanded counsel at his trial, and a gentleman from Bernalillo, who was by no means the worst lawyer in the world, appeared to defend him. The trial was conducted strictly in accord with legal procedure, Judge Abeita presiding, and the defendant received a sentence of forty days in the cárcel. It was useless for him to appeal to his Agent, since his Agent had prosecuted him. He appealed to the Commissioner of Indian Affairs, and to the Secretary of the Interior. Receiving no telegrams of sympathy, he was preparing a petition to the President of the United States when his sentence expired. He had served the entire period allotted him in literary work.

But let us examine another case. New Mexico has a law that should be styled "the peon's law." One who accepts employment to herd sheep, and who is installed as a herder on the range, may not quit his position of trust before having given "reasonable notice" to his employer. On the face of it, a very good law, protecting the owner of valuable live stock from discovering his flocks scattered because of the perfidy of the employed. But, as ever there is a jigger in it. The jigger in this particular custom is that once having employed uneducated men, such as Isleta Indians, as herders, the actual owner often kept himself entirely removed from the possibility of any such service of notice, reasonable or not — supplying the men from a distance; and so, when dissatisfaction arose from any cause, the herders could not quit — or, if they did, were liable to arrest and prosecution, it being a misde meanor punishable by fine and imprisonment to desert the sheep on the range.

Now came a notice to me that six Isleta Indians had maliciously and with malice aforethought done this very thing. The sheriff of Sandoval County, where the offense had been committed, appeared in my office and stated that he would proceed to the pueblo to serve his warrants. I requested him to delay his journey for a little, expecting to adjust the dispute quietly as I had on former occasions. He was willing to wait, but the complainants demanded the immediate arrest of the guilty men as an object lesson in civics and law. I then telephoned the pueblo, and the accused gave themselves up without protest. I said to the sheriff: —

"There is no reason to transport these men to Sandoval County. The Albuquerque chief of police always extends to this Agency the hospitality of his cells, and you may rest your prisoners there until I procure bonds."

"Very good," agreed the sheriff.

But he soon returned to my office, a look of dismay on his face. The complainants had insisted that he perform his full duty and bitterly incarcerate those prisoners in the Sandoval County jail, whence, if I were powerful enough, I could release them in accordance with the due processes of law. It was late in the day. I could not hope to procure bonds that evening.

"What am I to do?" the sheriff asked. He was one of the few New Mexican officials who did not welcome the opportunity to embarrass the Agency.

"Why, Mr. Sheriff! I see nothing for you to do, other than to imprison those men until I can arrange for their bail. I have offered to be responsible for them, and to deliver them promptly in court when

THE PEOPLE OF THE LITTLE ISLAND 327

wanted, but these complainants reject all idea of such courtesy."

So the sheriff departed into the dusk, leading his prisoners. The complainant was a prominent attorney of Albuquerque, one of those impeccable lights who shed a personal refulgence on any little town. He often sat at table with me at the Rotary Club, and made long orations whenever permitted. I planned to make an early start next morning — first to the Special Counsel's office, thence to friends for bail assurance, and thereafter to the precincts of the Sandoval County court. But it was not necessary. Before I had left the office, the telephone bell tinkled. It was a long-distance call. A bit of fear swept over me. I had counseled those Indians to submit themselves patiently. Was it possible that they had committed some foolish act — such as jail breaking?

"Yes; this is the Agent. Oh, the sheriff — they have n't given you the slip?"

"No," replied the officer, "the Indians are here, all right. I called you up to ask about feeding them."

"Feeding the prisoners, you mean?"

"Yes, those Isleta Indians. They had supper last night, and breakfast this morning, and — "

"Well! They 'll also require lunch, or dinner, according to the mode, and then again supper, and so on, three meals a day until — "

"But look here," challenged the sheriff, agitation in his voice, "I am not pressing the charges against these men. I offered to leave them in the Albuquerque jail, or to accept your word that they would be on hand for trial."

"Quite true. Nor am I prosecuting them. You have them, in your jail, as prisoners, and they will require three meals a day."

"But will you settle the meal account?" he queried anxiously.

"I! I did n't have those men arrested. They are a charge on Sandoval County; and please, Mr. Sheriff, permit me to counsel you — the United States will examine into this matter very carefully, so do not neglect to serve them three meals a day."

"No! They're not a charge on Sandoval County, either," he responded, heatedly. "They have become a charge on the sheriff of Sandoval County, and I do not see myself paying for their grub until you get ready to bail them out. Unless you agree to furnish them, I intend to open the jail door and boost them into the street."

"That will be perfectly satisfactory to me, Mr. Sheriff."

So he did, to the intense delight of everyone, including the Indians. The Special Pueblo Counsel said he had not heard the like since Mark Twain wrote a book. The matter was never brought to my attention again, for Sandoval County apparently was permanently out of meal money, and the case never came to trial.

And the pueblos of New Mexico have approximately 17,000 acres of land each, to the four winds, measured from the temple in the plaza; and so it was recorded by the Chairman of the House Committee in his report. Let us survey the actual Isleta domain on the Rio Grande: —

The original Isleta grant, confirmed by Act of Congress in 1854 . . . . 110,080 acres

About the year 1760 the Isletas purchased from the heirs of Lo an area that they call the "Lo de Padilla" grant, originally about 40,000 acres, from which they sold in about 1806 a tract of 15,000 acres. This is on the east side of the Rio Grande . . . . 25,000 acres

About the year 1775 they purchased what are known to them as the "Juaquin Sedillo" and "Antonio Gutierres" grants, west of the Rio Grande, from the heirs of those persons . . . . 27,000 acres

The above three "purchases" were confirmed to the Isleta pueblo by the Court of Private Land Claims in 1897. Between these areas is a tract known as the "Bosque de Pino." About 1825 a native citizen borrowed it to pasture mules thereon, and thereafter kept it. The Court of Private Land Claims not only confirmed him in this little matter, but added a small tract to it, about 700 acres west of the Bosque, formed by the Rio Grande in the process of changing its course during the years. This tract is now held by a district politician of the state of New Mexico, who should not be accused of having had anything to do with the condition of title. He simply inherited.

Because of error in the survey of the original east line, the pueblo was deprived for years of a tract, and fortunately protected from complete loss by its being included in a National Forest. Through the efforts of Assistant Secretary of the Interior Alexander Vogelsang, it was finally decided that the pueblo should have this territory, less those mining claims and patented homesteads that had been acquired by whites in the interval, and less all the grazing fees that had been collected by the Forestry Department.
Estimated roughly . . . . 12,000 acres

Thus the total land holdings of the Isleta pueblo are approximately 174,080 acres. Or, if you happen to be quick at mental arithmetic, just ten times the land surface of the usual Spanish grant to Indians (four square leagues) and held by the pueblo of Isleta under the terms of a treaty between sovereign nations — not a treaty made with conquered, inferior, and dependent Indians that the

Congress is not bound to respect, but the Treaty of Guadalupe Hidalgo, made with Mexico, and concerning in part its one-time subjects.

The religious calendar of the Isleta pueblo is similar to those observed by the other pueblos, but it has little distinctions of its own: —

January 6 begins a celebration of four days in honor of the newly commissioned pueblo officials. On the first day a dance occurs before their several houses, and the dancers expect that presents will be distributed among them.

February brings a day when the Indians dance as a petition to the Great Spirit for a good year in crops, rain, and game.

March sees the turning of water into the acequia (ditch), the Rio Grande then contributing its liquid gold, and this event is celebrated.

Palm Sunday is marked by a foot race for the little boys, aged from five to twelve years.

Easter brings the annual foot races, contested on three Sundays, the fourth Sunday being a challenge race like that Lummis has so vividly described in his *Land of Poco Tiempo*. When this race is finished there is a war dance.

In June (without a fixed date) a Mass is celebrated, and after the service the statue of San Agustín is carried by the Indians over the fields. When they return to the pueblo, the statue is placed in a shrine, and a dance continues until sunset.

August 28 is the Feast of San Agustín, the pueblo's patron, but because of many visitors to the church on this feast day, the actual fiesta is celebrated on the octave, or September 4, called "San Agustinito Day." It is a duplicate of the fiestas that have been described.

September is the occasion for an Evergreen Dance, taking place in the latter part of the month and explained as a rite of thanksgiving for a bountiful year.

THE PEOPLE OF THE LITTLE ISLAND 331

Christmas brings the four days of dances in honor of the Nativity. The last day, December 28, is commemorated as "Innocents Day," to memorialize the slaying of the newborn under Herod, and on that day only the little children dance.

The ancient scalp dance is now extinct, the practice no longer being observed by the Isletas and there seeming no good reason for its celebration. The last gruesome ceremony of this type occurred in February 1878, when the last Apache scalp was brought in.

In the great Revolt of 1680, Isleta, for a time, stood quiescent. As a portal on the Great South Road, the town served as a rendezvous for all those Spanish who fled the central pueblos. No doubt this influx interrupted communication between the Isletas and the insurrectionists in the north, and the inhabitants took no part in the massacre of colonists and priests.

At this time, in the neighborhood of Albuquerque — between the present Sandia and Isleta pueblos — were nineteen Spanish ranchos, haciendas, and so forth, indicating a considerable number of colonists settled along the Isleta highway. Albuquerque was not founded until 1706.

When Governor Otermin retreated from Santa Fe he found Isleta abandoned, as the earlier fugitives had preceded him southward. In 1681, when he sought to reconquer the Pueblo provinces, he first captured Isleta, and when he returned from the north, in January 1682, he took with him to El Paso del Norte 385 of the inhabitants of Isleta. The remainder of the population had scattered among the rebels, and, like the Sandias, some of them went to the Hopi country. Those that Otermin marched to El Paso were settled in a pueblo named "Isleta del Sur" (Isleta of the South). To-day, Isleta del Sur, where survivors of the Mansos tribe and some of the Piros were settled also, has lost its Indian significance.

When Oñate established the mission districts in 1598, Isleta, wherever it stood, fell to the pastorship of Fray Juan Claros, and this was its first contact with the Franciscans. The original church and monastery, erected by Fray Juan de Salas before July 1629, were regarded by Benavides and Vetancurt as especially fine for their day. Hodge states that the date of the reëstablishment of Isleta, after the revolt, is somewhat in doubt; but there is good evidence that Tihua families were assembled at the ruined pueblo in 1709, later to be joined by those who had fled to the Hopi country, and augmented by remnants of the Piros.

The present church is a huge building of very thick adobe walls supported by rounded buttresses. Its architectural value has suffered through repairs to roof and bell towers made in a modern manner, so that it resembles an old adobe fort crowned with two wooden towers. It is most unfortunate that the Franciscans have no funds available for the proper restoration of these historical monuments, for while Isleta has been a parish for many years in charge of a secular priest, the church is Franciscan and should accurately picture its past.

In my judgment, the most interesting feature of it to be remarked as late as 1922 was the padre's garden, the pride of aged Father Anton Docher, who served at Isleta thirty-five years and only recently retired because of failing sight. Father Docher first served at Bernalillo, and next at the pueblo of Taos. He came to the Isleta parish in 1891, and was a venerable man when I first met him. I shall always remember him as the bearded padre of the mission garden, where the bees droned among the cacti,

THE MISSION OF SAN AGUSTIN AT ISLETA

FATHER ANTON DOCHER IN HIS GARDEN

where the golden pheasants and parrots lived, and the aged magpie rasped its blessings or curses — one could never determine which. In his little office he would receive his friends, and, as a mark of special distinction, show his medals — that one gained in Morocco as a soldier, that one given him by the King of Belgium. A son of France, a trooper in Africa, then a padre among Indians in a Spanish atmosphere, heir to the ancient mission of Fray Juan de Salas, whose simple traditions he preserved for one third of a century! Isleta should not soon forget him.

Aside from stalking the Conquistadors and warring with Apaches de Navajo, Isleta has seen stirring times. What a wealth of world history has passed in review before this somnolent hamlet of adobes! Seventy years after its reëstablishment, it heard of war in the East, the founding of a new government on this continent, and a little later of a place called "Washington." But what effect could that have on Isleta, the dusty outpost of another nation? Another quarter of a century slipped away drowsily, when a cavalcade of Spanish troops, escorting a red-haired officer of these new Americans, passed through their pueblo on the road to the Spanish capital. A brave fellow, they no doubt said; and a prisoner — perhaps a spy. Fourteen more years and there was revolution in the south that cost the Spanish their northern New World colonies. The status of Isleta changed, and she passed from the red-and-gold banner that for two hundred and twenty-three years had dominated New Mexico to the Mexican flag. Twenty-five years under Mexican jefe politicos. Then Isleta heard that the long-feared Texans were advancing on Santa Fe; but that campaign ended in failure. Next the Americans were at San Miguel, at Santa Fe, and

Doniphan's column marched down the river to battle at Chihuahua, a campaign which was not a failure. Isleta realized that this new state of Washington had conquered Mexico. Another flag! — one of red and white, the Isleta colors, and many stars. Soon they were summoned to council with a new "Ah-hin-ti," one Calhoun, who had been sent to Santa Fe to rule them. Perhaps, if they thought anything about these events, they believed that General George himself had become aware of them and their problems. It would soon be a name to conjure with, — WASHINGTON! — only to be matched, within a few momentous years, by the name of LINCOLN!

They would have no more to do with kings. Charles I, great Philip II, who had sent forth the Armada; Philip III, Philip IV, Charles II, Philip V, grandson of Le Grand Monarque; Ferdinand VI, Charles III, Charles IV, Ferdinand VII, followed by that protégé of a whirlwind, Joseph Bonaparte; and then again Ferdinand VII until the Mexican colonies rebelled — all these had ruled over Isleta, and had disappeared into the twilight of time. Iturbide, clad in the last of the purple, followed them. They were to receive royal notice but once again, in 1919, when Albert, King of Belgium, paid them a call.

The celebration at Isleta pueblo in honor of Belgium's King was an affair stimulated by the citizens of Albuquerque. They had little to show the royal guest that he had not seen in other Southwest towns, but there was the ancient pueblo only thirteen miles away. So the hustling secretary for the Chamber of Commerce enlisted the interest of the Indian Agent, who pledged that Isleta plaza would furnish an historic stage, with the Franciscan cathedral as a back drop, and the entire Indian population as a colorful mob. In this plan the native governor and the padre joined, together with Superintendent Reuben Perry, of the Albuquerque Indian School, who would furnish an Indian band and two companies of Indian cadets to assist the city and pueblo police in preserving traffic regulations. The Indians constructed a dais in the plaza for their Majesties, covering it with rare Navajo blankets; they erected two flagpoles, that the Belgian flag might float side by side with the Stars and Stripes; they decorated the houses of the plaza with bunting, and agreed to appear fully arrayed in the national costume. Only the padre seemed at a loss for banners, and so that he might feel sufficiently patriotic, I dispatched an order to Denver for two large French and Belgian flags, being able to furnish him with the largest American flag ever seen in those parts. My idea was that the bell towers of the mission would be the proper places for the display of the French and Belgian ensigns, and that the very large American flag would show to best advantage if draped above the balcony across the front of the church.

My final concern was for the appearance of the Indian police. As Chief Officer Louis Abeita would rank as the commanding officer on the ground, it seemed to me that he should not stand out before those well-groomed Indian cadets in dingy khaki and red stripes. And I knew that Louis would never wear one of those contract sombreros, with a gilt string around it, that the Chicago warehouse sent us to serve as Stetsons. I wanted an officer who would look in keeping with Louis's record at the pueblos. So the Indian School tailor promptly built him a uniform of blue to correspond with those worn by the cadets, and the town hatter supplied a real Stetson of the proper frontier size, shape, and color. There was no prouder soldier on the field than this Indian, who, with ex-Service men and the city police, handled the crowd as if it were on parade. And it was a crowd. Please remember that a King and Queen are not common sights in the Southwest.

The pueblo gobernador, Señor J. Felipe Abeita, received the King and Queen with a speech in his native tongue that was translated by his official interpreter; and the King graciously decorated the Indian governor. Their Majesties were entertained, I hope, by an Indian dance, the stars of which had been imported from Laguna for the occasion; and then a frontier quadrille was performed by mounted cowmen. The band played "La Brabançonne," and then the padre met the royal guests at the mission door to escort them through the old church of the Franciscans, while the moving-picture men ground away at their camera cranks.

Standing in the plaza, I was approached by an American army officer of the King's escort, who said: —

"Crane, I have been about in various quarters of the world, and I had thought that I had seen nearly everything; but you have pulled a stunt here that stands alone."

Now this was more of praise than I had expected, and naturally I asked in what way our little fiesta scene took precedence over all those arranged for the boredom of the King and Queen. And the officer explained.

"Why," he said, "I have seen the American flag in all manner of situations; but never before have I seen the American flag raised above the cross on a Catholic church."

It was true! Old Father Docher had followed literally my instructions. He had placed the American flag in the centre of his church. Over one bell tower floated the flag of Belgium, over its companion waved the flag of

France; but high above them all, its staff supported by the cross itself, was the starry banner that had come west with Kearny and Doniphan. If this be treason, make the most of it.

A motley picture assembled before the King. He was escorted by the state governor, who was of the Spanish; welcomed by a Tihua-Indian gobernador; received in a Franciscan mission over which presided a French priest, who treasured the Moroccan medal and who had nailed an American flag to his cross; surrounded by native tribes and a frontier multitude, one half of which spoke the Mexican dialect. To me, aside from my chagrin at having caused Father Docher innocently to misuse the sacred symbol, there was one pathetic note in all this. In this old plaza, once an important station of the King's Highway, a place that had seen much of Spanish valor, there was no emblem of Spain. Then I remembered that when the royal retinue approached the pueblo its arrival had been vigorously announced by the mission bells, gifts of the Spanish kings.

XVI

LEGENDS AND LEASES

> "Have you seen the wooded ledges
> And the cliffs of San Diego —
> Where the Guadalupe murmurs
> And the Rio Jemez flows?
> There the padre, Juan de Jesus,
> Taught the Indians *Pater Nosters;*
> And for thanks they spoiled his altar,
> And for pence they gave him blows.
> Juan de Jesus, of Granada —
> Priest and pioneer and martyr!
> Sleeps in Santa Fe's old chapel,
> Deaf to savages and Kings!
> But the hour of *Matins* calls him
> To his walk, the Jemez Abbey;
>   To the solace of his garden
>   And the cadence of his choir,
>   Where the cliffs resound responses
>   And the Rio Jemez sings.
>
> —"Legend"

At several places in my narrative I have sought to suggest, as delicately as possible, that I am not filled with an overwhelming courage. I have scrambled about in Hopi villages, and a few Navajo camps, and through New Mexican pueblos by night, but never with a feeling of assurance. If one did not fall over the woodpile, he would into the ditch; in the Hopi country he could easily tumble off the mesa, and around Navajo camps some nervous seneschal, fearful of a *chinti*, might discharge a cannon and inventory the damage after daylight.

But, despite this natural timidity, I have always wanted to see a ghost. In the Pueblo provinces, where so much of history is buried, it seemed to me that I should have my ambition satisfied at some time or other. I am not particular about the sort or style of ghost, providing it is one possessing and exercising reasonable dignity — that is to say, not likely to proceed to extremes. At first I fancied that I might have the good fortune to view the shade of some long-forgotten padre going his rounds; and the spectre of a conquistador, clanking about in full panoply of armor and plumes, would have been worth telling about. I will not definitely assert that I longed to meet that native patriot, Popé, or his friend Catiti, brandishing either a scalp or a chalice; and Governor Perez, with his head under his arm, was no more inviting.

One winter's night at the Jemez pueblo I thought the long-nursed ambition would be satisfied. I had left an Indian's house, going from the light of his kerosene lamp into the pitch black suddenly, got turned around, fell into the community ditch, and was a long time struggling to my temporary quarters at the monastery, which, by the way, is situated at the farthest end of a long, narrow, very black lane completely filled with pueblo dogs. Perhaps these minor adventures had brought me to a fit condition for the ghostly encounter. Anyway, having turned in, I fell asleep, and in the night was aroused by a faint and anxious voice, calling from a great distance. A bitter winter storm had set in, with a howling wind, and sleet beating at the panes, and the night as black as the inside of a derby hat. Again came that voice, filled with anxiety and something like despair — a muffled voice, reaching out against the forces of the wind. And it was summoning me by name: —

"Crane! Oh, Crane!" accompanied by a dash of hail.

All I could see was the faint outline of the room's window, and now something was fumbling at the upper sash. I looked to see mistily a tall figure — outside the window — I was thankful for that — and it was vehemently demanding admittance. I was about to refuse firmly monastic shelter to this strange midnight guest, when — Pshaw! It proved to be Robinson. I had thought him in bed long ago; but he too had been belated, and had suffered adventures in the lane, and had found himself locked out in the storm, with the padres as deaf as adders, and I nearly as bad. Well! It was no ghost — not unless a tall angular government engineer may be considered one, whereas the Jemez pueblo country should be able to produce a number of more interesting apparitions to accompany its equally colorful legends.

One finds, though, that legends are too often constructed to fit the scenery, like that one concerning the departure of Fray Jesus Maria Casanes, victim of the short rebellion of 1696. This padre had both friends and enemies among the native people. It is related that he was called out at night to hear the confession of a sick man, and when responding to this duty was waylaid and beaten to death in the cemetery of the old Abbey.

This was but the culmination of the plan of revolt; but now we have a legend, to the end that the saintly padre had a premonition of the plot and secretly left the pueblo of San Diego, going by way of the Jemez Hot Springs. The Indians say that early on the morning of the day set for his death, his enemies surrounded the convento and waited for him to go to the celebration of the Mass. He did not appear. They then ventured to open his door, and found that his bed was untouched. Then they cautiously searched for him, intending to put him to death when found; but this had to be done without alarming the suspicions of his friends among the decent Indians. The rebels found his trail leading to the Springs. To their surprise, a fog of vapors was arising from the waters, and they heard sweet singing. The Springs that theretofore had been ordinary springs only were then discovered to be hot, and having medicinal qualities, the gift of this padre who had vanished; and they now say that each spring is typical of some virtue practised by the holy man, and will cure diseases of the soul as well as of the body.

A very nice legend, until one begins to examine its several parts, when we find that it has three principal points supported by the record, to wit: there was a Fray Jesus Maria Casanes — an entirely separate and distinct entity from Fray Juan de Jesus, who was martyred by the Jemez in 1680; and that he was killed by these rebellious Indians in 1696 somewhere in the San Diego Cañon not far from the old ruins; and that there are hot springs in that locality.

I suppose such a legend is sufficient for the relief of vacation time, when people are not critical; but my mind has a serious and practical bent, and in so far as any ghost or any legend is concerned I desire at least some fragments of data on which to build. So it seemed that my search would never discover any such treasure. The trouble was in my going abroad, unmindful of a sure-enough periodical ghost only thirteen miles from my doorstep. But for a magazine article, decked out with very old pictures to lend the appearance of age, I might never have stumbled across it. To be exact as to the geography, this persistent ghost frequented Isleta when in the mood for appearing, and I determined to investigate as did Doctor Johnson in Cock Lane. Certainly, if there were a standard ghost worthy of respect that had selected Isleta for its walks, either the Reverend Father Docher or Señor Pablo Abeita, perhaps both, would know of its habits. I interviewed the padre first, because this ghost was reported to be of the Franciscan Order with headquarters at the mission. Father Docher proved a poor directory for ghosts.

"I have heard about that ancient padre," he said, gravely; and then he smiled. "They say he is accommodating, in that he returns at regular intervals; but, alas! my son, he is now overdue. And if he comes back, at least I have not seen him —"

It was disappointing.

I crossed the plaza to the store of my Indian friend, Pablo, and we sat in his cool side room for a talk. Ordinarily we discussed pueblo affairs, such as when the Council would meet, and who was in jail, and just what our superiors at Washington should do about this and that; but on this occasion I plunged into the more important matter.

"What do you know of the old priest who comes back?"

"About as much as anyone," he replied, casually, "But I haven't seen the old gentleman in a long time."

"You have not seen him — in a long time —."

This was a startling confirmation.

"You mean to tell me that you have observed this perambulating padre who is not content with resting in his perfectly good grave?"

Pablo nodded, again seriously.

"I do," he said. "It was twenty-seven years ago when I saw him."

Suddenly it occurred to me that there was n't anything funny about it. Here sat a man, possessed, if I were any judge, of sound common sense — of course, I mean "Indian sense," a brand not always inferior to our white varieties of wisdom — who calmly, determinedly, and with the utmost gravity, asserted that he had seen the ghostly padre! Now Pablo usually laughed with me when there was anything to laugh about. The Pueblo Indians are a good-humored people, and, if they know you, pleasantry and smiles are customary. But Indians do not laugh about things that interest them deeply, and I could feel that this padre was no joking matter. Perhaps some clown had happened along to ridicule it.

"And you say that he returns, regularly?"

"There is evidence that Indians of the pueblo have seen him at different times. I saw him just once; but I believe that I could have seen him a second time if Father Docher had listened to me."

Here was my chance at last. A ghost! A real one — that had been seen, and, praise be! was expected to appear again on schedule.

"Pablo," I urged, earnestly, "tell me about it, and if you can figure out when the next public appearance will be, I want a ring-side seat."

He shook his head despondently. That chilled my enthusiasm. I knew there would be a jigger in it somewhere. There always is.

"I fear it will never occur again," he said. "The old man is nailed down. I helped to lay the new floor in the church, and I told Father Docher that we were holding Fray Juan de Padilla down with those spikes. I wanted to move the altar then, to satisfy ourselves about him. But I will tell you what I know of the case."

He lighted one of his special corn-husk cigarettes to keep me company, and related this strange thing: —

"It was twenty-seven years ago that Fray Juan de Padilla last appeared. In those days the wooden floor had become old and thin, and close to the altar the ground cracked. We called this to the attention of the priest, but he thought little of it. Then, about a week later, the crack had become large and was growing larger. Something was pushing up from below, and it looked like a coffin. And this thing pushing up was a coffin. Then the padre reported to his superiors, and they came to see for themselves. There were the Archbishop of Santa Fe, and a prelate from Baltimore, and another priest from this part of the country; and there were two doctors, also. Of the pueblo people present, there were José Chiguigui, who was our Governor then, and my brother, Marcelino, who was the Lieutenant Governor, and old Diego Abeita's son-in-law, whose name was Juan Andrés Zuñi; and there was my mother and myself. With all these witnesses, the business proceeded.

"This coffin in sight was the section of a cottonwood tree. It had been shaped and hollowed out with an axe or adze, and when we opened it I remember that they had left a place for the padre's pillow. The coffin was sound, even the splinters of it being hard.

"Within the coffin was the body of a friar, in vestments very much like those now worn by the Franciscans. He had on a small skull cap, with a fringe or tassel on the top. The appearance of this body was as if it had been dried; the features were plain, but like rawhide. The eyes were sunken and closed. There was a wound on the left side of the neck, just above the shoulder, and traditional history is to the effect that Juan de Padilla died of a wound like that. His left foot was broken off at the ankle, but this had occurred a long time after his death. We could see that. It came from handling the body at other times —."

At this point of his story my interest began to wane, for a mummified body did not seem half so interesting, nor one tenth as gruesome as the corpse I had myself exhumed in the old Acoma graveyard. Seismic disturbances could have accounted for the upward thrust of the cottonwood-log coffin, perhaps, although it did not seem likely without damage to other parts of the church. The dried condition of the body did not check up well with the fact that Isleta is raised but little above the Rio Grande, the water table of the entire valley at that time being reported by our engineers at an average of twenty-three inches. One could find seepage at six feet anywhere, even in Albuquerque. But the body could have been mummified at some distant place, before having been brought to Isleta. His mention of the first martyr, Juan de Padilla, did not move me to argument, because some such historical personage would naturally have been associated with such a legend, to lend it the highest color. Padilla died in what is now Kansas, and I had little idea that his body would have been packed all the way to Isleta for interment. In any case, there it was, — a good ghost story reduced to nothing, — the whole thing resolving itself into the prosaic business of opening an old coffin.

And friend Pablo continued: —

"Each of us who saw the body made a statement in writing, and these written statements, or affidavits, were then rolled up in corn husks first, and then in sabino bark, and placed in the coffin, along with pen, ink, and paper."

"Why the writing materials?" I interrupted.

"Well! Old Padilla was in the habit of coming back, and being received with courtesy; and, should there be a time when his coming did n't interest anybody, he might want to leave a message."

That revived my interest.

"You mean that this business had occurred before?"

"I do. The time I am speaking of now was twenty-seven years ago, or in 1894. Now old Diego Abeita — no kinsman of mine, for there are three sets of Abeitas at Isleta without their being related — this old man was one hundred and eighteen years old when he died. His death occurred about fifteen years ago. His eyesight was good and so was his hearing, until the very date of his death. Now he had been sacristan for the church from the time he was a boy of about ten years until within several years of his death. That would give him close to a hundred years of service as sacristan, would n't it? And he made oath that he had assisted in reburying the old padre five or six times during that period. Each time the coffin came up just as we saw it. Most of that time there was no wooden floor in the church. So — allowing him five times — that would mean a return every twenty years. And in the pueblo then were several persons who testified that they had seen the old padre at least once before the time I saw him.

"Twenty years after 1894, or in 1914, I helped to lay a new floor in the church. I went to the place at the altar and tried to force a saw down between the cracks of the old worn-out floor. It would go down eleven or twelve inches, and no farther, for it struck something solid. Then I told Father Docher that Fray Juan de Padilla was getting close to the top again; and I asked his permission to move the altar, just to see if he was coming around on time. But Father Docher did n't believe in such things, and he paid no attention, and we laid the new floor over the old one without learning any more about him. As for myself, I firmly believe the old man was getting to the top again; which would be according to his schedule, once every twenty years. This last time, I don't think he was given a good show for it."

"So, I am never likely to see him!" I said, disconsolately.

"Not with two floors over him, and the boards spiked down."

And there it went, higher than Gilderoy's kite, and my ambitions are still unsatisfied. The whole matter turned me decidedly against modern improvements in these old Franciscan missions. The padres may think me critical, but when one sees what has been done to the churches of Cochiti, San Ildefonsò, Isleta, and others, there is reason in my view. Towers of wood and gaunt corrugated iron roofs do not improve old relics, the artistic atmosphere of which should be preserved as sacred to our oldest ecclesiastical monuments, and should be as precious to the Southwest as is Independence Hall in the East. And, aside from art and reverence, when one permits a bunch of carpenters to destroy a perfectly good periodical ghost, it is sacrilege!

I like legends; but documented legends are elusive. For a long time I was watchful, and then, lo! I came full tilt on the portrait of San José, still hanging in the sanctuary of the Acoma Mission church, on the gospel side of the altar, dimmed beyond recognition, a venerated relic. Now here is something like! This legend is fairly old, and leads one through community quarrels, to threat of battle, to the courts. Judge Kirby Benedict, a robust figure of the early New Mexican Bar, put the official seal on this one, and his decision was affirmed by the Supreme Court of the Territory in 1857.

It is alleged that Fray Juan Ramirez, the first resident missionary to the Acomas, who journeyed to them about 1629, installed this picture in his first church as the gift of King Charles II of Spain. And it would appear that there is some belief that the first patron for Acoma was San José. Later it became San Estevan, then San Pedro (as is recorded on the bell), and again San Estevan. When Laguna received San José as its patron, Acoma being in possession of a rare painting of that saint, the Lagunas conceived the desire to possess the symbol. The case of the picture was finally adjudicated in 1857. But its militant history must have begun at least ten years before, since the briefs mention "the priest Lopez," and Fray Mariano de Jesus Lopez was the last of the Franciscans in New Mexico after the expulsion of them as an Order. He resided at Isleta, and had charge of Laguna and Acoma, from January 1846 to July 1847. During his time the controversy reached a boiling point.

The briefs recite that the Lagunas borrowed the painting for the celebration of Holy Week; and other records indicate that they petitioned Acoma to lend it as a temporary help against poor crops and much sickness that they were experiencing. If the Acomas actually acceded to a request on either ground, then they were in a charitable mood for once in their career, as they graciously lent the painting to their neighbors. But having obtained possession of it, the Lagunas neglected to return it. And with the more reason, as their crops improved and other distresses vanished. Behind the whole affair, however, there must have been some ground on which the Lagunas based a belief of actual ownership, since they maintained a claim of such ownership before the courts when appealing from Judge Benedict's decision. Quite likely this ground was the childlike theory that the Mission of San José de la Laguna should possess the image of San José, since the Acoma Mission was devoted to San Estevan. Why should not Acoma go forth into the art world and procure for itself a picture of its own patron, something in keeping with its sacred family? Why should the ancient clan of Browns treasure the ancestral portrait of a Jones?

But the Acoma people did not think so. They demanded the return of their property. They appealed to the padre, who directed that the painting should be returned to Acoma, and cited both pueblos to appear before him at that place. He proposed that they attend Mass, and after prayer to God and the Saint himself that justice and equity might prevail in this cause, they should expect some decision. To this the pueblos agreed. They no doubt prayed with earnestness and fervor, but no decision was handed down to them. The padre, very likely at his wits' end, for a large number of moody Indians were assembled to represent each claimant, suggested that they cast lots for the painting. This was agreed to. Twelve lots were prepared, all blank save one, and that one bearing the picture of San José. Two little Indian girls then drew for the two pueblos interested. The first, second, third, and fourth tickets drawn were blanks; then Acoma drew the fifth lot bearing the picture. The padre then said that God had decided the case, and that the decision should be accepted.

All Acoma and some of the Lagunas accepted it; but others of the Lagunas were dissatisfied with this adverse decision. They grouched for a while, and then appeared before the Acoma church in a body, and threatened to break down the doors if the Saint were not at once delivered to them. It looked very much as if the sacred precincts, and perhaps San José himself, would witness a Donnybrook Fair. Again the padre appeared, and, seeing the temper of the Laguna cohort, advised the Acomas to surrender the picture to avoid bloodshed. This was done.

But naturally an adjustment after this fashion did not suit Acoma. If this opéra bouffe occurred in 1847, — and the presence of "the priest Lopez" indicates that it did, — then the Acomas waited to present their plea to the first courts of the Americans. One witness swore that unless San José is with Acoma, the people thereof cannot prevail with God. The final decision in this strange case includes the following language, showing that the court was not unmindful of either the venerable religious aspects or the comic features involved: —

From the above testimony it is clearly deducible that said painting is an object of great veneration to the pueblo of Acoma, as well from its supposed spiritual protecting patronage as its high antiquity among them. . . .

The intrinsic value of the oil, paint, and cloth upon which San José is represented to the senses, it has been admitted in argument, probably would not amount to two bits, but this seemingly worthless painting has well-nigh cost these two pueblos a bloody and cruel struggle, and had it not been for weakness on the part of one of the pueblos, its history might have been written in blood. . . .

Finding that the courts would not sustain their claims to the painting, the Lagunas were somewhat abashed, if not ashamed, and the diplomatic ones among them began casting about for a method of relieving their foolish position. Receiving news of the final decision somewhat earlier than did the Acomas, they proceeded to carry the famous painting to a point in the desert about halfway between the two pueblos, and deposited San José under a tree by the trail. There the Acoma delegation, forwarded to escort the picture to its rightful home, happened to find it. Here was a miracle! Their patron had become so dissatisfied that he had started to walk back to Acoma!

In recent years, certain Fathers of the Church were interested in having the painting restored if possible. But the Acomas said, No! A most emphatic No! They lost him once; and it is not likely that they will ever run the risk of losing him again.

Thus we have fanciful legend, personal experience, and Court record from which to select. All are disappointing to those who may have expected an Indian Agent to unearth something more than a Cock Lane ghost. I can only say that an official has little time in which to collect old wives' tales, and that one who respects the reticence and privacy of his wards will not be likely to come away from them ballasted with a portfolio of Smithsonian papers or a Hans Christian Andersen supply of folk tales. It is no part of the duty of an Indian Agent to become interested in these things, no matter how engaging, so long as there are red lessees requiring grazing lands, and red patients needing medical attention, and red children lacking schools. Such sordid affairs demand his every day, and sometimes every hour, leaving him very little leisure — indeed, little unjaded mentality — for the consideration of romance. If you will accept a frank confession from me, it is the governmental farce that should, for sheer interest and involved construction, outrank anything the Indian country produces of history, folklore, or other phenomena, cultural or not.

Let us consider the farce of the Ready-made Lessees. The Lagunas have more cattle and sheep than any of the other pueblos, and their sales of wool are large enough to interest brokers operating on the Boston market. But to grow wool, one must have sheep, and to support sheep, one must control large grazing areas in the semiarid Southwest, where it requires from six to eight acres to maintain one head of healthful sheep. A sufficiency of such grazing the Lagunas did not possess; but they had friends who concerned themselves in an effort to improve their interests. Two Executive Orders resulted, one signed by President Taft in 1910 and the other by President Wilson in 1917, withdrawing and reserving for their benefit 146,879.57 acres.

Such an area, taken in connection with their original Spanish grant, and the Paguate, El Rito, Gigante, and San Juan Rancho "purchases," gave a grand total of nearly 265,000 acres (over 400 square miles). One might suspect that with such a tract the Indians had enough. But one should remember that 30,000 head of sheep (6 acres each), 3000 head of cattle, and 1000 head of horses (20 acres each) stock this area very thickly, leaving but a small remainder for pueblos and agricultural purposes. And this, considering the type of land, is the standard live-stock allowance.

The railroad, now the Santa Fe system, which in 1881 was built across New Mexico and Arizona to connect with the Pacific Coast, was an enormous venture financially, and the country between the Rocky Mountains and the Sierra Nevadas did not promise much. It was sparsely settled, and, judging from its surface advantages, if any, and the lack of water for drinking purposes, looked as if it never would attract people from the choicer lands of the Middle West. It was clearly up to the Government to encourage these railroad pioneers, and it did. It was necessary to negotiate with the various pueblos for rights of way across their Spanish grants, but the United States owned all the lands surrounding them. And thus the railroad, in those sections not controlled by the Pueblo Indians, acquired rights of way that varied from a few miles to forty miles, in alternate sections, each side of its track. In area it was nothing short of an empire, and until very recent times this possession made all sorts of grief for the Indians of the various tribes, for their Agents and, in an absent and mildly interested manner, for the Indian Bureau. I do not wish to charge the Indian Bureau with worrying about it; but the Bureau was forced, every now and again, to dust off the maps and stare at them in a helpless fashion. Thus we find this situation at Laguna:—

	COMPLETE AREA	LAND HELD UNDER RAILROAD TITLE
Executive Order, 1910	29,665.09 acres	1,453.47 acres
Executive Order, 1917	117,214.48 acres	36,602.39 acres
	146,879.57 acres	38,055.86 acres

That is to say, of the reservations made for the sustenance of the Laguna herds, the New Mexico and Arizona Land Company, a subsidiary company of the Santa Fe Railway, possessing the management of such lands, held title to more than twenty-five per cent. And this twenty-five per cent was checkerboarded over the whole area withdrawn, each alternate section being at the disposal of the railroad's representatives; so that during an afternoon an Indian shepherd would graze his flocks first on a section controlled by his tribe under the Agent's jurisdiction, and next on a section with which they had little to do. It was all legally "Indian country" for the purpose of controlling the liquor traffic; but in other ways had a string to it. Moreover, water — precious water — had not been arranged for by the Creator in accord with government surveys, Executive Orders, or railroad titles.

Now observe the niceties of the situation. The New Mexico and Arizona Land Company said, and perhaps justly: —

"These Indian people are in possession of our lands. They should pay for the use of them."

But the Land Company was not in position to rent those lands to others should the Indians decide not to use them, for that would have necessitated fencing each separate tract, since a white lessee would immediately become a trespasser on the Indian area unless his stock were controlled; and no stockman could hold his animals within a single section, for water might prove to be several sections away. The matter resolved itself simply into this: the Indian, since he was at home, and had by necessity to graze his stock over the entire area, was forced to become a trespasser *unless he leased the railroad sections.* Or he could avoid this unpleasant feature by going out of the stock business. Argal, the Indian was the only possible lessee, and to keep from becoming a trespasser, he had to lease. He was a lessee ready-made.

So the Indian stock owners leased the railroad lands, on the advice of their Agent, who thought that at no distant date the railroad company could be eliminated through exchange of lands — that is, by receiving other tracts elsewhere. Among others, Reverend Father Anselm Weber personally brought this matter to the attention of the Washington officials, and slowly the ponderous wheels began to grind. And in the meantime the Laguna stock owners dribbled their little fees into the wallet of the Land Company — to pay for benefits two Presidents had awarded them.

Remember, too, that these Indians had inhabited, cultivated, and otherwise used these lands two hundred years before the Land Company appeared on the horizon, and, for that matter, one hundred years before our Government began deciding anything. Also, a pertinent point in argument, the United States, through its Indian Bureau and its Agents, had educated these Indians and urged them — shoved them in a measure — into the position of stock owners.

But somehow or other — you know how these things happen in a great country, where everybody is busy attending to his own business — the lands were not exchanged. Eleven years had passed since the order from President Taft, and four years since the order from President Wilson. It was now 1921, with a feeble hope still glimmering at the Indian Agency and considerable unrest in the pueblo.

We have now arrived at the office of the Indian Agent on North Second Street in Albuquerque, New Mexico, a place removed several blocks from the office of the New Mexico and Arizona Land Company on South Second Street in Albuquerque, New Mexico. In the first-named office complaints were being received from the company that grazing fees were not being paid by the Indians, and Indians were being received complaining that they just could not raise the money. Also, the telephone brought notifications from the land company that still other Indians had not signed new leases to succeed those that were expiring. Thus, you will perceive, another factor had entered into the problem. The Indian Agent, a Federal official appointed for the guidance and protection of Indians, had become, first, a rounder-up of Indian lessees for the land company, and, second, a collection agency for the land company. And the attitude of the Indian Bureau could be expected to be, as ever: "Surely, Mr. Crane, the Laguna Indians would not refuse to pay their just and legal grazing-fee debts!" Because, if behind anything existed a law, or the distorted semblance of a law, we must accept the thing humbly, with a Christian humility that even the Franciscans did not possess. Dr. Johnson would never have found reason to say to the Indian Bureau: "I perceive, Sir, that you are a vile Whig." The Stamp Act would have gone unchallenged. Taxation is no tyranny! But the modern Englishman frequently sums up a situation like this in better words than I can summon:—

Justice existed when there was no need for judges; and mercy existed before any man was oppressed.

To add to the merriment, the representative of the land company became more or less peevish. I suppose that behind him too was an office, pressing for its doles. He found that the Pueblo Indians could not be sued successfully for debt — or, if some state court entered judgment against them, their stock and equipment, their homes and lands, could not be seized to satisfy the judgment. This was a terrible state of affairs. But all would be satisfactory if the Indian Agent would continue to act as whipper-in.

Now there was no way by which the Indian Agent could get around advising the Indians to pay promptly their

Photo. by H. F. Robinson

KIVA ENTRANCE AND SENTINEL, TAOS

just debts; but, on the other hand, he had no personal wish to urge them, much less authority to compel them, to lease the lands if they did not care to do so. Thousands had trespassed on Indian lands, and for centuries; and, in the face of an embarrassing debt, why not become a trespasser in return?

In the meantime, urgent representations to the Indian Bureau did not seem to click. The actual exchange of lands was a matter for the decision of the General Land Office, where the maps, schedules, and all other necessary papers had been transferred, and rested; but the Bureau did not seem to be able to bring any pressure to bear on the General Land Office, and the General Land Office invited one's pity, for it seemed that it had become paralyzed and could not function. Well, it was too bad!

Then to my office one day came a Laguna gentleman who was a rather cunning individual. Most Indians are frankly, bluntly, plainly honest, and a few Indians are frankly, bluntly, plainly crooked; but occasionally there exists one who has developed finesse to a degree, giving him a smooth, polished, and altogether deceptive personality. This one knew his way about. In whatever business he was engaged, I rather doubted the complete legitimacy of the proceedings, and I would have preferred any other of the 1800 Lagunas to have produced the bombshell that he packed in. For the purposes of this recital we will call him Andrew Johnson. He invited to my attention several dunning letters and statements of account from the land company.

"Yes," I said. "These, Andrew, are notices that you owe for the grazing use of sections blank and blank, on which you have sheep. It seems that the annual bill is due."

Andrew Johnson sat in the chair reserved for confidential visitors, smiled, shook his well-dressed ringlets, and said blandly: —

"I do not owe the money, for the reason that I have no lease."

"Did n't you lease those sections?"

"I leased them several years ago, and paid the fees; but this last year, the time covered by those notices, I did not lease. I get the papers just the same. They call me a trespasser unless I pay up. Do I have to pay them if I have no lease?"

Then the general tenor of Mr. Andrew Johnson's methods arose in my mind's eye, and I felt that caution should be exercised. I requested him to think, and to think hard, with view to refreshing his memory as to whether or not he had signed a lease for the period named. He assured me on his word of honor as a Laguna gentleman of the Queres tribe that he had signed no lease, unless he had done so in his sleep, and that he was not given to somnambulism. I called the company's office.

"This Andrew Johnson, said to be delinquent in paying grazing fees; he maintains that he has no lease on those lands."

"What! What! . . . Of course he has a lease. We have it right here in the files. And he has sheep on those lands; therefore he uses the lands."

"Will you please let me see the lease? I'll send a messenger for it. I wish to confront Mr. Johnson with the evidence."

Within a short time the document was brought in by the Agency runner. I unfolded one of those legal-looking papers that panic most Indians, observed the parties of the first and second parts, noted the description of lands, and turned to the spaces reserved for signatures and seals.

"Here, friend Andrew," I said, pointing to the dotted line.

But Andrew smiled, shook his ringlets again, and said:—

"I did n't sign that. Let me have a pen and paper, and I will write my name for you."

Which he forthwith did, signing his name with a legibility that would have put Spencer to shame. The two signatures resembled each other in no manner, shape, or form.

Within a short time there was a heated argument in the office of the land company. Its representative had found these leases, their various signatures, and their annual renewals troublesome and wearing. We exchanged some very plain thoughts on the subject of seeking to collect moneys from Indians who had not signed the fatal papers.

"What does it matter?" he argued. "It is common knowledge that they use the lands of this company, and they should pay for them."

In addition to this he informed me that he proposed to visit Washington in the near future — indeed, that he would go rather sooner than he had intended — and that he would make it his express business when there to get my job; not for himself, you will understand, but for the personal satisfaction of seeing me without it. In this mission I wished him Godspeed, telling him in rebuttal that there would be no more collections through my office, and that I meant to inform the Laguna Indian governor, by a direct manifesto signed by myself and not by someone else, that when leases expired they should not be renewed.

"We will then lease those lands to white cattlemen," he declared.

"An action that I cannot prevent; but the moment one hoof gets on to Indian territory I'll impound the stock and take your lessee into the Federal Court on a charge of trespass."

Apparently the gentleman made his journey, and arrived safely in the capital city; for immediately, or as soon thereafter as mails could be handled, came a terrific blast addressed to the Pueblo Indian Agent. Through the issuance of that manifesto to the ignorant people of Laguna, he had performed an act that savored of sedition, if not conspiracy. At once! At once, mark you! The infamous instructions should be withdrawn, annulled, and rendered innocuous by the Indian Agent's confessing, himself, to his ignorant charges, that he had been without authority in his attitude concerning the leasing of railroad lands within the Laguna Executive Order reservations. Moreover, he should never again issue such an order without first having imbibed wisdom from the font that gurgled in the Interior Department.

The aforesaid Pueblo Indian Agent did not believe that he should abase himself to the Laguna Indians. He then prepared another letter to the native governor, stating that by Indian Office direction the Indians could lease those railroad lands if they wished to.

A complete understanding of this seeming paradox involves a knowledge of the Indian character. The first impression always sticks longest. And within a short time, — indeed, one is justified in saying within an extraordinarily brief time, — in that same year of 1921, to be exact, *all* the railroad lands within the boundaries of the two Laguna reserves *were exchanged*. I make no categorical assertions with respect to this peculiar happening, but it would appear that some irreverent person had directly, and with vicious malice aforethought, hurled a blunt instrument into the whole delicate works.

XVII

THE INDIAN WHO GOT AWAY

> They that sit in the gate speak against me; and I was the song of the drunkards.
>
> — Psalm LXIX. 12

There is one art in which few Indian Agents become proficient; which, indeed, few Agents take the trouble to consider except as a matter of sordid routine. It is the understanding of Indian policemen. Imagine Napoleon as one who paid more attention to his dinner than to analyzing General Vandamme. It is recorded, I believe, that the Corsican once said: "Had I two Vandammes, I would shoot one." And very often the contemplation of neurasthenic school-teachers, or the struggle with some contract for plumbing, prevented me from giving this subject the attention it deserved.

In the course of fourteen years, I commissioned and sought to direct perhaps threescore native gendarmes — probably more, for one cannot remember those failures who lasted just long enough to spoil a uniform, and get fired. I can recall eight distinct individuals of the Navajo tribe, five of the Hopi, and two of the Tewa among the Hopi, in northern Arizona. There were three regular officers at my Agency in South Dakota — two plain, unadulterated Sioux and one Charles McBride, who struck me as having a good bit of Irish in his Indian composition, and so naturally drifted to the police force, where he wisely influenced native affairs and made himself generally and courteously useful. Among the Indians of the Lower Colorado River valley I had most faithful service from an old Mohave Apache scout, Peter Nelse, who as a young warrior had kept ahead of the regular troops, and I have no doubt accounted for more than one desert enemy. He had received a "regular's" training, and went through a monotonous routine of petty duties with the regularity of a clock. He bore a distinct resemblance to Marshal Hindenburg, and like that martinet carried out his orders, and sometimes his imaginations, with a crushing finality that was admirable. In the same district I observed a rare personality, garbed as a policeman, who often patrolled the railroad station at Needles, California, and who was diligent after his own peculiar fashion. He rejoiced in the name of Abraham Lincoln, and I think he would have interested Lincoln not a little.

Each individual of this small army was a separate and distinct problem. All wore uniforms, and some of them were as trim as troopers, while most were not; all carried the traditional six-gun of the Western heavy-artillery type; and several were not unskilled or diffident in the use of the weapon. As a bludgeon, it was damaging in its immediate effects. More than once I have worried for fear of finding a grim corpse on my official hands. They would come to me for cartridges, and when I dealt out the heavy lead slugs I would wonder what was in the chart of fate. But no one of these potential gunmen ever killed anybody, so my fears were without foundation.

Somehow, I had received the impression that the Pueblo Indians of New Mexico, who had enjoyed nearly four centuries of civilizing influences, would require little restraint; and there was that vision of a "native govern-

THE INDIAN WHO GOT AWAY

ment," admirably functioning, with a Governor pueblo, elected in a democratic manner and s. by a staff of fiscals and sheriffs. And I comfort self with an idea.

Then one morning a short, thickset, duck-legged . low reported to me, introducing himself as Louis Abeita, Chief of the Pueblo Indian Police. If he impressed me in any way at our first meeting, it was as a peculiar contrast to the many stalwart and stolid Indians I had seen in the same position.

"An odd little duck to be chief of police!" was my thought.

He had broad shoulders and a long, mature body on legs that should have carried lighter weight, and his arms appeared shorter than they should have been. With humped shoulders or a limp, he would have been a dwarf. His pleasant smile was the best sort of recommendation, however, for it brought one's attention immediately to his head. It was a large head, with a high and very broad forehead. There was a generous width between his eyes. And those eyes snapped brilliantly, like live coals, full of vigilance, along with good will and the intelligent quick-witted white man's instant appreciation of things. He possessed a white man's sense of humor, an engaging quality, because one so little expected it of an Indian; and too, on occasion, he could be abruptly and witheringly sarcastic. He was a character in the Pueblo provinces. He carried an automatic, and he bought his own cartridges.

I had not been in charge many days when the morning paper told me of a nocturnal affair at the railroad station of Isleta. A certain officer Abeita had counseled a suspicious looking traveler to pause and display his luggage

DESERT DRUMS

But Officer Abeita, if it were the same Louis Abeita of the Indians, the son of Juan Rey Abeita, had not reported this occurrence to the Agency, and the orders were mandatory that records should be faithfully kept of those arrested for violations of the law within the Indian country. I determined to call this slip to the attention of Officer Abeita when next he appeared, and to caution him that, whereas an automatic is an ingeniously constructed device capable of terrible effects and operating with lightning efficiency, he should keep it rather as an ornament than as an instrument of decision. Perhaps I had just received one of the Bureau's circulars devoted to moral suasion. In any event, on going down the street to lunch, I happened to meet the Albuquerque Chief of Police.

"Hello, Chief!" I called to him. "Tell me — this Officer Abeita, who jailed a Mexican last evening, is he one of your men?"

"Until you object," said the Chief.

"Oh! it was Louis, then!" I exclaimed. "I shall have to speak to him about using that gun he carries."

"Why?" asked the Chief.

"Well, he seems to be rather careless with it. One of these days he may seriously damage somebody, and there will be no end of trouble."

The Chief did not act as if annoyed, but he did tender the following official advice: —

"If I were you, and I were the Indian Agent, I'd let Louis Abeita alone. He's doing all right. Whenever he shoots anybody, the fellow deserves shooting. It may be in the regulations to speak kindly two or three times to Indians, but Louis, when working with my men, or when acting as deputy sheriff for the county, or as special officer for the Santa Fe Railway, has to go up against people who are not Pueblo Indians. We value Louis highly as an officer, and when he cuts loose on anyone you may be sure of two things — one, that the fellow is guilty of something warranting his arrest; and two, that the fellow is shot. Louis will get him from either hand. So I wouldn't make him timid and destroy his influence in the community."

So that was it. Louis Abeita was something more than an Indian policeman, and his judgment could be depended on, as well as his ability to hit smaller marks than barn doors, shooting with either hand. I made additional inquiries as to this duck-legged Louis Abeita, and two or three anecdotes turned up. Said one man: —

"Haven't you heard of the box-car thieves? It looked as if no one around this country could land them. The railroad cars were being robbed with an increasing frequency, and it became bothersome. Then Louis Abeita was put on the case, and he finished the gang. The feature of it was that while a judge handled the remnants of the affair, the coroner was needed first."

"You mean that Louis killed someone?"

"Dead as a stone hatchet, and a good job, too. You see, he and some deputies trailed them to a house, and told them to come out and be good. They came out, but they came out firing, and all bets were off. It saved the county some money."

"But he seems such a mild-mannered, good-natured little fellow," I said, doubtfully, the whole thing contrasting too abruptly with his physical make-up, and the expression of his eyes, and his smile.

"Oh! he is *now*. But before he became a police officer he was an awful boozer, and a tough egg. He reformed, and his present mission is to keep the world running in a straight and narrow path. Send him after someone — one of his relatives, for instance. Select his uncle. Once he has the warrant, friendship and tribal affiliations cease. The uncle will be delivered, or else you can have a Mass said for the repose of Louis's soul."

"I never expected to find such an Indian policeman," I commented.

"Don't worry about Louis," repeated my counselor.

That was the first of several mistakes that I have regretted ever since. I did not worry about Louis. The second and the third mistakes I charge to myself also. When next he appeared in the office, I said: —

"Do you carry a gun? If so, let me see it."

He did not reach for his belt, but went down into the side pocket of his reeferlike coat and produced a piece of artillery that had seen much service. It was a Colt's automatic, with the handles gone from the sides of the grip, and it operated with a double action; that is, one had to pull the trigger and squeeze the grip at the same time. Perhaps for that reason he had removed the handles, as his hands were small. And it was a .32.

"It is not heavy enough for serious work, Louis," I said. "If you must shoot criminals, you should have a .38, at least, and a single-action gun. The next trip we make together, I'll let you have one that would knock down a cow, and then you can turn this one in."

THE INDIAN WHO GOT AWAY

He smiled and said he would like to have a heavier gun.

Came the second mistake, for, while I permitted him to carry the heavier weapon for a period, I once again became timid and withdrew it. It was a dangerous gun, with no safety lock, and nothing to prevent the firing of eight slugs as from a gatling. And the third mistake of mine was recorded when I did not telephone him to kill a man quickly, and to make a report of it later.

But in the meantime, we had many adventures. To my amazement, while he had traveled over much of the United States, he had not visited all the pueblos of his people. It was necessary that I go to them frequently, and seldom it was that some police matter did not arise. The usual method is for the Indian Agent to visit his stations unhampered by any retinue. When he has reached a point fifty to one hundred miles from his headquarters, he may discover some affair crying aloud for investigation and settlement. He then returns home, issues warrants, and has his police apprehend the evildoers sometime during the next three months, if indeed they are brought to book at all. The widely scattered pueblos of the jurisdiction invited procrastination, and the entire moral effect of prompt arrest and trial was often lost. Moreover, once the agent had returned to his headquarters, dusty and tired, the accumulated business would distract his attention from the distant pueblo disorders. Punitive measures were too frequently neglected, until a fresh occasion superseded them.

Always requiring a voice, I would take Louis, who thus served in several capacities. He was guide, interpreter, sheriff, court bailiff, and chaperon for those who failed to beat the case. He was an instructor also, in that he told me of the Indians on those long rides across the desert, and of his adventures once he had reformed and became a monitor for the District. But he would not talk of the box-car thieves. That subject was taboo. There was no boasting in Louis Abeita.

One day I issued to him the annual commission as a deputy special officer of the Liquor Service. He smiled, and said: —

"I got the first of these blue cards that time they were after the bootlegger beyond Grants. Whiskey had been coming down the line for a long time. Indians were getting it, too. The railroad officials wanted the fellow caught, but they could n't manage it. I said to Pablo: 'Why don't you get me a blue card, and I'll go after that Mexican?' So Pablo got the Agent and the Chief Special Officer to arrange it. They sent one of those white men Special Officers out with me, I guess to see that I did n't lay down on my job; but I told him to go on to the hotel when we reached the station, and to pay no attention to me. I said: 'Don't register for too long a time.'

"But you see, I had n't gone up there with Special Officer written all over me. No! I got myself good and dirty first, let my beard grow out, and wore my oldest clothes. I had a roll of bedding along. Pretty bum roll it was, too. And when I got off that train, I was a vagrant sheep herder looking for work on the range. I did n't go to a hotel. I lay around the corrals for a little, and then drifted off up the road to a place I had suspected, where sheep herders and Indians would be likely to hang out. I got the Mexican, all right."

The actual occurrence, as related by others, is to this effect. A small boy came running to the hotel and cried out that a man was fighting with some Navajo. The roadside shack found Louis Abeita sitting on two Navajo Indians. He explained that he had arrived a short time before, and had bought some whiskey, and had idled about to see three Navajo barter for a jug of it. One of the Indians had made good his escape; two were securely in hand.

"But," said the Special Officer, despairingly, "you should have arrested the man who was selling the liquor to the Indians."

"Oh! that fellow!" said Louis. "He's in the rear room."

Going to the door of this rear room, the officer found the whiskey peddler embracing one of the posts of a bed. Examination showed that he was securely handcuffed to it. Louis had quietly attended to his case first.

When the Judge asked Louis how it was that he managed the affair so quickly, he replied: —

"Judge, I drank so much of that stuff in my time, I can smell it two miles off."

And more than one supported this testimony, for Louis had been the horrible example of the pueblo of Isleta. One Indian has stated that Louis, in his palmy days, consumed more fire water than any three heavy drinkers of the pueblo. He had been the first drunk and disorderly case presented before Judge Pablo on his appointment to the Indian Court.

"He used to laugh later at seeing his name first on my old docket."

But suddenly he achieved grace in some manner and braced up, and sought an Agency position — not as interpreter, not as handy man, not as resident farmer; neither did he seek the job of Indian Agent, which so many Indians believe they could handle with success. No!

He wished to be an Indian policeman, for the purpose of breaking up the liquor habit among his people. The Isletas were great vintners. They kept wine on hand in quantities, and there were few among them who did not imbibe. Perhaps the responsibility for this should date back to those two Franciscans, Fray Antonio de Arteaga, and Fray García de San Francisco y Zúñiga, who founded the missions of Senecu and Socorro (1630), and planted a vineyard, thus introducing the grape into New Mexico.

One morning in the year 1917 this new officer, at whom many laughed, appeared at the pueblo in a suit of tan clothing, having little red pipes down the pants' seams, and red straps on the shoulders. That day a large number of his old compadres at the jug found themselves standing before the Judge. Louis had not arrested them. He had simply invited them to the courthouse for a friendly chat.

"Now," he warned them, with a sober fanatical intensity, "this is the end of drunkenness in this pueblo. You were my old drinking friends, but when I see you drunk again, you are my enemies. I will arrest you and lock you up, first. Then I will swear out a complaint against you, and prosecute you, even my own brother, to the limit."

He kept his word. From that morning in 1917 until another morning in 1921, no careless imbiber was safe in the pueblo of Isleta. He had no reverence for the sacred things of the tribe. When cunning ones secreted their jugs among the ceremonial masks, and implored him not to desecrate the symbols of their ancient religion, Louis was obdurate. The masks were unharmed, but the jugs went into the ditch, and the owners went to jail.

As for his ability to scent out liquor, I can give only one incident. He proceeded with me one night to the pueblo

THE INDIAN WHO GOT AWAY

of Santo Domingo, forty-odd miles from Albuquerque. It was fiesta time, and the Santo Domingos would generously entertain many visitors. The car had scarcely stopped in the pueblo before Louis espied a group of Mexicans, and without parley arrested one of them. Did the man have liquor? He did. His brand fitted nicely with the pueblo scenery, for it was labeled "Old Mission Rye Whiskey," and had a neat representation of a Franciscan monastery with church and bell towers as a recommendation. But a cautious sniff of the bottle's contents convinced one that it was a subtle concoction of Battle-Ax Tobacco and prune juice, cut with sulphuric acid.

Now this was a pretty pass. Properly to jail this miscreant would require a return to Albuquerque, forty-odd more miles, and the giving up of fiesta supervision for the evening. We had gone there expecting to find the Santo Domingos gambling in the booths after midnight, or at least permitting gambling games to flourish under the direction of the concessionaires.

"Hold him right here," said Louis. "These Domingos have some old tool house that will serve for a jail. I'll get their keys."

The Governor of the pueblo pointed out an old adobe, with barred windows, where perhaps the native Inquisition had installed its victims at times.

"But," I said quietly to Louis, "that will never hold him. Look at the chimney. Two men could scramble through it."

"Leave it to me," said Louis, confidently. He placed the man inside, lingered there a moment or two, and then locked the door.

"He'll be there in the morning," assured Louis; and the man was there at daylight. After we had deposited him in Albuquerque, I asked this little dynamo how it was that the Mexican had not escaped from the impromptu prison; for we had not watched it, going our ways to the climax of the evening, when Louis demolished several games of chance that had sprouted when innocent pleasures became boring.

"It was easy," explained Louis. "I put him inside. I showed him the bars on the windows, and then I showed him the open chimney. I said: 'Go right up the chimney, my friend, whenever you get ready. You can get out that way. But remember! I will be outside — and the second your head appears above the top of that chimney, you're a dead man!'"

So the Mexican sat down on a pile of old implements, and patiently waited for daylight. He had heard of Louis Abeita.

He knew how to appeal to Indians, too. It was not all rough stuff with him. Again he accompanied me to Santo Domingo, this time for the purpose of rounding up pupils at the opening of the fall school term. All the older children had departed for the boarding school at Santa Fe. Having sent away so many, the Indians preferred keeping the youngsters at home. The day school was only a short distance away, at the edge of the pueblo, but if a child did not enroll the first day of school perhaps he would be permitted to drift as a truant for several days, and be forgotten. Just as among the Hopi, the villagers began secreting the children; and it was necessary to go into the houses after them, a thing that had not been done vigorously at Santo Domingo before this, and that was not relished. Finally the teacher's list was checked off, with the exceptions of two growing lads, who had been seen scuttling around, from alley to street, but who were no longer in sight.

"They are in the kiva," said Louis. "Let me handle it."

To tell the truth, I was perfectly willing to let him handle it. I had gone into many Indian kivas, and had some rather stern discussions in their depths, but those kivas were not at Santo Domingo, and I had no idea how cordially I should be received.

Louis climbed the long flight of adobe steps leading to the drumlike roof, and then disappeared down the kiva ladder. He was inside some little time. To my relief, he reappeared with the two boys and took them to the school.

When I related a scene of this kind in my last book, there were several tender sentimentalists who expressed their disapproval of such a proceeding. I think Miss Mary Austin termed it, "the rape of the Hotevillas!" I regret having caused Miss Austin any mental discomfort, and hope to be absolved in this instance by relating that the only person at Santo Domingo to protest strenuously against our efforts was that gentleman of quasi Orders, the sacristan. It seems on the face of the testimony that the Indian religion and ancient forms of spirituality had not this time been offended. The sacristan was training his son to be a sacristan, also, like old Diego Abeita at Isleta, who had held his pontifical post for one hundred years. The mere matter of three R's could be dispensed with. Nevertheless, we took the son of the sacristan to school, very much to the old gentleman's disgust. The Franciscan Fathers did not object. There have been times, I do not doubt, when certain of the devout Fathers, perhaps just returning from Retreat, have found themselves sorely tempted to apply the toe of the ecclesiastical boot to certain sacristans, who, when the spirit moved them, stopped only short of celebrating the Mass.

I asked Louis what had been his adventure in the kiva.

"Oh! it did n't amount to much," he related. "They met me on the ladder, and said that I could n't come in. Then they backed down the ladder, because I was coming down it, and they stopped at the foot with more words about what might happen to me. So I sat down on one of the rungs, and talked to them. I said: 'You fellows are making a mistake. I won't spoil your kiva, because I am an Indian. It does n't matter if I come down. But we must have those two boys for the school. If I take them, it will be an Indian doing it. But if I go back without them, then that Agent will surely come up here, and he will come into your kiva, *and he is a white man!*'"

Louis grinned.

"I knew they did n't want you spoiling their kiva. So I waited a little bit, and they thought it over, and they said it was best for an Indian to do the job."

Moral suasion, mixed with mysticism and Tihua finesse.

But occasionally Louis would indulge in an adventure that proved temporarily embarrassing — to others, not to him. The pueblo lands of Isleta form a barricade across the valley of the Rio Grande, south of Albuquerque. The lands stretch from the Manzanos Mountains to the River, and then west of the river into the barren sand-dune desert. All main roads run through the pueblo lands. When going anywhere north or south along the Rio Grande, one must proceed through this little Indian domain.

So when anything disappears from the pueblo, such as live stock, it will have crossed the south boundary or the north boundary only, and to a skillful tracker, such as Louis, could easily be traced up or down the river, frequently being found at one or the other of the Mexican settlements in the neighborhood.

Some horses were lost, strayed, or stolen, and Louis followed their tracks south to a little Mexican hamlet. He discovered the animals in a barn, and found that there would be opposition to giving them up. The deputy sheriff appointed for that district and the local justice of the peace were inclined to sympathize with the holders of the stock, and they did not relish this Tihua Indian smooching about in their bailiwick. So they sought to dissuade Louis from seizing the team.

Louis explained that he was a deputy sheriff also, and had four or five badges that he wore only on special occasions, this not being one of them. Some of the badges were engraved with the words: "Special Officer"; others had a defiant eagle spread across the top over the words: "Chief of Indian Police." And apart from these trinkets, he explained that the Pueblo Indian Judge had directed him to find the stock, which he had done, and that it was the sworn duty of all officers like themselves to assist him in the performance of his duty. He showed them the brands, which had been duly registered. He said that he did not propose to arrest or to prosecute anyone in this matter; but that he did intend, and that without any delay, to return the team to the pueblo and to its rightful owner.

"Now," said Louis, firmly, "you will see me go into the barn, and come out with the horses. That's what I came down here for."

"Do you have a gun, my friend?" asked the native-citizen deputy.

"Haven't you a gun?" said Louis.

"No."

"Well, then, you go home and get your gun. I will sit here on the fence until you return with it; because, if you mean to interfere with me, you should have a gun. You will need it."

But they continued to argue with him, and because of this hopeless discussion Louis became annoyed. Very little love is lost between the full-blooded Indian of the pueblos and the fellow who prefers to call himself "a native citizen," and who for years has dwelt within squatting distance of the pueblos. Some of them had drifted across the lines and were to be found on the wrong side. Perhaps Louis was not feeling well that morning, or again he may have had some personal reason for disliking the two gentlemen whose forbears had assisted in conquering and colonizing the lands of his fathers. At any rate, something happened to produce hostilities. I could never learn whether he engaged them single-handed and managed to handcuff them together, although he was very deft at that, or whether he held them up at his gun's point and so compelled their submission. But the fact is that a short time thereafter one could have seen this native citizen deputy sheriff and native citizen justice of the peace, with gyves upon their wrists, walking ahead of Louis Abeita in the dusty road leading to Isleta. Louis rode one of the horses and surveyed his captives grimly.

"Where are you taking us?" they asked him.

"To the Isleta jail."

"But what have we done?"

"Interfered with an officer in the discharge of his duty."

THE INDIAN WHO GOT AWAY

On arrival at the pueblo, Louis marched them before Judge Pablo, and the judge was very much confused, not to say dismayed. He took Louis to one side, and engaged him in conversation, thus: —

"This is a terrible thing that you have done."

"What's terrible about it? Did n't I have your direction to go about finding and recovering stolen property, and did n't they seek to prevent me from taking possession of it when found? Is n't that a Pueblo team? You know those brands, and the owner of those horses."

"Yes, Louis; but these men are county officials. We are constantly complaining that they interfere with Indian affairs, and now. . . . No! there is no use in my telephoning to the Agent about it. He would blow up the pair of us for a thing like this. No, no! this will never do. Leave it to me, though, and I will try to get you out of it."

Then Judge Pablo had the handcuffs removed, put on his spectacles, and assumed his most solemn judicial air, proceeding to read the Riot Act to the unfortunates, and solemnly sentencing them to dismissal from the Pueblo limits, with a warning that they should never come back. And they never did. What is more, they were so impressed by the apparent gravity of the affair, and the probability of being hanged for the next offense, that they forgot to report the matter to any higher official of the state.

The Pueblo Agency possessed a squad of police, natives selected from and assigned to the different pueblos, but for the most part they were nice boys who assisted the resident farmers, and who carried messages very faithfully. Louis Abeita preferred to operate alone. When support was necessary, he was fortunate in that I possessed one strange complement to him. At the Pueblo of San Felipe Señor Juan Chavez was employed, a pleasant and hospitable man in his home, and a zealous government employee. Juan was commissioned as a special deputy of the Liquor Service, and was thus authorized to act as a policeman within the Indian country. He was of considerable importance and influence among his own "native citizen" people, and had once represented them in the state legislature. Garbed in a helmet and cuirass, Chavez would have made a good figure as a conqueror; and he had the courage of one, with a single-track mind devoted solely to his duty as an official of the United States. Threats involving the loss of life and limb had failed utterly to divorce him from his appointed pueblo station, and a former superintendent stated that the San Felipe day school might never have been built but for Juan Chavez. Showers of stones had lacerated his scalp, but the mail went through the pueblo despite "secret dances"; and on several historic occasions, when Señor Chavez lost his solemn calm and his temper at the same time, the unreasoning proletariat had suffered extreme pain coupled with an earnest desire to escape elsewhere. Louis Abeita was not much over four feet in height; Chavez towered above him into the snow line of six feet. Separated, each was formidable; combined, they were invincible. These two then, an Isleta Indian of the Tihua, and a Spanish Mexican of Algodones, bore the burden of preserving the peace in the Pueblo provinces. Their courage and their faults, however, no longer count in the scheme of things along the Rio Grande.

And this suggests the last adventure of Louis Abeita. The man who enjoys a first adventure will inevitably reach a last one. I can fancy certain critics, who have

JUDGE JOHN DIXON OF COCHITI

JOHN CHAVEZ: A LAGUNA POLICEMAN AND INTERPRETER
Not to be confused with Juan Chavez

THE INDIAN WHO GOT AWAY

never possessed any, lamenting about a shred of brief authority. One must have images; and the policeman presents a disagreeable one to the cloistered mind. Indeed, I have found that life produces but two classes of people: those who live and breed and die legally, and those who do not. It is the selfish first class who produce all the trouble, and make policemen necessary. But for a fancy that they must have security in order to conduct their biological processes in a dull routine of monotony, the generous second class could wend a primrose way, carelessly brave, full of high spirits, with something of interest happening every minute, and no time clocks to be punched or taxes to be paid. Incongruous as it may seem, reflection proves that it is the kill-joy policeman who fetches up the 9:15; who guarantees that coffee and hot cakes may be had in cafés, that the doctor makes his rounds, that certain "Ostermoors" vend bedding to a lot of drones who waste one third their precious time in sleep.

And it came to pass that a negro must select the Albuquerque railroad station for running amuck, and shooting several people who displeased him, one of whom promptly died. At midnight the Sheriff made a trip to the Isleta pueblo, and warned Louis Abeita that this desperate fellow was still free to go and come. The next morning's papers all indicated that the outlaw had fled eastward to the mountains, which would have taken him completely out of the Pueblo country. I should have done two things. I should at once have carried to Louis Abeita the heavy automatic, well oiled, and with magazine clips filled; and I should have instructed him to shoot fugitive negroes first and to investigate afterward. But no one believed that the quarry would turn up at Isleta, in the peaceful midst of nine hundred Indians. Officers were searching for him in all other directions, save southerly. And yet, that is exactly where he appeared.

"Come along, Louis," said a workman, "and help me fix this pump."

"In a minute," replied Louis, "after I arrest this coon."

Down the railroad track came a man in an overcoat, and he was black, and there was something furtive about him.

It was my morning for being shaved in Albuquerque, and Jim, the barber, had about half completed the operation when a man entered the shop with news of a fight at Isleta. He said that an officer had been wounded, and was being brought on a special train to Albuquerque. It was but a jump from the barber's chair to a telephone. The chief of city police reported that Louis had arrested the negro, and disarmed him of one gun, only to find that the outlaw had two weapons, the second secreted in his overcoat. The affair had occurred on the railroad embankment at the pueblo. The negro had taken a desperate chance for his liberty after relinquishing the first gun, by dropping and rolling to the foot of the embankment. From that position he fired at the officer. Louis fired at him once before being struck in the right arm. He switched the automatic to his left hand, and it jammed. Then a bullet struck him in the abdomen.

At these shots, the word spread like magic through the pueblo streets. It was all right to hiss at Louis Abeita for being a policeman who interfered with pueblo drinking parties; but, on the other hand, when one shot Louis Abeita, he had shot a Tihua Indian. The entire community, arming themselves en route, turned out in a man hunt. The negro fled to the swamps along the river front, and there the Indians surrounded him. He would go no

THE INDIAN WHO GOT AWAY

farther. When he sought to cross the river, a thin line of watchers appeared on the far bank of it. It was an old game with them. In the swamp they kept him until commissioned officers could be summoned by telephone. And these officers arrived from Albuquerque in a very short time, carrying high-powered rifles, and very promptly sent this lonesome individual to whatever hunting grounds his kind possess. No one tried to crawl up to him with words of moral suasion. That part of it was soon over.

A special engine of the Santa Fe happened to be on the Isleta switch, and but for this Louis would have bled to death. It came to the city in record time, and then I found him on the operating table at the Saint Joseph's hospital with two surgeons about to see what could be done for him. A nurse was holding an ether cone over his face as I entered the room. Hearing my voice, he immediately began a choking report of the happening. So I told him that everything was going nicely at the pueblo, and that he should lie quiet and go to sleep.

"It's a bad piece of business," said the chief surgeon. "What chance has he?"

"About one in a thousand. He will require special nurses, day and night, and with good luck — well, that's all we can do for him."

I went back to the office and dispatched a telegram to the Bureau, relating the circumstances and requesting authority to cover these unusual expenses. Being a trifle too keyed up to sit at a desk, I went down street to file the message. My route led past one of the banks, and a director asked me as to Abeita's condition and his chances for recovery. I told him it looked rather discouraging.

"I suppose the Government will see him through?" he asked.

"Well! I mean to get for him anything that Albuquerque has; but you know how these things are. I am just wiring for the money."

"We all knew Abeita. Plucky Indian. Should you find any sympathy lacking in this matter, come to the bank."

That was some consolation, for in answer to my telegram I received a brief wire of instructions, reading: "Turn wounded officer over to Public Health Service." Did anyone suggest "Ice Water"!

No! I did not turn Louis Abeita over to the Public Health Service. So that I could make an honest report about it, along with the other things I wrote, I investigated to learn how much of a Public Health Service there was in Albuquerque at that time, and found an office, locked, the incumbent thereof being on some distant mission. The special surgeon, and the house physician, and the relays of special nurses at the hospital were not disturbed.

When Louis came from under the influence of the ether, it was necessary to tell him that the negro had been killed long since, for he insisted on getting up, out, and after him. Then he grew quieter in mind and for several days rested easily. His family were brought from the pueblo, his sons from the school, the physicians saying that they could do him no harm. They were all stunned; and his little son, Nicolas, spent his time in the hospital hallway, weeping, and would not be comforted.

Then came a morning when the patient did not seem so clear in mind.

"We must go after that fellow," he said. "You get me

a new uniform. The old one is covered with blood. And then we'll go. ..."

"Yes, Louis; but in the morning. We'll take an early train. And it's pretty cold these days."

"That's good. You get the tickets. You say it's cold — well! I have a sheep-lined coat for it."

Some time after this he reached up with an effort, caught my arm, and struggled to lift himself.

"Get me outside, please," he pleaded. "Not with this nurse, but — just you. ... We'll walk up and down outside. ..."

"This afternoon, Louis; it's very windy now."

I knew then that we should make no more trips together. He wanted to get into the open. They always do. The crisp sparkle had now left his eyes. He said nothing more of that mythical journey we were to have arranged, yet he seemed conscious of some distant mission. Another Indian, a big fellow, one of those you would think could scarcely be affected by anything, stood wrapped in a blanket at the foot of the bed. The nurse busied herself with stimulants. For some minutes Louis Abeita stared beyond us, then slowly he fixed his great dark questioning eyes on me, and suddenly he was gone.

I turned to the bed's foot.

"Horrible!" said the Indian who remained.

Such things are nerve-shredding, tragic; and they were followed by unpleasant duties. The gentleman who contracted to bury my Indian dead was consulted, and we decided that the usual arrangements, always in accord with decency, would be a bit bare, not to say shabby, for this brave little fellow. Somehow his forty years had sloughed away from him, and only youth showed in his calm, masklike face. The new uniform caused him to resemble one of the School's cadets. And I would have to take him home to the pueblo.

"That is a heluva fuss to kick up over a dead Indian," said a man on the street corner, as the Albuquerque police walked beside the hearse to the station.

"My friend," countered an equally frank bystander, "when you 're half as white inside as he was, we 'll kick up a heluva fuss over you."

The local train slowed at the Isleta station, and Indian police took the gray casket to the little Indian home. Until this time I had not thought of any more distressing scenes. There would be the simple Mass in the old church on the plaza, and after that a few people at the grave. But I had forgotten that most of the affecting things had occurred in the city, in a hospital, and that these people—those who had laughed at and hissed him, those Peublo who had respected and loved him—until now had had no opportunity for an expression of their grief. The little house filled to suffocation, and outside it more humanity packed around the door. There were few men. These were the women of the pueblo in their scarlet shawls. I thought it would be best for the Indian police to stand very close to his coffin when it was opened.

Then all suppressed feeling burst forth in a series of piercing screams that could be heard across the Rio Grande. It was a symphony of despair; the frenzied unreasoning emotion of a grief-stricken mob; and they surged up to and against the coffin. But for those big fellows fencing it. . . . And this wild shrilling continued and continued. Only the members of the man's family were quiet.

And then, when the terrible display of grief had partially subsided, came exactly what I had expected. There was discussion, led by persons who had little interest in the matter, as to the manner of his burial.

It would never do, they said, for him to be buried with his fathers in that official garb. He was no longer a white man; he was no longer an Indian policeman; he was dead, and he had returned at last to his Indian people. All evidences of his former apostacy must be torn away, that he might be buried as an Indian.

Now I had seen the bodies of educated students torn from their caskets that they might have the rites of a tribal funeral. Once or twice I had tried to prevent it. And I had seen that man we had disturbed in the old Acoma churchyard.

Louis Abeita had told me his own point of view when living, and of the plans he had formed for his family. There had been nothing in the last four years of his life to indicate that he clung in the slightest to the ancient ways of his people. From the hospital, he had sent for the padre.

His eldest son, a very bright lad, was summoned.

"What do you, and your mother, wish about this?" I asked him.

"My father lived that way," he said, without hesitation. "I want him to be buried just as he lived."

It was a decided relief to receive this decision, for I had determined that the growling and grumbling multitude should not be indulged in their fancy.

Next morning, there was the Mass in the church, a service attended by many officials, and the pueblo people, and their neighbors from the near-by Spanish towns. Breaking pueblo precedent, the padres went to the grave.

Louis was not left entirely unequipped for his journey to the Spirit World. During the night that had been attended to, and his casket was very heavy. When the last of the earth was being filled in, an old Indian woman made her way through the crowd and broke an olla of water at the head of his grave.

Then I went back to my office to engage in the inevitable wrangle about the cost of his passing, the value of his coffin, and what I should have done in the premises; the whole sordid business of it lasting through some several months. In a little while — of course after the subject had been brought up and persons in official life reminded of the circumstances — such a pension as the law permitted was granted to his widow, with little monthly additions for the children who had not reached eighteen years. I seem to recall that it totaled all of thirty-three dollars a month. And the man was dead.

When next Jim the barber eased me back in the chair, he stropped his razor thoughtfully, and said: —

"So your Indian got away."

I did not at once catch the meaning of his expression; then its full import flashed to me. There was no longer a Louis Abeita to summon for disagreeable service, to go and to come without counting the hours, patient, cheerful, tireless.

"Yes," I admitted, "he got away."

XVIII

"MAÑANA, AND MAÑANA, AND MAÑANA..."

> WHEN they speak of gifts and profits, you remember that
>   the Psalms
> Say: "Put not your trust in Princes!" they have often
>   itching palms;
> Watch your ballot-seeking Masters — they are serving soon
>   and late
> For a chance to go to market, just to peddle real-estate.
> — "Lincoln's Counsel"

THE Pueblo provinces are not without their natural beauties, and I have often envied the student or the tourist who could spare time for them. There is the dreaming hill country surrounding Cochiti, its bluffs overlooking the sometimes sleepy, sometimes turbulent Rio Grande, ringed by a diadem of mountains, blue and silver, which are shaded by fleecy clouds and often capped with snow. Close at hand rises O-ku, the "Sacred Turtle," as the Tewa name the lone Sandias, that monument of deaths and legends; and farther away the solemn splendor of the Sangre de Cristos. There are the multicolored screens of the San Diego Cañon of the Jemez, its wooded heights on one side of a babbling mountain stream, and its bare and painted cliffs in the alcoves; its hot springs, its woodland silences, and the ruined grandeur of the Jemez Abbey, like a symbol of the Middle Ages transported to crude America. There is the gaunt and fantastic scenery in that distant lonely country of the Acomas. There are the pastoral settings of the Laguna pueblos, the mediæval atmosphere at San Felipe, the purely Indian impression at Santo Domingo, and the Spanish color at Isleta. Journey brings one to the edge of that vast domain of the "Apaches de Navajo," so interesting to old Father Benavides, to the shadow of San Mateo, the turquoise mountain of the south, to Cabezon, the severed head of Yei Tso, the most terrible of all the alien gods; but the Navajo encountered on the Pueblo borders is a Spanish-type Indian, different from his Tartar-like brother of the Painted Desert steppes.

Generally, in comparison with that desert which extends from Fort Defiance, still a frontier outpost, to the Grand Cañon of the Colorado, the Pueblo country, notwithstanding all its historic associations and the indefinably mysterious atmosphere of its pueblos, lacks something to one who has lived for years in the broader Arizona scene. The Pueblo country has lost the glamour of magnificent distances. Nothing is lost behind the ranges of it. The white man has found everything, and is greedily cataloguing the havens of the pueblos for more. The foreign influences — first the crusading Spaniard, then the colonizing Mexican, and last our own hurried vital people, devoted to gasoline and cattle and real estate, have wrought a peculiar insidious change in the Indian drama — one that makes small appeal to sentiment and inspires little admiration. These adobe towns were once as ethnologically important as those of their obdurate kindred, the Hopi, or the camps of their old enemies, the Navajo, still happy uncivilized men of the desert treasuring untainted tribal songs. What a strange thing to find so sharply defined a line of demarcation between the

THE MISSION OF SAN GERONIMO, TAOS
Founded about 1617

MUSEUM AND ART GALLERY, SANTA FE

native people of the one great empire. Wherever the Spanish influences halted or turned aside, to-day the original native is encountered, changed very little in customs, in thought, or in daily modes from what he was when Juan de Oñate mapped this Province of New Spain; and yet, wherever the Spanish influences prevailed, we find something less than civilization. The Pueblo drums are still throbbing, but the Pueblo Indian has become distinctly the product of a garbled environment, and is to-day neither don nor chief, neither savage nor peon. Perhaps this will the sooner make of him a mediocre citizen of the United States; but certainly, except for a few striking personalities, and except for whatever survives in the secrecy of his lodges, his character as "an Indian" is expiring.

As for the future of these people, I am reminded of another experiment in civilization similar to theirs in a milder land; one much younger in its evolution, and that has nearly perished from the earth. In 1879 Robert Louis Stevenson saw the pathetic dregs of it, pictured in his classic *Across the Plains:* —

The Carmel runs by many pleasant farms, a clear and shallow river, loved by wading kine; and at last, as it is falling toward a quicksand and the great Pacific, passes a ruined mission on a hill. The roof has fallen; the ground-squirrel scampers on the graves; the holy bell of Saint Charles is long dismounted; yet one day every year the church awakes from silence, and the Indians return to worship in the church of their converted fathers. I have seen them trooping thither, young and old . . . with those strange, handsome, melancholy features which seem predestined to a national calamity, and it was notable to hear the old Latin words and the old Gregorian music sung . . . by a trained chorus of red Indian men and women. An old blind man was their leader. . . . He had seen changes in the world since first he sang that music sixty years ago, when there was no gold and no Yankees, and he and his people lived in plenty under the wing of the kind priests.

Of course, this is pure sentimentality; so let us leave it. If the Pueblo Indians had ever a season of such felicity, it was before 1821, though I doubt that the Franciscans were successful in redeeming them so far from their desert gods. But there is enough of truth and sentiment in Stevenson's sketch, and enough of parallel to serve as a horrible vision.

As for the nonsentimental side of their picture, that portion of it that belongs in law courts and committee rooms, you may reasonably ask: Why all this pother? Was not the Bursum Bill outlawed after being dismembered by Congress? Were not the Pueblo Indians, thanks to their disinterested friends, once more triumphant? And have they not managed to labor through several centuries of distant statesmanship and local skullduggery to achieve this present proud position in the sun? Are they not surrounded by a perfect hedge of protecting officials — two Agents, a supervising supervisor of superintendents, a special attorney, supported on the flanks by a Bureau of Indian Research, to say nothing of that flicker of genius "The Council of One Hundred"! And now, have they not a Lands Board to find and adjust their boundaries, press their suits for clearance of title, and docket their losses?

Ah, true! These are all honorable gentlemen, who will earnestly salvage whatever it is possible to recover from the wreck. But let us hope that their security may be assured before some new piratical craft, having been careened and scraped and disguised in the backwaters of New Mexico, swims into the offing. A recent Act of Congress bestowed on them the status of citizens at last, but untaxed Indians in New Mexico are denied suffrage. Shall we permit the Pueblo Indians to be taxed as corporations that they may exercise this splendid privilege of the white man's democracy?

Whatever sails may yet be dragged from the old loft, the justification will be sufficient unto the day: To protect the Pueblo Indians from themselves by furnishing a means of local control superior to the court's vision of "Internal Affairs;" to provide relief from the petty business of struggling with their misdemeanors; to saddle on others the duty of ministering to the health of the ignorant; to permit the state of New Mexico to share in the cost of Indian education in exchange for Indian suffrage and corporate taxes; to pay for an expensive dam in the Rio Grande, or to help finance their participation in the benefits of a dam that will be expensive; to recover some part of those "gifts," advanced in the form of reimbursable loans when, foolishly, no security was demanded; to adjust matters to the Act of 1921 so that five per cent may be charged as interest on irrigation construction costs and secured by a lien on the land improved; *and*, since there will be no other way, to do all this, or as much thereof as may be necessary, through a change in Title. The Pueblo Indians are dependent peoples, ever hungry for benefits, and "they have never rendered any service, or given anything to the United States." The Supreme Court has been their sanctuary; but the Supreme Court has been known to change its mind.

In his last Annual Report to the President, transmitted November 30, 1927, the present Secretary ventures hopes and beliefs that conferences already arranged with certain state officials will hasten the time when the states will accept larger responsibility (in education, health, medical, and welfare work) to prepare Indians for complete citizenship. Wherever there are "colonists" to be satisfied, such conferences will be welcomed whenever arranged. And would it not be equitable? See the money we have spent, distributed impartially from Moencopi to Tres Ritos. Are we to drain and recover to posterity 3000 acres of land at Sandia, on a splendid highway and but thirteen miles from a metropolis of the growing Southwest, to have this money-breeding domain monopolized by ninety-two or less of dance-contriving natives? Unthinkable! The surplus Isleta lands may yet attract someone who piously wishes to found and endow a dude ranch.

Then allotment, or partition, as you will, carrying with it patents in fee according to the South Dakota mode. Of course, for charity's sake, put this off until mañana — twenty years hence, at the suggestion of some tender-hearted Secretary who would rather have his successor face the whirlwind. I fancy an echo from the Bureau's incredible optimism: —

"But, surely, Mr. Crane, we would not do this!"

Considering the record of the past, why "surely"? I am visioning the to-morrow of some new Congress, as little informed and as little interested as were the old ones; a time of new officials — new agents with jobs to hold, a new attorney with a patron or a padrone to commend him, a new argument, the ghosts of old infamies having been exorcised into oblivion. Old advocates, old reports of hearings, old books will have disappeared; only visible will be the old eternal land, and the old lust for it.

And should time prove this but the fancy of imagination, you may safely comment: —

> I had rather have a fool to make me merry than experience to make me sad.